Nefertiti: The Mystery Queen

By Burnham Holmes

A
cpi
Book

STECK-VAUGHN
C O M P A N Y
A Subsidiary of National Education Corporation

First Steck-Vaughn Edition 1992

Copyright © 1977 Contemporary Perspectives, Inc.

Art and Photo Credits

Cover photo, John Bennett Dobbins/Photo Trends
Photo on page 6, The Museum of Fine Arts, Boston
Photos on page 10, 12, and 29, The Metropolitan Museum of Art
Photo on page 15, J. Alex Langley/dpi
Photo on page 16, Harry Burton/The Metropolitan Museum of Art
Photo on page 19, The Metropolitan Museum of Art, gift of Edward S. Harkness, 1921
Photo on page 20, The Brooklyn Museum, Charles Edwin Wilbour Fund
Photo on page 25, Jeffrey Foxx/Woodfin Camp & Associates
Photo on page 26, The Metropolitan Museum of Art, gift of J. Pierpont Morgan, 1917
Photo on page 30, Brian Brake/Photo Researchers, Inc.
Illustration on page 36, N.Y. Public Library Picture Collection
Photo on page 39, The Metropolitan Museum of Art, The Theodore M. Davis Collection. Bequest of Theodore M. Davis, 1915.
Photo on page 43, Wide World Photos, Inc.
Photo on page 44, George Holton/Photo Researchers, Inc.
Photo on page 45, The Metropolitan Museum of Art, gift of Mr. and Mrs. Everit Macy, 1923.
Photo on page 47, The Metropolitan Museum of Art, Rogers Fund, 1925
All photo research for this book was provided by Roberta Guerrette.
Every effort has been made to trace the ownership of all copyright material in this book and to obtain permission for its use.

Library of Congress Number: 77-10445

Library of Congress Cataloging in Publication Data

Holmes, Burnham, 1942-
　Nefertiti: the mystery queen.

　SUMMARY: The life of Nefertiti concentrating on the period during which her husband, Amenhotep IV, struggled to change the ancient forms of worship in Egypt from many gods to one, the sun god.
　1. Egypt—History—To 332 B.C.—Juvenile literature. 2. Nefertiti, Queen of Egypt, 14th cent. B.C.—Juvenile literature. 3. Amenhotep IV, King of Egypt, 1388–1358 B.C.—Juvenile literature.
　[1. Nefertiti, Queen of Egypt, 14th cent. B.C. 2. Queens. 3. Egypt—History—To 332 B.C.] I. Title.
DT87.45.H64　　932'01'0924 [B] [92]　　77-10445

ISBN 0-8172-1056-3 hardcover library binding

ISBN 0-8114-6863-1 softcover binding

16 17 18 19 20 21　97 96 95 94 93 92 91

CONTENTS

Chapter 1

THE SEARCH BEGINS

The year was 1912. The setting was the ancient ruins of Tell el-Amarna in Middle Egypt. A group of German archeologists was digging to find the ancient city named Akhetaton.

Finding a stone tablet, the archeologists stopped to translate the picture writings on its face. The tablet told them they were presently in the workroom of Tuthmose, "the Chief Craftsman, Sculptor, and Favorite of the King." This room had been built more than 3,000 years ago!

Suddenly one of the archeologists struck something hard with his shovel. Perhaps the scientists were getting close to their ancient city.

The picture writings on stone tablets from Tell el-Amarna
describe much of what we know about the ancient Egyptians.

The other workers gathered around to scrape
the sand away. What they saw astonished them.
First a flesh-colored neck appeared. Then they
saw the face of a woman—her eyes of rock crystal stared up at them. On her head was a blue
crown. The crown was decorated with an Egyptian cobra—the symbol of Egyptian royalty.

The German scientists soon learned that they had made one of the most important discoveries of their time. The stone head they had uncovered was indeed a royal one. It was the face of Nefertiti, ancient Egypt's mystery queen. Their find raised many questions all over the world. Little if anything was known about this beautiful queen. No one was sure she ever really lived at all! She lived and died quite mysteriously. Now, perhaps, more of her secrets would be revealed. Who was Queen Nefertiti? When did she live? Why was she so important and yet so mysterious? What really happened to her?

Nefertiti's name never appeared in official Egyptian records. It was thought she lived only in Egyptian stories. Since the stone head was found, Egyptian experts tried to put together the puzzle of her life.

Here is Nefertiti's story—the story of an Egyptian queen. It is told as if she were telling it today.

Chapter 2

NEFERTITI SPEAKS

I lived during a good age for my country, more than 3,000 years ago.

We had strong leaders and strong priests. Our armies and navies won wars with foreign lands. Egypt overflowed with gold. Our artists built huge, beautiful temples for the gods. Great tombs honored our dead kings and their families. It seemed as if Egypt ruled the world. At least as much of the world as we knew.

I was born in 1384 B.C. in the royal city of Thebes. My name, Nefertiti, means "the Beautiful One Has Come." My mother, Tiy, was the Royal Nurse for the family of King Amenhotep

III and Queen Tiy. But my mother was more than just their nurse. She and the Queen were very close friends. Both of them came from poor families. (As you have probably noticed, my mother's name was the same as the Queen's. She did this to honor the Queen.)

My father's name was Aye. Although few have heard of him, Aye was a very important person in the history of ancient Egypt.

My father started out simply enough. He had no wealth or family title. He searched for a career and decided to become a scribe, a writer for the King's important records. Scribes were very important in our day because few people could read or write. It took my father years to learn *hieroglyphics*—a system of pictures that stood for words in ancient Egypt.

When he finished his schooling, my father went to work for King Amenhotep III. Aye was very good at his work and soon became the chief scribe. This allowed him to sit in on every important decision the King made.

Aye was smart and hardworking. It wasn't long before Amenhotep III appointed him Grand Vizier (which was like a minister of state).

My father-in-law, Amenhotep III, is pictured in a wall painting with his mother.

My father was no longer just writing down the King's laws, he was *making* them!

Our family (which now included my younger sister, Nezemmut) lived near the palace of the King. My childhood was spent playing in and around the royal palace and by the banks of the Nile with my best friend, Amenhotep. He was the King's son.

Amenhotep was a year older than I and had the same name as his father. He was the oldest son and would someday be the king. As you might imagine, this was a big responsibility even when he was a young prince. Not that he didn't like to play. He enjoyed watching a new litter of royal kittens or trying to spear the quick, darting bolti fish as much as I did. But as time passed, he spent more time with his father and less with me. Amenhotep had much to learn if he was to be a good king in the future.

In addition to being the King's scribe and Grand Vizier, my father was also the Commander of Horse. This meant that he was in charge of all the King's chariots. The Commander of Horse was saluted by those entering the palace. The visitors would first salute the

Amenhotep and I enjoyed long hours together hunting wild birds and spearing bolti fish.

King and Queen, then the Commander and his chariots and horses.

Oh yes, before I forget, my father was also the Prince's tutor. There was no one in the kingdom as able to give him a good education as my father. And Amenhotep was a good student. He was always asking questions. As far as I know, he always received an answer.

Chapter 3

GROOMED TO BE QUEEN

I was very young when the Queen and my mother realized that I might very well marry Prince Amenhotep. We loved each other as brother and sister. So, although I didn't receive much formal education (certainly not like the Prince's), I was groomed to be the future queen.

When I put away my playthings for the last time, there were many women of the court to wait on me. They would bathe me, apply make-up, and dress me for the day. This took many hours. The Egyptians thought women should always look beautiful. Everyone wanted to make sure that I was as beautiful as the meaning of my name.

During this time, I could go anywhere, even into the busy streets of Thebes. Unlike the old days, Egyptian women were now allowed to appear alone in public, to own property, and to be on an equal basis with men. King Amenhotep III had a lot to do with these new rights of women. I'm glad his son also felt the same way. And why not? Two of the most important people in his life were women, Queen Tiy and I!

Thebes, the royal city where we lived, was beautiful. But King Amenhotep III wanted to make it even more beautiful. He needed someone to plan and carry out the many building projects he had in mind. And the perfect man to do this was my father. Aye had studied geometry and science to become a scribe and was always interested in designing and building. Aye's most impressive buildings were the *Colossi of Memnon*, the *Temple of Luxor*, and the burial tomb called *Kom el Haitan*.

The Colossi of Memnon were statues of Amenhotep III and Queen Tiy carved of stone and over 50 feet high. We had hundreds of gods in those days, and the Temple of Luxor was built to honor the god of our city—the sun god Amon. Not only was the Temple of Luxor holy, it was also beautiful. It was connected to Queen Tiy's palace by a garden that was over a mile long and full of trees and flowers.

Kom el Haitan was located in the Valley of the Kings, where many kings of the past were buried. The building of burial tombs began during a king's lifetime. Death was a very important event for us. We loved life and wanted to enjoy it forever. We believed we could live again in a new life after death. To protect our treasures and bodies, we had great tombs built. The tombs of our most important kings were built

My father, Aye, was proud of the Temple of Luxor, built to honor the sun-god Amon.

Both Amenhotep III and Queen Tiy had giant tombs built in the Valley of the Kings.

into the Pyramids. Some of these giant stone triangle-shaped buildings remain standing even today.

Not only were the tombs built to last, but they were supplied with everything the king and his royal family would need in the other world. There were food, wine, and treasures such as you've never seen.

Many of my people spent all their lives in "the city of the dead." Their job was to prepare the royal bodies for the new life after death. This was not an easy job. It took great skill and training. The vital organs were removed from the body. These organs were placed in large decorated jars. Carved stones in the shape of beetles were put into the body in place of the organs. The stones had holy writings on them. The bodies were then drained, treated with chemicals, and wrapped in cloth. All this was done to preserve the bodies for all time. Some of our mummies are still in perfect shape and can be seen in modern museums—*thousands of years after death.*

After the long burial process, the dead were ready to meet the god *Osiris.* The person who had led a good life and done good works could join Osiris and live forever.

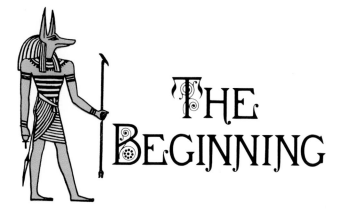

Chapter 4

THE
BEGINNING

In 1372 B.C., the health of Amenhotep III was beginning to fail. He asked his 13-year-old son to rule with him. In ancient Egypt, children had to grow up quickly. When we were in our early teens, we were looked upon as adults.

Young Amenhotep readily learned the role of a king. Each day people came to the palace to have their arguments settled. Amenhotep settled more and more of these disputes with patience, good sense, and fairness. His father was pleased. The prince was wise beyond his years.

One day as I entered the throne room I knew something had changed. King Amenhotep III was nowhere to be seen. Then Queen Tiy

The new King—Amenhotep IV.

told me that he had decided to step down from the throne. His son, now called Amenhotep IV, was to be the sole ruler of Egypt. The year was 1369 B.C.

The coronation of a king was an elaborate and solemn occasion. It was held in the Temple of Amon. The incense was so thick you could see it. First, the priests of Amon, dressed in white robes and leopard skins, entered carrying the golden statue of Amon. My father, Aye, was among them. Then the old King and the new King came into view. I couldn't take my eyes off Amenhotep.

The new King was dressed from head to foot in gold. He even wore a gold beard. At the end of the ceremony, his father placed the crown on his head and kissed his cheek. *Amenhotep IV was now king.* As they moved to the palace, you could hear the people of Thebes shouting, "Long live the King! Long live the King!" All Egypt celebrated for days.

One evening my father entered my chamber and told me that the King wanted to see me. Aye looked happy but said no more. When we entered the palace, Amenhotep IV was seated on his throne. Standing nearby were his parents

When Amenhotep IV and I were married, royal portraits were made.

and my mother. King Amenhotep IV looked over to me and smiled. He told me that he had just been reading the writing on the holy stone from his parent's wedding. It said: "Amenhotep, son of the Sun, ruler of Thebes, living eternally, and the King's great wife Tiy, the immortal."

Amenhotep IV had decided to marry. I, Nefertiti, was his choice. Believe it or not, Amenhotep IV was just 16, and I was only 15!

We were married in the Temple of Amon. The ceremony lasted several days, but it seemed a short time to me. We were entertained with dancing, singing, and much feasting. The rich and powerful toasted us with wine. We could hear the people in the streets singing, "May your marriage last a million, million years." For the second time in a row, a king was marrying a commoner. *Hathor,* the goddess of love and joy, had been most kind to me. I was grateful and so happy. *Little did I know what fate awaited me!*

In the months that followed, we sat proudly on our thrones. I had trouble remembering we were not only royalty now; we were also like gods. To the people of Egypt, we had become divine.

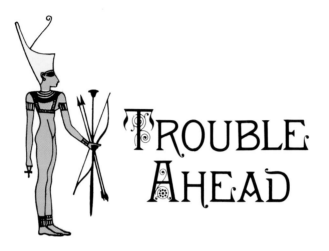

Chapter 5

TROUBLE AHEAD

During this time, Amenhotep IV became very interested in religion. He spent hours discussing the role of the gods with Aye. He wanted to know more about *Re*, a sun god. Amenhotep began to worry the important members of his court. He had odd ideas for a king. Why was he interested in sun worship through a new god and not in Amon? Then Amenhotep announced that he now believed the supreme god was not Amon at all, but a god named *Aton*—the sun itself. *This new belief got us all into a lot of trouble.*

The more the King talked, the more I believed he might be right—Aton, not Amon, could be the most powerful of the gods. You can imagine how the priests of Amon started to worry. The priests knew that this new thinking might be their end. They tried to discourage the King but couldn't. They even tried to convince me, but I agreed with Amenhotep because I knew his secret. He told me why he believed in the new god.

Amenhotep IV wanted a sign from the gods. One night he went to the Temple of Amon. He stood in front of the statue of Amon. Nothing happened. He returned and spent a sleepless night, wondering why a new king would not have a message from the most powerful of the Egyptian gods.

Amenhotep woke me just before dawn. We walked out onto the balcony. Only a few guards were on duty. The city was still deep in sleep. Then in the east, the edge of the sun came into view. The sun seemed to be the only thing in all the world, other than us. Amenhotep was very excited. It was the sign. He was sure. Aton, the sun itself, was the true god of kings. He took my hand in his and said, "Nefertiti, now that I am King, many things will change." Amenhotep later wrote of this new feeling:

Thou appearest beautifully on
the horizon of heaven,
Thou living Aton, the beginning of life!

Amenhotep IV ordered that a Temple of
Aton be built at Karnak. The priests of Amon
didn't like it. They said it would upset the way
things were. But Amenhotep IV commanded
that the city of Thebes be known as "No-Aton,
the City of Aton."

Amenhotep IV changed his name from
Amenhotep ("Amon Is Satisfied") to *Akhenaton*
("He Who Is Beneficial to Aton"). He gave me
the name of *Neferneferuaton* ("Beautiful Is the
Beauty of Aton"). The priests were beside them-
selves. This was the final insult.

I tried to reason with the priests. After all,
what was the difference between Amon and
Aton? One was the sun god. The other was the
sun itself. "The difference," I said, "is small."
But I knew it wasn't. The King was saying that
Aton was the one true god, *the only god.*

For centuries, the Egyptians had been wor-
shipping *hundreds* of gods. Even the crocodile
was holy to us. The priests knew that if there

were only one god, everything the Egyptians had believed was now open to question.

My husband went even further. Akhenaton was upset. Just building a temple for Aton at Karnak wasn't good enough. Every important god had a special place. Karnak was located in Thebes and Amon was already the god of Thebes. Memphis had Sekhmet, a woman with the head of a lion. Akhenaton wanted the same for Aton—a special place that belonged only to this god. The King left by chariot with some new priests of Aton to search for just such a place.

Giant statues lined the Avenue of the Sphinx at Karnak.

There are stories that he drove his golden chariot until the sun was directly overhead. And then he stopped. But I know that Akhenaton chose the place because it was so beautiful. It was bounded on one side by the Nile and on the other side by cliffs.

There he drove wood stakes to mark the place where the new city—Akhetaton—would stand. On one of the stakes, he wrote, "I have made Akhetaton for my father, Aton, forever and ever."

And a good omen soon appeared. We had a baby—a beautiful baby girl. We named her Meritaton ("Beloved of Aton").

Akhenaton drove his golden chariot to find a place to build the city of Akhetaton.

Chapter 6

AKHETATON

Akhenaton returned to Thebes bursting with ideas for his new city. He chose a man named Bek to be his royal architect. Together they drew up the plans. The city was to be two miles long and a half-mile wide. The first thing to be built was, of course, a temple for Aton. Next would come the Great Palace and then palaces for Akhenaton's family.

Through the center of the city would run the King's Highway. Akhetaton would be the first *planned* city in history.

It was the spring of 1368 B.C. We were busy with preparations for building the new city. Workers and supplies would have to be moved there. A fleet of barges was loaded with people and goods for the 240-mile trip down the Nile River. From his throne on the royal barge, Akhenaton announced: "Whoever has purpose with the King must come to Aton's city."

The busy port of Thebes was now still. Thebes was no longer the City of Kings. A city yet to be built down river was now the capital of Egypt. As the barges, under their colorful flags, drifted down the muddy river, the priests of Amon watched their power slowly slipping away. My father was the only cheerful priest in the city. Aye was now a priest of Aton.

When we arrived, a large town of tents was set up and work began immediately. Workers went off to the nearby cliffs to cut stone. Others cleared the land. From the shade of the royal tent, I watched the work with Meritaton and our second daughter, Meketaton ("Virtue of Aton"). The blocks were fitted together for the Temple of Aton.

"The House of the Sun," as it was often called, was a tremendous building a half-mile

Akhenaton and I made special offerings to our great god Aton.

These few stone blocks are all that remain of the once-great temple of Akhenaton at Karnak.

long, ringed with columns and filled with altars and tables for making offerings. When it was completed, Akhenaton and I led the people inside. We both made offerings to Aton and my name appeared alongside the King's on monuments. Meritaton shook a *sistrum* (the rattle used in religious ceremonies), and I placed lotus blossoms on the altar. Akhenaton led the people in prayer: "The living Aton, the lord of all that the sun encircles, he who illuminates Egypt, the lord of sunbeams."

Some time afterwards, the Great Palace was ready for us. The walls were made of dried blocks of mud from the Nile. They were painted with scenes of all that Aton shone upon. Everything in the palace—from a wall painting of an antelope to the sun-shaped mirrors—was fashioned by our artists.

When the royal family appeared at the "window of appearances," the crowds below greeted us. As the cheering faded, Akhenaton spoke: "Grant a great age to the Queen Nefertiti, long years may she keep the hand of the King. Grant a great age to the royal daughter Meritaton and to the royal daughter Meketaton and to their children; may they keep the hand of the Queen, their mother, forever."

Afterwards we all stood on the bridge between the Great Palace and the King's house and watched the many chariots below. To the south, men were already at work on a smaller temple, the "Mansion of the Aton." We crossed the bridge to the garden so that the princesses could play near the lake. They would try to catch bolti fish with their bare hands as their father and I had when we were children. It was a glorious day.

Another palace, the North Palace, was built especially for me. And off in the distance, our tombs were underway.

For the rich people of our city there were private estates. The workers too had houses. Everyone in Akhetaton had a place to live. It was the most beautiful city the world had ever seen. There may *never* be a more beautiful one.

There was even a special section of the city for the many artists who decorated every part of the city with their work. The most well-known of these artists was Tuthmose, who lived on the Street of Sculptors. He carved and molded statue after statue of royalty, the wealthy, and even the poor. I was particularly pleased with one he did of me and I gave him a lotus *amulet* (or charm) to bring him good luck and long life.

Our artists were given great new freedom. Before our time, artists showed kings as great military leaders and as gods on earth. Akhenaton didn't pretend to be either.

Our artists were allowed to show things as they really were. So there were portraits of Akhenaton that were not very flatttering—flat head, big belly, things like that. And they showed our family as we really were. We were a family who enjoyed each other and expressed affection. Akhenaton and I sitting on the same size stools. Our children, drawn not as small adults, but as children, with their loving parents.

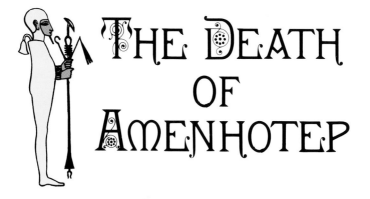

Chapter 7

The Death of Amenhotep

In 1361 B.C., Amenhotep III, my husband's father, died. Akhenaton returned to Thebes. I stayed behind in Akhetaton to care for the princesses. We now had four beautiful daughters, but we were still hoping for a son. Akhenaton was very unhappy with me. He so wanted an heir to the throne.

It was sad to receive Akhenaton's messages about how Queen Tiy and the people of Thebes poured dust over their heads in their grief. He sent word to me that the priests of Amon were now openly enemies of their King. They hated our new city and our worship of Aton. Akhenaton even heard them discussing the time when a *true king* would once again rule the land from Thebes. I was a little afraid for Akhenaton's safety.

After the two months of mourning for his father, Akhenaton came back to his beloved city. While he was away, I had ordered a prayer carved in the stone of a nearby cliff: "Grant to thy son who loves thee, life and truth to the lord of the land, that he may live united with thee in eternity. As for his wife, the Queen Nefertiti, may she live forever eternally by his side, well pleasing to thee; she admires what thou hast created day by day."

Akhenaton was overjoyed to be back. Once again we turned to a life spent in the worship of Aton and the building of his holy city.

But the beginnings of bad fortune were upon us. Once started, our bad luck never ceased. Death visited us once again. Our daughter Meketaton died. The King and I suffered great grief. We buried Meketaton in the unfinished Royal Tomb. Even when we had two more children, the Princesses Baqtaton and Setepenaton, our grief lingered on.

The priests of Amon did not approve of Akhenaton's belief in only one god. They plotted to destroy Akhenaton's power.

Akhenaton, in his great sadness, could no longer allow the worship of the false god, Amon. He ordered the destruction of Amon's name all over Egypt. It was a dangerous thing to do. The priests of Amon called Akhenaton a traitor. I feared what the outcome of my husband's actions might be. We soon found out.

All over Egypt the priests of Amon were growing in strength. They were plotting against Akhenaton. The enemies of Egypt, upon hearing of this religious dispute, were growing bolder in their attacks on Egypt's lands. I warned Akhenaton of the danger. Even Aye, whom he had trusted throughout his life, was unable to persuade Akhenaton of the danger.

The people of Egypt did not side with Akhenaton. Even though he told them that the true way was to worship Aton, they wouldn't change. How, they asked, could one god take over for their hundreds of gods? They wanted another king—one like Akhenaton's father. They wanted a king who was a warrior and statesman, not a religious man. A revolution was growing in Egypt. I could *feel* it!

In 1359 B.C., Queen Tiy's body returned to Thebes on a funeral barge to join her husband in his tomb. It was a very sad time for us all.

In 1356 B.C., Akhenaton was only 29 years old. But already there were many who posed threats to his reign. My father and I warned Akhenaton of the many dangers to him and to Egypt. The Hittites were taking over lands formerly held by Egypt. Foreign kings sent messages to the "Lord of the Two Lands" beseeching him to "bring help, before it is too late." But the King ignored all warnings.

One day as we walked to the sunshade temples, we heard of the rebellion in the army. Soldiers were fighting with their officers. That night Aye talked to Akhenaton. He told him that Egypt was about to collapse.

Somehow the King would have to get back the confidence of the military and the priests of Amon. Akhenaton was very upset. "Does that mean," he asked, "that the royal city will be moved from Akhetaton to Thebes? Will Thebes once again be 'No-Amon,' the City of Amon?" The look in my father's eyes told him the answer he did not want to hear. Akhenaton said nothing. He just turned and walked slowly back to the Temple of Aton.

All around us I saw our world crumbling. One daughter was dead. Another daughter had moved far away to Babylonia where she married the prince. Our daughter, Meritaton, turned against her father and me. She went to Thebes, where the priests of Amon tried to make her the Queen of Egypt in my place.

The more troubled times became, the less Akhenaton was able to do anything about it. I remember his once saying that he wished he could have been a priest. That, he said, would have

Our daughter Meritaton's head, as it was carved for the lid of a stone jar.

made him happy. He wanted to be left alone. He wanted to talk not with me but only his god Aton.

Not knowing what else to do, I left Akhenaton and went to live in the North Palace with my youngest daughter. When I got there, a lady-in-waiting told me that my daughter Meritaton's name had replaced mine in my own sunshade temple.

Chapter 8

THE END

Years passed. It was 1353 B.C. Akhenaton finally came to live with me. It was heartbreaking to see him such a beaten man. None of his old enthusiasm remained. One afternoon he stood looking out to the fields. "All cattle are at peace in their pasture," he said. These were the last words I heard him speak. He died soon afterwards. He was only 32 years old when he was placed in his tomb. I made sure his long poem, "Hymn to Aton," was carved on the walls where he could read it:

When thou settest in the western horizon,
Thy land is in darkness, in the
manner of death.

Before the tomb was sealed, I placed a figure of a bolti fish next to him to remind him of the good days.

In 1352 B.C., I proclaimed a young boy of our city—Tutankhaton—King of Egypt. He would take my youngest daughter—Ankhesenaton—as his queen. They would have to move to Thebes to try to bring the country back together again. I would never again see my child or her husband, the King.

Aye also returned to Thebes and even took up the leopard skin of a priest of Amon. Once again, he became the Grand Vizier. With pressure from the priests of Amon, King Tutankhaton changed his name to Tutankhamon and Ankhesenaton changed her name to Ankhesenamon. Throughout Egypt the god Amon replaced Aton. Only in our city of Akhetaton was Aton worshipped.

The next eight years in Akhetaton were difficult ones. Barges no longer stopped at our docks and the King's Highway was deserted. There were no longer artists busy at work. Weeds, rather than flowers, grew in the parks. Almost everyone had returned to Thebes.

In 1344 B.C., young King Tutankhamon died. My father looked around for the next king. I was out of favor and unmarried. There were no male heirs. So, Aye chose himself to be king. His claim to the throne was that he was related to a queen. Certainly no one in Egypt was more qualified to be king.

The mask of the boy king, Tutankhamon, was discovered in his tomb in the Valley of the Kings.

Much of our life in ancient Egypt can be seen in the wall paintings in our tombs.

Just as he tried to keep alive our family rule, Aye tried to keep alive the memory of Akhenaton. As King, he added on to the Temple of Aton started by Akhenaton at Karnak so long ago. But by this time, Aye was old. He wouldn't be able to stay in power long.

I felt that there was only one thing to do. I wrote to the Hittite king, our archenemy, and asked if I or my daughter could marry one of his sons. It was a desperate move, but it seemed the only way to save the kingdom. A prince was sent, but he was killed by Harmhab's troops. Harmhab wanted the throne for himself.

44

My father died in 1342 B.C. After over 50 years of faithful service to four kings, my father, as King himself, was dead. He was buried in the Valley of the Kings.

A favorite of the priests of Amon, Harmhab, took over the throne. He tore down the Temple of Aton at Karnak and built two towers in front

Harmhab,
the commander-in-chief
of Tutankhamon's armies.

of the Temple of Amon. With the backing of the priests, he declared that he had actually been king since 1369 B.C.—as if Akhenaton, Tutankhamon, and Aye had never existed. *As if I, Nefertiti, had never lived.*

One afternoon a messenger ran up to me, bowed low, and told me that troops of Harmhab were on their way to wreck the city of Akhetaton. They had vowed to level it to the sands of the desert. After he left, I walked to the Temple of Aton. In the west, the sun was just fading over the Nile. "Oh, Aton, sun of the heavens and the earth. When thou settest in the western horizon, Thy land is in darkness in the manner of death."

Now I am dead these 3,000 years. Nothing more is known about me, about my husband, or my children. I went to my tomb with the secrets of my life . . . *and my death.* In the last years of my husband's life, he was angry with me. I couldn't produce a male heir. Not only that, I had begged his sworn enemy to marry me. Those last years of my life made me do things I will always regret.

In 1912, German archaeologists discovered the statue of Queen
Nefertiti, Egypt's Queen of Mystery.

The tombs and mummies of Akhenaton and Nefertiti have never been found. It was once reported that a villager was seen carrying a golden coffin down a mountainside. Soon afterwards, jewelry bearing Nefertiti's name was being sold in local shops. But apparently, it is only a legend.

Perhaps someday someone will discover her tomb. And then the final chapter on Queen Nefertiti, Egypt's Queen of Mystery, can be written. Now we can only guess.

Was Nefertiti's walk to the temple her *last* walk? How did Nefertiti die? Was she killed by her own hand? Or was it at the hands of others? Was Nefertiti a religious traitor? These questions remain unanswered. But the search for Nefertiti continues.

THE CARD

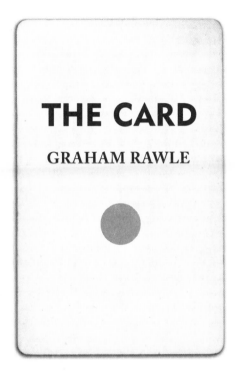

THE CARD

GRAHAM RAWLE

ATLANTIC BOOKS
LONDON

First published in hardback in Great Britain in 2012 by
Atlantic Books, an imprint of Atlantic Books Ltd.

1 2 3 4 5 6 7 8 9

A CIP catalogue record for this book is available
from the British Library.

Hardback ISBN: 978 085789 124 2
Standard E-Book ISBN: 978 085789 764 0
Colour E-Book ISBN: 978 085789 846 3

Designed and illustrated by Graham Rawle
www.grahamrawle.com

Printed by Ten Brink in Meppel, The Netherlands

Atlantic Books
An imprint of Atlantic Books Ltd
Ormond House
26–27 Boswell Street
London
WC1N 3JZ

www.atlantic-books.co.uk

In memory of my lovely dad

DENIS LESLIE RAWLE

1924—2010

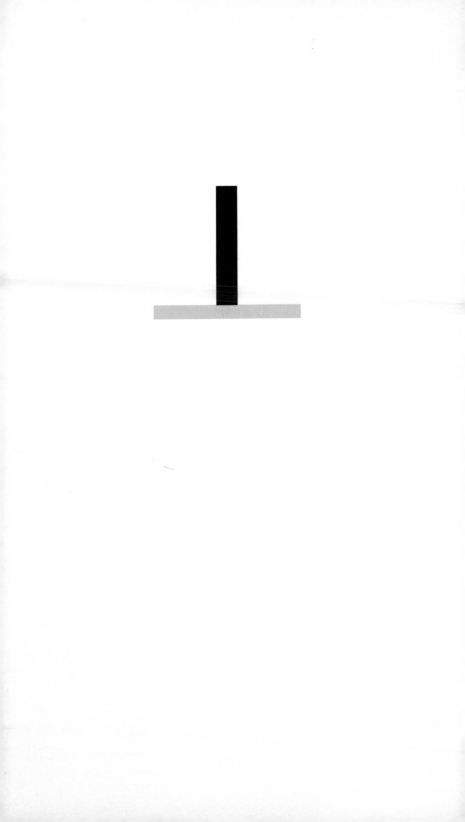

ONE

THIS IS THE way I see things.

1967. A young man, cigarette in mouth, works a sheet-fed offset printing press. Two older men are busy in the background. Machines and noise. The young man wipes his hands on a dirty rag as he watches a pretty secretary in a mini-skirt pass through the print shop. He's a family man, but she seems nice. Given that this is the swinging sixties you might expect him to be sporting a mod Carnaby Street hairdo and 'If You're Going to San Francisco' moustache, but he actually has more of an Elvis look about him. Some might put him closer to Engelbert Humperdinck, but his co-workers opt for the more obvious reference. His hair is longish, in the modern trend, but it retains the toppling teddy-boy quiff of his teenage years, along with the wide, flaring sideburns, like miniature trouser legs straddling his face. He's dark and handsome—but where Elvis glows with flawless Max Factor gold, the printer's complexion is lardy and pitted with inky blackheads.

Sheets of card stock fall one atop the other as they clatter through the machine. The noise is relentless. A Vitalis-slick swag of hair falls like a curtain across the Elvis brow as he leans over to check the job. The machine rhythmically pumps the sheets out one by one. The job in progress is for Chad Ltd, a bubble-gum card series of photo stills from the popular TV show, *Mission: Impossible*. The colourful, playing-card-sized pictures sit in neat rows, six images by eight: the entire series of forty-eight printed on one sheet, ready to be guillotined, mixed and packed, five cards at a time, along with a thin rectangle of pink bubble-gum in a deliciously slippery wax-pack wrapper. The constant blurring movement as each subsequent sheet slides into place frustrates any attempt to focus on a particular image.

The boss enters and strains to make himself heard. Elvis turns. The boss points at the press and then strokes his index finger across his throat. Understanding the mime, Elvis touches the greasy button and kills the machine. Less noise now, but other machines continue to shake, rattle and roll.

"What's up, Mr Greenwood?"

"How many have you done?"

"Just these." Elvis indicates the thick wad of printed sheets.

"They're withdrawing one of the cards."

"Why?"

"God knows, but we've got to start again with a new plate. They're sending replacement artwork. There must be some legal issue because Chad wants all prints from this run to be destroyed. Get Sid to cut them through on the guillotine before you bin them."

"Which card is it?"

"They didn't say. Anyway, get rid of this lot and start on that Burton's job."

The boss starts to leave. Elvis calls him back. "Is it all right if I take a sheet home for my lad? He loves *Mission: Impossible*"

"No, it bloody isn't."

"I'll make sure it doesn't leave the house, Mr Greenwood."

"Absolutely not. If that cancelled card surfaces somewhere, I don't want Chad blaming us."

The boss leaves. Elvis stacks the printed sheets on a trolley and wheels them over to the guillotine. Sid, one of the older workers, is busily stacking postcards, whistling loudly. There's a tune playing on the tinny transistor radio, but it's not the same one. Elvis realizes that his co-worker hasn't seen him. Seizing the opportunity, he checks to make sure that no one else is watching before sliding a sheet from the top of the pile and tucking it surreptitiously behind one of the machines. Sid turns and Elvis hands him the pile, leaning in to his ear to pass on Mr Greenwood's instructions.

Late afternoon. Elvis bids goodnight to various co-workers as he leaves for home. He moves a little self-consciously as he passes the boss's office. The secretary glances at him discreetly, but nobody notices that protruding from one of Elvis's raincoat sleeves is a stiff white cuff of rolled cardboard.

Later the same evening. The *Mission: Impossible* sheet lying flat on a bedroom carpet. Elvis crouches beside a ten-year-old boy who kneels prayer-like before it, poring with wonder over the colourful pictures.

"Can I cut it up into cards?"

"Wouldn't you rather keep it as a poster? Put it on the wall? It would look great over your bed."

"No, I want them as cards so I can take them to school."

"Oh no, son, you can't do that. You'd get me fired. This series isn't even out yet. You must keep it here in your bedroom. Promise?" Elvis points a warning finger to show that he is serious. The boy reluctantly agrees. They shake. It's a pact.

Next day. A huddle in the school playground. The boy's hands dealing through a set of *Mission: Impossible* cards with inexpertly

550

cut edges. Other boys gather round the coveted collection. Blazers jostle, grubby fingers prod and paw; things are getting out of control. *Cor, where d'you get them? Give us a look. Do you want to swap?* The boy shakes his head and tries to return the cards to his pocket, hoping to put an end to it, but as he does, someone makes a grab for them, knocking the cards from his grasp. They scatter to the ground and the ravenous pack pounce, scrabbling to pick them up. The anguished boy struggles to assert ownership.

880

Well, that's no good. I've just done a word count: 880 so far, and I've only told the very beginning of the lost-card story. *The Lost Card.* That's quite good. I might use that as the title for my piece. Or maybe just *The Card.* The editor told me 2,000 words maximum and there's a long way to go.

The article is for *Card Collector Monthly*, a specialist magazine for collectors of cigarette cards, trade and bubble-gum cards. I've written to the editor, Michael Mallinsay, on numerous occasions before, usually to point out factual errors or to suggest features on specific bubble-gum series, but most recently to propose my contributing a thesis on the origin and mysterious disappearance, thirty years ago, of the now legendary **card number 19** from the 1967 *Mission: Impossible* series. He wrote back saying he'd be delighted to consider such a piece for publication for their *Readers Writes* section, which I took to mean that there would be no fee involved. The first part of my story, covering the genesis of the card—how it became the sole surviving example, and the circumstances that launched it into general circulation—is probably too long, but I want to give the readers something of the flavour and atmosphere of the period before I get on to the factual stuff.

I'd been so engrossed in writing my article that I'd missed a call from Hector Goodall, who had left a message on my answering machine. An item he thought might interest me had come in. It's probably nothing special, but you never know.

There's usually a bloke with a wagon outside the Queen's Head on **R**ookery **R**oad, selling cockles and whelks, but he wasn't there today. In his place, a ruddy-faced man in a grey tracksuit stood behind a wallpaper-pasting table selling little polythene red white and blue Union Jacks, perhaps anticipating that a bout of lunchtime drinking might induce flag-waving patriotism in the pub's customers. *Five for a pound, your flags.* He shouted the price to nobody in particular as he stabbed their plastic poles into an offcut of white polystyrene. I noticed he was selling disposable cigarette lighters as a sideline—also five for a pound.

A poster in the window of Books Etc announced that one of the so-called stars of *Coronation Street* has written a book, *Life on the Street*, a candid account of her twenty years as Britain's best-loved soap queen, and that the store will be hosting a book-signing event next Thursday at 2.00 p.m. Suddenly everyone on television is an author; the real writers no longer get a look-in. To get on the bestseller list today, Dostoevsky would need to have his own daytime TV show, or become a regular on *Ready, Steady, Cook.*

I shan't be going. I'm no stranger to celebrity, so I tend to be less easily impressed than most. I've met dozens of famous stars, like **Bob Monkhouse**, merry master of mirth, and the lovely **Katie Boyle**. You'll remember her, of course, as the iconic presenter of the Eurovision Song Contest in the sixties and seventies, as well as for her television adverts for Pink Camay beauty soap with the creamy rich lather. Later on, she had breast reduction surgery; I read about it in one of the magazines. Not sure why. They didn't seem especially big to me.

Members of the public will be familiar with **B**ob **M**onkhouse as the veteran comedian and popular TV game show host,

X but might not be aware of his interest in calligraphy. It was a surprise to me too, but when he signed my **autograph** book, he used a proper fountain pen and he had beautiful handwriting. Celebrities generally use whatever pen you give them, but Bob produced his own from the inside pocket of his sleek suit jacket. It had evidently perspired a little under the hot stage lights of the Futurist Theatre, Scarborough, because when he came to sign, he accidentally made an ink smudge on the facing page. Bob suggested I save that one for his comedy rival, **Jimmy Tarbuck**. Bob's a real joker. **F**ay **F**oyne or Toyne or something, a tennis player—can't read her writing. I met these people when I was just a kid, and long before **B**arry **M**anilow burst into the charts with his 1975 hit, 'Mandy'. Can you imagine the look on **B**ob **M**onkhouse's face today if I told him that **Barry Manilow**, the greatest singer-songwriter in the world, is actually my cousin? If he knew that, Bob might whip out his fountain pen and ask *me* for *my* autograph instead!

I don't collect autographs any more. Living in London, you see people off the telly all the time.—**David Soul** from *Starsky and Hutch*; I almost didn't recognize him. Moustache, fat cigar and big bulging sunglasses that made him look like a blowfly. He had a sweater tied round his neck and one arm draped over the thin shoulders of a young woman wearing **Nancy Sinatra** go-go boots. He must have spotted me trying to locate his eyes behind the reflective lenses because he nodded and said, "All right, pal." His accent sounded more Yorkshire than American, but I'm pretty sure it was him.

Then there was **Lulu**, waiting to get served in the circle bar at the Albery Theatre during the interval of *Blood Brothers*. We stood next to each other for ages because the bar was busy and under-staffed. I could smell her perfume. I made a point not to look directly at her because of her celebrity status, like not staring directly into the sun during an eclipse, but there was a mirror behind the bar so I could watch her without fear of permanent eye damage. Later, when she went to stand with her friends, I noticed that her petite, girlish torso was supported by surprisingly short legs and that she had a larger-than-average-sized head, lending her the bodily proportions of a ventriloquist's dummy. I could have gone over, sat her on my knee and congratulated her on being (joint) winner of the Eurovision Song Contest back in '69 with 'Boom Bang-a-Bang', but decided not to bother her. Famous people don't always want to chat with the public and I'm familiar enough with the world of showbiz to know when to hold back, even though there was the obvious connection with me having met **Katie Boyle** who had hosted the event. Celebrities need their personal space. Barry's the same; he yearns for privacy. It's up to the fans to respect that, but how many of them do? I'm not sure if Barry knows **Lulu**. Even though they share superstar status in the music industry, and Barry has sung duets with just about everyone going, I couldn't say for sure whether their celebrity career paths have ever crossed.

The general consensus among dealers, Hector Goodall included, is that **card 19** from the 1967 *Mission: Impossible* series is a myth, that it doesn't exist and it never did, but a number of us avid collectors are convinced that it's still out there somewhere.

Why a replacement for No. 19 was never issued remains a mystery. At the time, the manufacturers, Chad, were accused of deliberately withholding the card to encourage collectors to buy more. But in 1967 there was no Advertising Standards Authority to monitor such things, or if there was, they chose to do nothing about it.

A card may be withdrawn because of a factual error or in response to complaints that its image is considered likely to corrupt the mind of the juvenile collector. The offending card is quickly replaced by an alternative, and the original becomes collectable, its scarcity depending on how early in the print run the substitution is made. There can be production-error cards too: wrongbacks, where the front and back are misaligned, and blankfronts, where the back is printed as normal but the front has not printed at all and therefore remains blank. Why a collector would pay top price for something like this beats me. Yes, it may be a rarity, but *there's nothing on it*! I have complete sets of nearly all the series that were issued in the 1960s: footballers, pop stars, flags, war, TV detectives, etc., including many of the original cards I collected as a boy—bought with my pocket-money from Morrissey's, the local sweet shop, in packs of four or five cards at threepence a time. I have most of the alternative cards too, but only if the variation is of interest. Blankfronts are for losers. However, the notion of a properly printed card that is the only one in existence, the missing card that completes a series, is the collector's dream. No wonder **M**ichael **M**allinsay is so eager to publish my piece on it. The *Mission: Impossible* **card 19** must be the most sought-after collector card in the world—certainly in the UK. (In America, there are rare baseball cards that fetch over a million dollars. People will kill for a lot less.) The fact that no one knows why the card was recalled makes it even more intriguing. For those who believe it does exist, the big question is whether it has survived the thirty years. Did it end up on a bonfire or at the bottom of a landfill? Does it lie forgotten in an old desk drawer or stowed amongst comics and toys in someone's attic? That's why I enjoy *Antiques Roadshow*; it tends to bring items like this out of hiding. Imagine the experts' faces if someone turned up with it for evaluation. What would this card be worth today, in 1997? That's what everybody on the programme wants to know, isn't it? Well, it's like anything else;

it depends what someone is prepared to pay for it. What would I pay? I couldn't say. I'm not interested in its monetary value; I'm a collector, not a dealer. Who knows, if I don't find it, maybe one day I'll get lucky and the card will find me.

On my way back from Hector's I stopped off at Nell's for a spot of lunch. Nell's a big Manilow fan so I knew she'd be interested.

"Been shopping?" she said brightly.

The carrier bag was a precaution against the unexpected rain that had been forecast. I ordered a tea. While she poured, I showed her what was inside. "Ooh, what's this?" she said, glancing up.

"A rare copy of *Manilow Magic: The Best of Barry Manilow*—signed by Barry himself."

"When are you going to get that autographed picture for me?" Nell turned to the wall behind her as if imagining where it would go. "You've been promising me for ages."

That's the trouble with being related to a celebrity: everyone is always asking for stuff. It's embarrassing. She doesn't have any celebrity pictures apart from one of **Les Dennis** standing in front of the counter, but it's very blurry and you can't really see who it is. It isn't even signed. She did once see *Davy Jones* from The Monkees apparently, walking on the beach in some little seaside town, but she didn't think to ask for his autograph. There's also a printed ten-by-eight promo flier of Coffee and Cream, a local interracial cabaret duo, but I'd hardly call them celebrities. The picture is signed with the practised hand of the not very famous. You can always spot them; they write far too neatly. It's as if the time and effort that goes into the inscription is in inverse proportion to their celebrity status. Barry is just a scrawl.

"It's not that easy, Nell. I can't go bothering him every two minutes for signed photos. I've got loads of people asking for them. He's very busy at the moment; he's got a big European tour coming up."

Nell was keeping the counter ship-shape with a damp J-cloth. "He's got time to sign records for you though."

"I didn't get this from Barry; I got this from Hector Goodall."

"Who's Hector Goodall?"

"Hector Goodall's Emporium on Essex Road. He deals mostly in film and TV memorabilia, but he has quite a lot of records too."

"Why didn't you get Barry to sign it in person, write a personal dedication? I thought he was your cousin."

"He's not in the UK very often. He lives in Palm Springs with his long-time partner, Linda Allen. I told you that."

"So you had to shell out good money?"

"I don't mind paying if it gives Barry a bit of peace and quiet before the tour."

She gazed dreamily at the picture of him on the cover. "Ooh, I'd love to meet him."

That's the funny thing. I can never quite see why Barry's female fans are so attracted to him, especially Nell; she must be nearly fifty now, but was obviously a real looker in her day.

"Well, don't forget to watch him," I said. "Eight o'clock Wednesday. ITV."

"Ooh, yes. Must remember to get a new tape."

She wrote the word 'tape' on her order pad and underlined it three times. "Can't you get me a little photo, Riley? It can't take him a second to sign his name."

It was true; I had promised. And she's a good friend—extra chips and what-have-you and always time to chat. I handed her the record. "Here, Nell. You have it."

"Me?"

"Yes."

"I can't take that, love. It's yours."

"Go on. I want you to have it. Put it up on the wall; it'll look good. I'll get Barry to sign me another one next time I see him."

She seemed genuinely moved by the gesture. "But it must have cost a bit. Let me pay you for it." She opened the till.

I raised my hands in protest. "Forget it. It wasn't that expensive; the record's got a big scratch on side two."

Most people are surprised to discover I'm a **Barry Manilow** fan (or 'Fanilow' as we're sometimes called). To tell you the truth, it's quite a surprise to me too because he's not really my style of entertainer. I probably wouldn't have given him much thought if I hadn't discovered that we are related. But the more you listen, the more the Manilow magic gets hold of you. I don't like everything he does, I'm not one of Barry's 'Maniloonies', and neither is Nell, but I think everyone agrees that 'Could It Be Magic?' is a great song. Even if Chopin did write it first. Then there's the Latinesque 'Copacabana'. And, of course, 'Mandy'. He writes wonderful songs that make the whole world sing, as Barry himself proudly boasts in 'I Write The Songs'. Except he didn't actually write that one; a chap called Bruce Johnston wrote it— which is quite ironic, I suppose.

I noticed that all of the components of today's lunch special began with the letter P: **P**ork, **P**arsnips, **P**otatoes and **P**eas. You don't often see it in restaurants so I decided to order it. Nell asked if I wanted gravy with it and I said no because gravy begins with a G. She didn't get it. It's quite easy to create an alliteration-themed meal at home: **C**hicken with **C**auliflower **C**heese; **B**acon, **B**read and **B**utter, **B**eans. I'm not obsessive about it, but once you start noticing the connections, it can be hard to break the habit. Last night it was **T**urkey and **T**inned **T**omatoes on **T**oast with **T**iramisu. You can get some terrible combinations. Sometimes I wish I'd never started it. I often opt for a straightforward single-plate dish: lasagne or risotto, just to make things easier. For a while, the accompanying drink had to fit too. I don't do that now. **V**enison with a **V**elouté and **V**egetables is delicious with a glass of **V**iognier or a **V**ouvray, but if you're in a place where they don't serve alcohol you're stuck with **V**imto, which I quite like, but makes your breath smell of sick.

I sat at my usual table. Taking my writing pad out of the bag, I began to formulate my third letter of complaint. It had been several weeks since the big swindle, but from time to time the anger and indignation would resurface. That so-called dealer still had my money and was completely ignoring my demands for a full refund. I would lie awake at night getting myself into a lather about it, plotting vengeance. If he lived in London I'd have paid him a visit by now, but the address he had given me was in Leeds. I wasn't prepared to travel two hundred miles to find that his address, like the card, was fake.

I should never have trusted him. The card he had created looked genuine in the photocopy he sent, but without seeing the real thing up close it's impossible to tell. Counterfeit cards are easily identified through direct comparison to the original. Of course, since **card 19** is unique and there is no known documentation of it, the forger is given a huge amount of leeway. Only a handful of people are likely to have seen it and there is much speculation amongst collectors about the card's subject, leaving the forger free to use any image he chooses from *Mission: Impossible* TV production stills, so long as it fits within the style of the other cards in the series. The forger's choice was believable enough: the Impossible Missions Force team leader receiving assignment instructions from a miniature tape recorder, a scene that introduced every episode. The card was authentically yellowed with age, suggesting that it had been printed on real vintage card stock. Clever. The fraudulence, however, was revealed through the dot pattern on the colour printing. The original cards were printed by four-colour-process at around 200 dots per square inch, while this card had been printed on a consumer inkjet printer, creating an entirely different arbitrary dot-matrix pattern—a dead giveaway when viewed through a magnifying loupe. This was further compounded, upon close inspection of the type on the back, by the fact that the letters had the wobble-soft edges of an inkjet printer instead of the characteristically crisp edges created by an offset litho printing process. The clincher, though, was the cleanly cut edges. No awkwardly scissored jagged bits or skewed parallels. The card looked guillotine-perfect. Fake.

I was just getting into my stride with the letter when Nell set down the lunch special in front of me and I had to stow the writing pad in my carrier bag to finish later.

"What are you writing? A love letter?"

"Far from it. It's a letter of complaint. Somebody sold me a fake card."

"Blimey. Another one? They must see you coming."

There had been one or two other forgeries in the past. "I *am* writing something else though, as a matter of fact," I said. "Something proper. I've been commissioned by the editor of *Card Collector Monthly* to write an article for them. Two thousand words."

"Really? Is it going to be in the magazine? With your name on it?"

I nodded. "There might even be a picture."

"Ooh. You'll be famous," she said. "I'll type it up for you if you like. Bring it round when you've finished it."

"I didn't know you could type."

"Ah," she said with playful beguilement. "There's a lot about me you don't know."

The food was good, but a little dry. It could have done with a drop of gravy, actually. By the time I'd finished eating, a table had opened up by the window so I went and sat there. It was then that I spotted him—the man off *Mission: Impossible*. The same one from the fake card—what was his name, the one with the prematurely grey hair? He was wearing a **Prince of Wales** check jacket like in the picture, grey slacks and treacle-toffee brogues. His hair looked soft and freshly shampooed like the girl off the Timotei advert. There he stood, on the edge of the pavement, looking down the street as if waiting for a taxi. I was amazed by the coincidence. I called Nell over.

"Here, quick, Nell."

She was delivering all-day breakfasts to four workmen on table two.

"Quick."

"What?"

"Come and see who's outside."

"Who?"

"Look."

She reluctantly came over.

"It's that bloke off *Mission: Impossible*."

"Tom Cruise?"

"No, not the film, the TV series. *Mission: Impossible*. The one who plays Jim What's-His-Name."—She looked blankly.—"You know. *Your mission, Jim, should you decide to accept it… This tape will self-destruct in five seconds.* Jim Phelps. That was his name."

"Oh yeah. Where? I can't see him."

"There. The bloke with the grey hair," I said, pointing through the window.

"That's not him."

"It is."

"That series came out about thirty years ago. He'd be ninety by now."

"No, he wouldn't. He'd only be in his fifties. Late fifties, maybe."

"How can you tell it's him? You can't see his face."

She rapped sharply on the window with a fifty-pence piece that had been left as a tip by a customer. The man inclined his head slightly, as if unable to locate the source of the tapping. Not enough to show his face, but enough for me to be sure.

"There you are."

"That's not him, you daft sod."

"It is."

Outside on the street the man looked at his watch before setting off towards the junction with Albion Road. Uninterested, Nell turned back to her customers. On an impulse, I decided to follow the man, more to prove to Nell that I was right than anything. She had sounded so dismissive.

I could see him up ahead, moving at quite a lick. He was obviously on a mission and needed to be somewhere in a hurry. I was on a mission too, but my path was suddenly blocked by a middle-aged woman with a clipboard.

"I don't know if you've heard about the Pitch-and-Putt in Mirfield Park." She was wearing a blue nylon tabard over an expensive-looking coat with fur trim.

"The what?" I was trying to keep an eye on Jim Phelps. I could have walked away, but you don't like to seem rude, do you?

"The Pitch-and-Putt mini-golf course in the park. The council are planning to close it down to build a skateboard park in its place."

"Are they?"

"We feel that the mini-golf offers recreation for all ages whereas a skateboard park caters mainly for teenagers, which discriminates against the elderly. And, er, middle-aged."

"Yes, I can see that."

"Will you sign?"

"Sign?"

"Our petition? We've already got nearly a hundred signatures." She turned the clipboard towards me and offered her pen. "All we need is your name and address."

"Yes. I don't see why not. I rather enjoy a game of golf," I said, adding my *signature*. I hadn't played for years, but on several occasions Nell had offered to take me on a proper course like you see on television. She plays at least once a week with her girlfriends. I think she's quite good at it. Besides, it seemed churlish not to support this woman's campaign, in spite of the urgent nature of my quest. Luckily I still had Mr Phelps in my sights.

Down Milton Road. Past Sainsbury's. Up to the shops by the station. I kept my distance, concerned that he might see me and consider my following him a nuisance; I didn't want to look like I was stalking him. I wasn't sure what I was planning to say when I caught up with him. I didn't have a camera to take a photo and I could hardly expect a big American celebrity like him to march down to the post office with me so that we could sit together on the little stool in the passport–photo booth. Nevertheless, an autograph would have been nice and it would prove to Nell that I was right. I had pen and paper, but I was now rather regretting having returned the **card 19** forgery. Even on a fake card, a genuine *signature* would have made a handsome keepsake.

There's an alleyway that runs between a row of houses and You've Been Framed, the picture framers on the corner. I'd never been down there so had no idea where it led. Jim Phelps must have known because he headed straight for it. I hung back at first, watching to see where he went.

Halfway along he stopped, perhaps sensing that he was being followed. I stopped too and tried to appear nonchalant in case he should turn around to confront me, but he didn't; he just stood there, barely moving, as though waiting for something. Then he did an extraordinary thing: he reached into his jacket pocket, took out what looked like a card and tossed it on the ground. With that, he continued walking, heading left into an adjoining alley.

I wasn't sure what he'd dropped—a calling card of some kind? Whatever it was, it seemed important. I suppose it could have been rubbish: some piece of worthless detritus he'd found in his pocket and decided to get rid of while he thought no one was looking—yet it was hard to think of Jim Phelps as a 'litter lout'. Besides, because of the *Mission: Impossible* coincidence, a thought had already occurred to me—that the card he had dropped might somehow be the famous missing No. 19 from the series. The real one, this time. Why would I think this? I don't know. There was no logical reason why it *should* be, but after so many years in pursuit of it, I often imagined that if the coveted card ever *did* fall into my hands, it would be through extraordinary circumstances such as these.

I'd become so engrossed in watching Phelps that it wasn't until he'd gone that I realized I, too, was being watched. The owner of You've Been Framed was eyeing me curiously from inside his shop and had come to the window to get a better look. He stood with his hands on his hips, unashamedly staring at me. Caught off guard, I went through a series of gestures I thought might justify my lurking presence: checking my pockets, looking at my watch, peering up at a For Sale sign on a nearby building. Having established what I felt was a plausible reason for being there, I headed purposefully into the alley and out of the nosy shopkeeper's line of sight.

Once I reached the card I paused for a moment to check the adjoining alleyway in case Phelps was still around, but there was no one there. Twenty yards ahead the alley came to a sudden dead end with a high wall, so I couldn't figure out where he'd gone. There were windowless buildings on either side that seemed to serve as workshops or storage units for the shops that backed on to the alley. Phelps might have slipped into one of these, but as far as I could see, all the doors appeared to be secured by padlocks. Jim Phelps, it seemed, had simply vanished.

The card lay face down on the ground where Phelps had discarded it. From the pattern on the back I could tell straight away that it wasn't **card 19**; it looked like an ordinary playing card. I bent down to pick it up and when I turned it over in my hand I saw that it was the **queen of hearts**. I could find no connection with *Mission: Impossible*, or with anything else, so I'm not entirely sure why I put the card in my pocket. Perhaps because there had been something about the deliberate way he had dropped it—as if it were meant for me.

TWO

I GET MY HAIR CUT at Mr Vann's. He's a highly skilled *hairdresser* who keeps abreast of modern trends while maintaining an unpretentious hairstyling service at down-to-earth prices. What I like most about Mr Vann's set-up is that he doesn't pander to a celebrity clientele like some of the hairdressers you see on television. (No names mentioned, **Nicky Clarke, Trevor Sorbie**.) You won't find any famous heads among the portraits in Mr Vann's window; no boastful claims to have trimmed the goatee of a television newsreader or blow-dried a personality from the world of light entertainment. And even though Mr Vann is well aware of my 'Manilow connection', he treats me just like any other customer.

My appointment was at two thirty so there had been no time to go home and work on my magazine article, but while I waited for my turn in Mr Vann's chair I started thinking about how I might gradually introduce some more general thoughts on card collecting into the piece: card rarities and alternatives, fakes and forgeries, different types of collector—that sort of thing. For the moment though, following the specific story of **card 19**, its origins and subsequent journey, seemed to be gathering momentum so I decided that when I next had the chance to put pen to paper I would continue in that vein.

1967. The boy clutches a pile of *Mission: Impossible* **cards as he sits on a sofa with his Elvisly styled father. They stare straight ahead, mesmerized by the flickering light from the television. The theme from** *Mission: Impossible* **starts up.**

Dat-dah. Dut dut. Dat-dah. Dut dut. **Dad sings along as he taps out the five-four beat on his knees with his hands.**

The boy glances at him and tuts his disapproval. His father meets the rebuke with an added vocal rendition of the brass section. *Diddle dah. Diddle dah. Diddle dah. Daddut.*

The boy gives him a disparaging look, but is unable to suppress a giggle. His father pounces on the betrayed weakness and grips his son's knee sharply in the jaws of his hand, making him yelp with giddy excitement.

1,000

Once the hair maestro had the nylon cape secured round my neck and the little sailor's collar of paper towel tucked in place, I explained how I fancied a bit of a change—a creation of my own based loosely on a style I'd seen **David Bowie** sporting in a recent magazine feature. Mr Vann says it's actually very helpful when customers bring in pictures of a style they have in mind.— I had taken several. Once briefed, Mr Vann set about the task with an air of professional efficiency, leaving the way open for light conversation.

"Has Jack been in this week?" I asked casually.

"Jack who?"

"*Jack Douglas*."

"Who's Jack Douglas?"

Perhaps I'd overstepped the mark in terms of protocol. In the mirror I eyed the waiting clientele, ever anxious for any titbit of insider celebrity gossip. I lowered my voice so that only Mr Vann would hear. "**Jack Douglas**. You know. From the *Carry On* films. He does that character Alf Ippitittimus with the nervous tic where his cap falls off."

"Oh, I know who you mean. No. He doesn't come in here."

"He does. You cut his hair."

"No, no. That was years ago when I shared the business with my brother. He came in once, but it was my brother who cut his hair, not me."

"Did you get his *autograph*?"

"No. I didn't recognise him. My brother told me later who he was."

"I don't bother with autographs either. It's silly, isn't it, asking someone to sign a piece of paper?"

There was a pause before I started things up again.

"I've met **Bob Monkhouse**."

"Yes, I remember you saying."

"I expect he and Jack know each other. Bob was in the very first *Carry On* film, *Carry On Sergeant*."

"Bob Monkhouse? Was he in that?" Mr Vann seemed distracted by something outside the window.

"Oh yes. People think of him as a game show host now, but in the early days he was in lots of comedy films. Charming man. Really friendly and very funny. He'd have you in stitches. I wish I could remember some of his jokes. Of course **Dora Bryan** was in *Carry On Sergeant* as well."

"I don't think I know her."

"You do. She was in *Hello Dolly*."

"I thought that was Barbra Streisand."

"No. The stage musical. Drury Lane. That's where I saw her. I didn't actually meet her, but she waved to me from her car."

Mr Vann shook his head. I'd lost him. I waited while he studied my hair in the mirror. The style I'd requested was beginning to take shape.

On the wall next to the mirror there was an old-fashioned advert for a product called **Silver Fox**, which claimed to restore natural colour to grey hair. *You control the amount of grey.* The man in the picture had chosen to control all of the grey except the little distinguished tufts at his temples. He was pictured from above, looking down on his neatly parted hair as if photographed by a man on horseback.

"Yes, I suppose I've met a lot of famous people really," I said.

Mr Vann held my head firmly between his fingertips and thrust it forward so that my chin rested on my chest. He began to tease the hair at the nape of my neck. It was hard to speak with my jaw wedged shut, and I could no longer see him in the mirror to gauge his reaction, but I decided to 'carry on regardless'.

"As a matter of fact, I've just bumped into the star of *Mission: Impossible*. That advert reminded me. You know—the main one with the grey hair." Mr Vann was trying to place him. "I'm not talking about the film; I'm talking about the TV series. Jim Phelps, the leader of the Impossible Missions Force. Prematurely grey. I can't remember his real name."

Still nothing. I'm not sure that Mr Vann was listening. He takes his work very seriously and can become lost in concentration when he's involved in creating a special hairstyle.

"Yes. He seemed like a very nice man," I added. "He gave me his card, actually."

Just then a policeman popped his head round the door. "Does anyone know who this transit van belongs to?"

Nobody did.

By the time I got outside, they were lifting it on to a flat-bed lorry. Most of the cars in the street had gone. There were traffic cones lining the kerb and a lot of policemen and women standing around. Something was clearly *going down*. I wondered if they were filming an episode of *The Bill* and for a while thought I recognized one or two of the actors, but they turned out to be real police preparing for a VIP visit to the hospice.

"Who's coming then?" I asked one of the policewomen.

"You can't go that way, sir. You'll have to go round," she said.

There were people standing on the other side of some galvanized steel barriers.

"Why can't I just go through the gap?"

She shook her head. "You'll have to go round the block and join the crowd from the other side."

"I don't want to join the crowd; I just want to get through. Who's coming anyway? Is it **David Jason**?"

"Who?"

"From *Only Fools and Horses*."

"Could you go that way please, sir?" She nodded towards the adjacent street.

"—Only I know he does quite a bit of charity work. —For hospices and things. You might know him better as Detective Inspector Jack Frost."

"You'll have to move, sir. It's a security measure."

"Why, is there a bomb?"

She gave me a stern look. It was only a joke.

"I'll just…" I lifted the barrier to create enough of a gap to slip through. She moved it straight back again. Stubborn.

"That way, sir, please. I won't tell you again." She held out her arms as if directing traffic. Her tone had become defiant; there was no arguing with her. Her bulky fluorescent yellow jacket was all puffed up with importance. It annoyed me that she had assumed I was just one of the punters, desperate to catch a glimpse of a minor celebrity.—Well, not so minor as it turned out.

I didn't need to be told the identity of the very important person; when I looked more closely, the crowd on the other side of the barriers provided all the clues. They were mostly mothers and their children, all of them in a gaggle of excitement, holding little **Union Jack** flags and posies of flowers. These are the women who believe that the Royal Family *do a really valuable job* and think that the *Queen Mum* is *smashing*. I'm not anti-royalist particularly, but really... The *Diana Ten Years On* souvenir from the *Daily Mail* that someone had brought, various glossy photographs, and a woman holding a commemorative plate with a picture of the Princess on it were further confirmation. I'd never been much of a fan myself, so I left them to it and headed off to visit Mr Rose, High Class Family Butcher, to get something for my dinner.

Unlike other families who would religiously sit through the Queen's Christmas Day speech on television, and who throughout the year saved cuttings from newspapers and magazines to paste into special Royal Family scrapbooks, there was little in our house to suggest any real allegiance to the monarchy. I remember an old toffee tin full of rusty screws in the garage that had the **Queen** and **Prince Philip** on its lid, and we had a jigsaw commemorating the 1953 coronation, but that was probably more by accident than design. We had all kinds of jigsaws. There was one of **Christopher Columbus**, but we never thought much of him either.

We always did a big one at Christmas—it was a nice way to bring the family together—and though we'd usually opt for a seasonal scene to keep us in the Christmas spirit, sometimes Columbus or the coronation puzzle would offer respite from large areas of white snow and featureless blue skies.

Once a jigsaw was finished, we found it hard to break it apart again and return it to its box. It would be left out for several days so that from time to time we would admire our handiwork, proudly smoothing the wobbly surface with a flat hand, until lack of space would eventually force someone to make the cruel decision to dismantle it. My dad's reluctance to destroy what had been so lovingly created (as far as jigsaws went, at least) would have him carefully trying to fold the completed puzzle like a table napkin so that sections of it remained linked inside the box. Why did he do that? So that next time, we'd have half of it done before we started? Wasn't *doing* it the whole point? Sometimes he'd go so far as to glue the completed puzzle, piece by piece, on to the board, and subsequently frame the whole thing behind glass. We had several of them hanging up around the house. They were never particularly lovely pictures to look at, spoiled, at least to my mind, by the squiggly jigsaw lines where the pieces joined. Still, it was something we had created together, and that's what mattered.

We each fought to be the one to put the last piece in the puzzle; the sense of satisfaction this brought was a much-sought-after Christmas bonus. Towards the point of completion it became a common family practice to hold one of the jigsaw pieces back and hide it in a pocket or up a sleeve, producing it at the last minute to gain the coveted honour. The ploy was to pretend to have suddenly found it under the table or behind the Christmas cards, saying, *Oh look, here it is.* I think it was my dad who started it, but over the years we got wise to his ruse and all joined in. It became a battle to see who would hold out longest, as we went through the motions of searching under the rug or checking the box lid, never quite sure whether any pieces really were lost. *Come on, you've got it. I haven't, honestly. You have. Come on, hand it over*—the accusations met with outraged denial and poorly acted self-righteous innocence as we tried not to betray ourselves by laughing.

The appropriated jigsaw piece had to be important, noticeable by its absence, and the best puzzle to demonstrate this was the Queen's coronation, a formal portrait of Her Majesty in blue sash and tiara against swags of plush curtaining. The scale of the picture was such that with a single jigsaw piece it was possible to withhold an important facial feature: an eye, a nose or a mouth. The one *between* the nose and mouth worked well, especially on a dark baseboard, because the gap that remained would give her a wiggly Hitler moustache. My favourite, however, was the piece that held the left eye which, once removed, made her look like she was wearing a pirate's eyepatch.

One Christmas—I must have been nine or ten—we were down to the last piece and, having by then surrendered their own pilfered pieces, the family turned to me. I'd previously hidden the Queen's eye in my back pocket, intending to suddenly 'find' it on the rug or behind the fruit bowl once the rest of the puzzle was complete, but now I was being watched, there was no opportunity to retrieve it without implicating myself.

The joke went too far and my father got cross, demanding that I hand it over. Loath to confess, I went on protesting my innocence. I think my mum was starting to believe me, but my dad knew me better and continued his accusatory assault. In a final showdown, I managed to stand my ground, though I was hot with shame. "Right!" said Dad and stormed out, carrying the jigsaw with him. We could hear him out in the garage, though none of us dared go and see what he was doing. The next thing we knew, the Alpine snow-scene jigsaw from the previous year that hung over the mantelpiece was being replaced by Queen Elizabeth, framed behind glass with the crucial eyepiece still missing. Nobody said anything, all of us remembering how angry Dad had been. He was not given to losing his temper, and I think he was embarrassed at how he had reacted, so the picture stayed put and was never referred to again. Looking back, visitors to our house seeing the meticulously framed portrait must have assumed we had a predilection for surrealist art, or had somehow stumbled across an undiscovered work by **Marcel Duchamp**.

It was something Mr Rose, the butcher, said that made me go back to wait for the Princess. If it had been **David Jason**, I probably wouldn't have bothered, but as he pointed out, royalty—well, that's history, isn't it? One day this woman would be Queen of England and how many people can say they've seen a real monarch in the flesh? He was right.

Getting close enough to the front required a great deal of manoeuvring. *Excuse me, but do you know how long we've been waiting?* said one woman. *No, I have no idea.* Why was she asking me? People can get quite nasty, and once one starts pushing, they all join in. Everyone kept saying we should let the children stand at the front. I noticed several more women clutching commemorative porcelain. Why would you bring that with you? To attract the Princess's attention, perhaps? *Here, Your Highness! Look at this. Your face on a plate.*

There was a lot of waiting. Forty-five minutes at least. If I hadn't been penned in by the crowd, I might have left. Eventually the car turned up. It was a wide, grey saloon type, a Jaguar or something like that, and it had a little flag on the front above the left headlight, like something you might stick into a sandcastle. The arrival all happened very quickly. Two other cars behind. Men in suits got out while it was still moving. Someone opened the back door and **Princess Diana** emerged. Everyone seemed to be racing for the door as if they were late. Cameras flashed. There was cheering and flag-waving, with people shouting in an attempt to get her attention: 'Di! Di! Di! Di!' An older man in a fancy uniform appeared from nowhere, partially blocking my view with his big fat epaulettes. I only caught a glimpse. She was wearing an all-white suit with a white sailor-type hat more commonly seen on people making pizza or serving ice cream. Black handbag and shoes. A couple of handshakes and she was inside the building. Was that it? Was that what everyone had been waiting for?

Royalty aren't proper celebrities like people off the telly. They can't *do* anything—tell jokes like **B**ob **M**onkhouse or juggle crockery. They'd be rubbish on *Stars in their Eyes* and I doubt if any one of them would have the discipline to sit in front of the mirror perfecting sleight-of-hand illusions, let alone possess the dexterity to pull them off in front of an audience. These people are famous merely by accident of birth, rather than by having real showbiz talent. I could never be accused of leaning on my lineage.

It would have been a lot easier if Dad had been there to answer questions, but I didn't get interested in genealogy until after he left home. Mum knew a bit about his side of the family, information she reluctantly imparted: she knew that his father, Arthur, was born in Bristol and that his mother's maiden name was Salt. It was enough to get me started. Dad's surname was Pincus; I don't think Mum ever liked it. You can see how going from Jean Richardson, as she was before they married, to Jean Pincus must have seemed like a step in the wrong direction, name-wise, like a Hollywood starlet being groomed for obscurity. So after Dad left, she reverted to her maiden name and she changed mine by deed poll while she was at it. "That's the end of it now. The name Pincus has gone for good," she said bitterly. I didn't mind; I hated being called Pinky at school and even at the age of ten I could see that **R**iley **R**ichardson was destined for greatness, whereas Riley Pincus was not. Plus, my new initials were on the front of every **R**olls-**R**oyce, the car favoured by Lady Penelope in *Thunderbirds*. The Pinky nickname stuck until

I went to grammar school where I briefly became Old Mother Riley, but this didn't last long as it was too much of a mouthful.

It turned out that Arthur was the second son of my great-grandfather, George Arthur Pincus, whose older brother, Gifford, emigrated to America, settling in Brooklyn, New York, in 1895. A little side shuffle as we edge along this particular branch of the family tree, and this is where it gets interesting as we follow the line forwards. Now, Gifford met and married Frances and they had several children, one of whom, Joseph Pincus, married someone called Esther, a schoolteacher. Their firstborn was named Harold. And who did Harold grow up to marry? Edna Manilow. They produced a son, Barry Alan Pincus, who was born on 17 June 1943. Have you got it yet? Not quite? Well, according to the biographies, Harold Pincus walked out when Barry was little, leaving his wife, Edna, to bring up the baby on her own with the support of her father. Like my mum, Edna decided to reclaim her maiden name, which she also bestowed on her son, Barry, on the occasion of his bar mitzvah.

Barry Pincus became **Barry Manilow**
at about the same age as
Riley Pincus became **Riley Richardson**.

So there you have it. Extraordinary as it may seem, Barry Manilow really is my cousin. Dad never mentioned it, so he can't have known anything about the family connection. He'd have got a real kick out of that.

Being on opposite sides of the Atlantic—Barry busy with recording and Las Vegas shows, me busy with my various pursuits—means we don't get together as often as some might think. Most people find it hard to believe we are related because, to be honest, we don't look anything like each other. I'm dark-haired and pale like my dad, whereas Barry has more of a golden-faced look, his skin flawless like polished walnut. I try to dress well, but my wardrobe can sometimes let me down, whereas Barry seems to have a perfect new outfit for every occasion, scaled-up versions of the kind that might come displayed flat in its own special packaging, designed for pop star Ken, Barbie's perfect superstar date.

About twenty minutes later, Her Royal Highness came out again. Men in suits who had been hanging around by the door moved into position. Press photographers in a penned-in area of their own aimed their massive lenses, like an artillery of rocket launchers. Standing in line on the steps were the chosen few, minor dignitaries waiting to be introduced. She shook hands with each of them and most of them bowed; a lady in a pink suit and matching hat tried a curtsy. One man wore a shirt and tie, no jacket. The thin bit of his tie was much longer than the fat bit. You'd have thought he'd have got that right for such an occasion. Then she approached her eager fans on the other side of the street. People whistled and clapped; this was what they'd been waiting for. Some men from a nearby building site had elevated themselves above the crowd by sitting in the raised scooping bucket of a bulldozer. When she gave a little wave in their direction, they cheered and punched the air as if they were at a football match. Everyone was thrusting out their hands in the hope of touching her, like they do at Barry's concerts. Lots of flowers, small bouquets mostly. She accepted so many that she was having trouble holding them all. A very camp young man kissed her hand and wouldn't let go. She was smiling, but I could see her trying to pull it away. More flag-waving. Babies were offered. The Princess smiled and chucked their tiny chins.

She was taller than I had imagined, and her legs seemed unusually long. Her skirt, a good deal shorter than is customarily worn by stuffier female members of the Royal Family, revealed a tantalizing glimpse of her shapely knees while remaining (to my mind, at least) firmly on the side of good taste. Sophisticated, elegant and poised, she looked like a princess, which, of course, she was.

She stooped a lot, anxious to maintain eye contact with the women in the crowd, but they were clearly not on her level. **The Princess** was from another world, sleek and groomed like a thoroughbred racehorse. On the other side of the barrier, the squat and shabbily dressed beamed in unison at seeing their favourite royal up close, but whenever she approached them, they would hide their faces behind raised cameras. It seemed rude and ignorant. She was only a few feet away, but instead of engaging with her, they'd be fiddling with the flash or winding the film on, intent on documenting the occasion rather than experiencing it.

Her impatient bodyguards were trying to lead her back to the car, but she realized that she had completely ignored the people on our side, so, in the interest of fairness, she headed in our direction. A little cheer went up, as if we'd won her from the others, like on *Family Fortunes*. She handed the flowers she had gathered to a man who put them in the boot of the car. As she approached, her hands clasped in front of her and her hand-bag tucked under her arm, I sensed that she was intentionally heading straight for me, and, astonishing though it now seems, she was. Before I could adjust to what was happening, she was standing right in front of me. I faltered, not knowing what to say.

"I hope you haven't had to wait too long," she said.

"Since about two thirty," the woman next to me answered. "I had to drop my grandson off at school first. I'm looking after him while his mum's away. She's in Edinburgh."—Stupid woman. The Princess didn't want to hear all that rubbish. You could tell the woman had never met anyone famous before. No sense of celebrity decorum.

Diana's hair was perfect, with deeply furrowed ridges as if it had been recently ploughed. I was glad I'd had my hair cut. Her complexion was perfect, too, with a healthy schoolgirl flush to her cheeks like she'd just been playing netball or lacrosse. There was more hand-shaking and then the Princess said, "Do you have friends or relatives in the hospice?"

"No," came the collective reply, all of them gushing radiantly as they shook their heads. Nobody gave a toss about anyone in the hospice. Someone said, "How's Charles?" She didn't answer. Everyone talked at once. She nodded and smiled. Someone behind piped up: "We saw you when you visited the Isle of Wight." There was nothing to say to that.

She shook more hands and accepted more **flowers**, but she didn't move along the line as she had on the other side. It was as if she was waiting for me to speak. She was less than three feet away from me now. Without thinking, I held out my hand and I could feel her shaking it. Her hand was slim and surprisingly clammy.

"I didn't bring any flowers; I didn't know you were coming." The words were out before I knew what I was saying.

"I think I've got quite enough," she laughed.

Beautiful teeth. I offered her the plastic bag.

"What is it?"

"It's a **P**ork **P**ie from our local butchers. He makes them himself. He's won awards."

"Thank you. I'll take it home for my boys. They adore pork pies."

The crowd chuckled at this intimate snapshot of royal domestic life. She took the plastic carrier from me and one of her aides relieved her of it almost at once. He wrapped the bag round the pie to make a discreet parcel and held it against his hip like a lady's clutch purse.

She had spoken to me. She had actually spoken to me. We'd had a conversation. Me and the future Queen of England, the most famous woman in the world. I didn't even get that close to **Dora Bryan**.

"Fancy giving her a pork pie. You embarrassed her." The woman with the Diana plate was obviously talking to me, though her eyes remained fixed on Diana, who had moved further along the barrier to talk to others.

"Why would that embarrass her?"

"She's a vegetarian, you stupid idiot."

"Is she?"

"Of course she is. Don't you know *anything* about her?"

I felt a bit ashamed. I *didn't* know anything about her.

Further down towards her car a row of elderly wheelchair users sat in front of the barrier. The Princess said something to a frail-looking lady with a flowery shawl over her shoulders, bending over to shake her hand. As she did so, she instinctively touched the woman's cheek with the flat of her hand; the kind of gesture Jesus is often seen making in religious illustrations. Overwhelmed by the blessing, the woman shifted her spectacles to wipe away a tear.

It was time to go. Diana turned and waved farewell before slipping into the back seat of the car. As he closed the door for her, the suited man touched his left shoulder and then his right hip, presumably to remind the Princess to fasten her seatbelt. As he moved round the back of the car I saw him toss my **P**ork **P**ie into the boot with the flowers before slamming it shut.

She was gone and now it didn't seem real, like she'd never been there. Her car wouldn't have got further than the Old Street roundabout, but she was already a million miles away. The barriers were moved and the crowd began to disperse, but the gaggle of women around me was still in a froth of excitement

about their recent acquaintance with **Her Royal Highness**. I felt
like **Richard Dreyfuss** at the end of *Close Encounters of the Third
Kind*, not initially selected as one of the team to meet the aliens,
but instead, chosen specially from among the multitude by the
mother alien herself. None of the women around me recognized
that their encounter had not been as significant or as meaningful
as mine. If it hadn't been for the men in suits I might have been
invited to board the mother ship, guided towards the interior
light of her car by children with big prosthetic heads.

"Ooh, I can't believe she came so close. I'm literally shaking."
Literally shaking? The women around me were still in a spin.
"Isn't she beautiful? Lovely teeth. She looks like a supermodel."
"Gorgeous smile. She's so natural, isn't she?"
"She touched me," I said. But they all ignored me. They were
clearly jealous.
"What a lovely girl," cooed one woman.
"Ooh, yes. She's so caring. You can see it in her eyes. No
wonder they call her the Queen of Hearts."

Until that moment, I had been in a bit of a daze, unable to
shake myself back to reality. The Queen of Hearts? I don't know
if I said it out loud; nobody bothered to answer me.

Once I was a safe distance away from the crowd, I took the
playing card out of my breast pocket and looked at it again. Of
course. That's what everyone called her: **the Queen of Hearts**.

I couldn't see anything unusual about the card; it looked like it
had come from an ordinary deck. I assumed that the court card
designs were traditional and therefore pretty standard—a queen
from one pack looking much the same as any other, but it just
goes to show that you don't really look. I'd never noticed the
queen of hearts holding a flower in her right hand. I thought
at first this might be significant because **Princess Diana** had

also been carrying flowers so I took out the pack from my desk drawer, just to compare it, and found that the flower was on that one too. The cards were much the same except for one big difference: on the card I had found in the alley, the queen's face was in profile, whereas in the one from my pack she was seen face on.

I must have woken Nell up.

"Riley? Oh, what time is it?"

"It's only eight thirty. Were you in bed?"

"No, I must have fallen asleep. I was watching a film. Why are you ringing? Was there some minute detail you forgot to mention?"

There was a trace of sarcasm in her voice. I'd called in again at the café, just as she was closing, to tell her my incredible story about meeting the Princess. Although outside the hospice I'd been surrounded by people, in a strange way it had seemed an intensely private moment and I found that the only person I really wanted to share it with was Nell. It was too precious an experience to risk on the the insensitive ears of Mr Rose or Mr Vann, who often seemed indifferent to such celebrity encounters. Even Nell made out that I had gone on about it too much—perhaps she was a touch jealous—but I knew that deep down she was as excited as I was. If Nell had met a royal, no one would ever hear the end of it.

"Have you got a pack of cards?"

"A pack of cards? Yeah, I think so. Why?"

I hadn't mentioned anything about Jim Phelps and the queen of hearts; I'd wanted to find out what it was all about first.

"Can you get them?" I said.

"You want me to find them now? This isn't one of your magic tricks, is it?"

"No, it isn't. Go on. I just want you to check something."

"Hang on."

There was a pause and I could hear the television in the background. It was *Double Indemnity*. Nineteen forty-four. Fantastic film. I've got it on tape. Fred MacMurray as insurance salesman Walter Neff, and Barbara Stanwyck as the young bride planning to collect on her husband's life insurance policy. From the dialogue I could tell it was the scene towards the end when it's all gone wrong and Fred MacMurray goes to the house to 'say goodbye', not knowing that that Barbara Stanwyck, who turns out to be rotten through and through, has a gun hidden under her seat cushion. He was just making his speech about 'getting off the trolley car before the end of the line' when Nell picked up the receiver again.

"Yeah, go on."

"Can you find the queen of hearts?"

"Queen of hearts? Hang on. Yeah."

"Which way is she facing?"

"What do you mean? Which way is she facing? Straight on."

"She's not in profile, looking off to one side?"

"No. Why?"

"Interesting."

"Why d'you want to know?"

"Er. Pub quiz question."

"Hey, that's cheating. You're not allowed to 'phone a friend', you know. Whose team are you on anyway?"

In the pause before I could think of an answer I heard the crack of gunfire down the line. Barbara Stanwyck had just shot Fred MacMurray.

THREE

BY THE TIME I GOT off the phone with Nell it was nearly nine, so I popped out to Mr Orhy's. Having given my **P**ork **P**ie to the Princess, I needed something for dinner. He seldom has anything I want—Mr Orhy sells everything and nothing—but it's the only shop nearby that stays open late. I like Mr Orhy. He's always very pleasant and calls me Mr Riley. I don't know whether he thinks Riley is my surname; perhaps he simply feels uncomfortable with anything so familiar as a first name. He has dark, liquid boot-polish eyes, like **Omar Sharif** in *Dr Zhivago*, that make him look as though he's perpetually holding back tears of regret about his tragic love affair with **Julie Christie**.

In spite of my misgivings, I found myself telling him about my meeting with Princess Diana. He didn't seem to understand.

"She was on *EastEnders*, was it?"

"*EastEnders*? No, I don't think so. I'm talking about

Diana, the Princess of Wales."

"Wales? Yes, I think it is a real place? What is it? Walford? Where is that?"

"Um. I don't think it's a real place; I think it's like a film set."

"Yes? In London?"

"Yes, in London. Anyway I met the Princess today."

"In London?"

"Yes."

He nodded and smiled. It was going nowhere. I remembered the rigmarole of trying to explain who **Barry Manilow** was.

Nothing in Mr Orhy's worryingly overstocked freezer took my fancy and the few vegetables in his little wire rack looked like somebody might have already thrown them out once. I decided to make do with **C**heese and **C**rackers at home. Since he does carry a few magazines at the back of the shop, I was hoping he might have a souvenir special or something about **Princess Diana**—there always seems to be a million of them about, but I couldn't find anything. Perhaps the royal visit had generated a surge of interest amongst the locals and they'd snapped up all the Diana literature. Most of the stuff seemed hopelessly out of date: puzzle magazines and cheap colouring books for children. There was a crafts magazine and a few flimsy pop magazines printed on shiny paper. Mr Orhy offered me the puzzle books at half-price, but I told him that wasn't really what I was after. He asked if he could help me to find something, but I didn't want to have to try and explain what I was looking for and he left me to it.

One of the joys of summer is the introduction of new maga-zine partworks. Partworks are those magazines that *build week by week into a unique collection that you will treasure for ever*. It's a familiar formula. My dad had a multi-volume encyclopaedia, bought by his Great-Uncle Harry, all held together in special binders. There are hundreds of partworks and nowadays they often come with something attached to the cover: a **Delia Smith** cake-decorating nozzle or part of a scale model of the Flying Scotsman.—Something to build piece by piece. They're a con, of course, exploiting the public's natural urge to collect. Miss one issue and you're left with a wingless Lancaster Bomber or a Tyrannosaurus Rex minus its lower jaw. They never tell you how many parts there are going to be and rarely mention the huge price increase after you have been suckered in by the initial introductory discounts. I've never been foolish enough to subscribe to a partwork myself. Not for the whole series anyway. It doesn't take the **B**rain of **B**ritain to work out that at four or five pounds per issue, you're going to end up spending hundreds on what will eventually amount to nothing more than a book and an Airfix kit. Great-Uncle Harry could have gone out and bought an encyclopaedia in a shop for a fraction of the cost. Still, the idea of collecting the series has understandable appeal and perhaps for my dad the excitement of receiving a new issue each week was worth it.

Mr Orhy had Part 3 of what looked like a long-defunct series called *Infamous Murders*. On its cover was a mug shot of President Kennedy's assassin, **Lee Harvey Oswald**, holding a little badge showing his Dallas police booking number. I picked it up and leafed through it. A couple of customers had come in; I sensed someone looking over my shoulder.

"You're not thinking of buying that, are you?" It was Steve, my new neighbour. I'd met him a few times on the stairs. He seemed pleasant enough, but his boorish manner put me on edge. From what I understood, Steve had been in the Territorial Army and was currently working in what he enigmatically referred to as 'a branch of security'.

"If you want stuff on Oswald," he said, "I've got a fantastic book that blows the lid on the lone gunman theory once and for all."

"I was just looking." I put the magazine back on the rack to show I wasn't really interested.

"The CIA masterminded the whole thing, but they needed a scapegoat. Oswald was just a patsy."

I nodded. It's a funny word, 'patsy'. There's the actress, **Patsy Kensit**, and country-and-western legend **Patsy Cline**, as well as **Patsy Rowlands** and **Patsy Palmer** from *EastEnders*. Each one of them was just a **Patsy** too, but they didn't seem to mind.

Steve leaned over to the chilled section and reached for a Scotch egg.

"There's no way Oswald could have fired off that number of rounds in the time," he continued. "They had US Marine sniper instructors reconstruct the whole thing: the angle, same range, moving target, time limit, obstacles—everything. Not one of them could do what the Warren Commission claimed Oswald did. Now, if those guys couldn't do it, how did Oswald, who barely qualified as a 'marksman', do it?"

"Yes, I've heard that theory. The second shooter on the grassy knoll."

"What do you mean, *that theory*? It's fact. I'll lend you the book."

"Great. Thanks."

"Are you walking back?" he said.

I wasn't sure I wanted to listen to more about **Oswald** and I certainly didn't want Steve's big army boots trampling all over my recent Diana experience.

"No. I'm calling round to see a friend," I said.

"Which way are you going?"

"Er. The other way."

Steve headed for the till with his Scotch egg and some Mr Muscle spray cleaner. He took out a banknote to pay. His wallet, I noticed, was attached to a belt loop of his combat trousers by a steel chain thick enough to restrain an angry bull. Another shopper stood behind him to form a queue. I recognized him at once. It was Jim Phelps, the Silver Fox. He had his back to me, but it was definitely the man I had followed earlier. Same jacket, same shoes, same grey hair. Steve was oblivious and walked out without turning round. Phelps stepped up with his wire basket to be served and waited while Mr Orhy transferred each item from the basket to a thin blue plastic carrier as he rang it up on the till. I watched from the back of the shop, pretending to read the label on a packet of **M**uesli. He was less than twenty feet away. I could have easily approached him, but as I've said already I never like to barge into a celebrity's personal space.—Not like some people do. I prefer the encounter to happen naturally. I realized that Phelps probably wasn't holding **card 19**. Why would he be? Nevertheless, when he left the shop, I decided to follow so that I could accidentally bump into him on the street. There, having made sure it really was him, I would shake his hand and say how much I enjoyed his television programme; perhaps even tell him of my magazine article about the missing *Mission: Impossible* bubble-gum card. I was certain he'd be fascinated to hear about that.

I paid Mr Orhy for the cereal and exchanged a few polite words. It was no use asking him if the customer he had just served was the man off *Mission: Impossible*; he didn't even know who **Barry Manilow** was.

Outside, I looked left and right, but couldn't see Phelps. Where could he have gone? Had he got into a car or hopped on a bus? No buses in sight. A woman with a pushchair-buggy-thing was struggling to get into the shop so I held the door open for her. She looked vaguely familiar, but I couldn't think where I'd seen her before. As I watched her line up the wheels, I spotted another card on the pavement. I could see that it wasn't a playing card because it was smaller and there was writing on the back, but it seemed significant because it looked old. Had Jim Phelps

Nº 27

GREAT BRITISH
TRADITIONS
SERIES OF 50

May Day.

Every year, on the first of May, the May
Queen, usually a local teenage girl, is
selected to ride or walk at the front of a
parade for May Day celebrations. She
wears a white gown to symbolize purity
and a tiara or crown of flowers. Her duty
is to open the May Day celebrations and
make a speech before the dancing
begins. Children dance round a maypole
celebrating youth and the springtime.
According to popular British folklore,
the tradition once had a sinister twist, in
that the May Queen was put to death
once the festivities were over. The
veracity of this belief is difficult to
establish, and in truth it might just be
an example of anti-pagan propaganda.

ISSUED BY
GALLAHER LTD
BELFAST & LONDON.

dropped it? When the woman was safely inside, I bent down to pick it up.

It was issued by Gallaher's, in the 1950s I would guess, as part of a cigarette card series. I think there was a similar set entitled *Strange Customs of Britain*, given free with Typhoo Tea in the 1970s. It was certainly unusual to see something like this among the litter on the street. Could it have got there by chance? It seemed unlikely that anyone would throw a card like that away, and even less likely that they would have chosen to do so on the pavement right outside Mr Orhy's shop on this particular night. And if it had been there earlier, wouldn't I have spotted it on my way in?

On the back of the card it said: *Every year, on the first of May, the May Queen, usually a local teenage girl, is selected to ride or walk at the front of a parade for May Day celebrations. She wears a white gown to symbolize purity and a tiara or crown of flowers. Her duty is to open the May Day celebrations and make a speech before*

*the dancing begins. Children dance round a maypole celebrating
youth and the springtime. According to popular British folklore, the
tradition once had a sinister twist, in that the May Queen was put
to death once the festivities were over. The veracity of this belief is
difficult to establish, and in truth it might just be an example of anti-
pagan propaganda.*

The May Day story seemed to be mostly about the May
Queen. Two queens: **Queen** of Hearts, **Queen** of the May.
Surely something more than mere coincidence? But what did the
May Queen have to do with **Princess Diana**? At first I couldn't
see the connection. There was the white dress and the flowers,
obviously, but I'd never heard **Princess Diana** referred to as the
May Queen. I wondered if it was another nickname invented by
her adoring public, perhaps with reference to her purity? More
puzzling was what all this had to do with *Mission: Impossible*.

Steve was back again. I thought he'd gone, but it was
apparently only as far as the off-licence. He was holding a can of
Stella.

"Who's that, your girlfriend?" he said, looking at the picture
on the card.

"It's a cigarette card. I just found it on the ground." I started
to put it in my pocket.

"Let's have a look." He took it from me, setting his beer
down on Mr Orhy's window ledge. "It looks old."

"It's from the fifties."

He turned the card over and glanced at the text, then cupped
his hand to his mouth and pinched his nose to imitate a nasal
upper-class voice. "*Mayday. Mayday. Mayday. Calling all rescue.
This is HMS* Pinafore. *Come in, please. This is an emergency. Over.*"
Laughing at what he thought was a piece of brilliantly conceived
satire, he handed the card back and took a swig from the can.

The use of 'mayday' as a radio emergency call had not until

then occurred to me, though I was familiar with it from films and television programmes. "Why do they say 'mayday'? What's it got to do with May Day?" I asked.

"It's not *May Day*, you berk, where little kids go dancing round the maypole. *Mayday* is the international distress signal. It means 'in grave and imminent danger'. You're supposed to say it three times. *Mayday, mayday, mayday.* It's from the French *m'aidez*, meaning *help me*. Didn't you know that? It's always coming up in pub quizzes."

"I don't go in much for quizzes."

"That's why you don't know anything." Steve finished his beer, crushed the can and belched before speaking again. "In 1929, Donald F. Duncan introduced a toy based on a weapon used by sixteenth-century Filipino hunters. What was it called?"

I shrugged.

Steve coughed up a K sound and shook his head in disbelief that I didn't know. "Yo-yo," he said.

I wasn't sure if it was the answer or an insult.

To avoid spending more time with Steve, I headed in the opposite direction to home and took a detour via the alley where Phelps had dropped the first card. I don't know what I was hoping to find: some clue perhaps as to where he had gone, or something to explain the significance of the cards. Perhaps Phelps had an apartment in one of the workshop units—a little pied-à-terre in town that opened on to the alley—which might explain how he had disappeared so quickly that morning.

As I was passing the bus shelter by Argos, I noticed that someone had left a newspaper on the seat. On the front page there was a photo of the Princess. It was too soon to have been taken during her visit to the hospice, but I made a mental note to check the papers the following day. It had crossed my mind that perhaps one of the journalists might have snapped the two of us in conversation.—That would be one for my hall of fame. As it turned out, the picture on today's paper was a close-up of her looking rather anguished. It was a side of her that I had not seen earlier, but then I expect she's become pretty good at putting on a brave face. The headline read:

DIANA'S CRY FOR HELP

I headed over to the shops by the tube station, retracing my steps from earlier that day. At You've Been Framed I turned the corner and made my way into the alley. It was quite dark down there by this time. Luckily, I had my little torch with me: the Maglite flashlight, no bigger than a lipstick and chosen by professionals the world over. Precision-machined high-strength aluminium alloy case, and a high-intensity spot-to-flood beam, adjustable with a twist of the wrist. I took it out and shone it around. Nothing. When I checked, there was a dull orange glow from the bulb but it was next to useless. The battery was on its last legs; I must have left it on by mistake. What I really needed was one of those big powerful things with a fierce white search-light beam like they use in *X-Files*. Would they sell something like that at the petrol station on the corner?

It's open twenty-four hours, and inside there's a mini-supermarket section selling various grocery basics, but after nine they shut the door and you have to shout your order through a little security window. It soon became clear that the young woman on duty didn't speak English.

"Do you sell torches? Torches?" I pointed to my Maglite. "Like this, but bigger?" She shook her head. "No? OK. Do you have batteries?" She looked puzzled so I unscrewed the end and removed the battery. "Battery." I said. "Like this." She nodded and produced a pack of Duracell AAA batteries. I needed AA's. "No. Too small. You have bigger?" No. She didn't have bigger.

"What about candles? You sell candles?" She had no idea what I was talking about. "Candles." I tried to think of a mime, like you would when playing charades. I'm usually pretty good at this; I once did *How Green Was My Valley* in seventeen seconds. But acting out candles is a hard one. In the end, I sang a bit of 'Happy Birthday to You' and mimed blowing out the candles on a cake. Her face lit up and she set off down one of the aisles. She came back with a Mr Kipling Viennese sponge.

"No, not cake. Candles. For birthday. Go on top of cake." I was starting to sound like Tarzan. *Me need fire.* When I blew the candles out again, she got it. She came back with a little packet of drip-free cake candles, half pink, half blue. I grinned and gave the thumbs-up. Is the thumbs-up a universal sign? It must be; she smiled back.

"Yes, OK, but do you have bigger? Bigger? *Grande?*" I tried to explain that I wanted household candles: "Bigger, about this long," but she was shaking her head. She smiled resignedly at not being able to help and was about to return the cake candles so I called her back. "Yes, yes. I'll have those." I nodded enthusiastically as I pointed at the packet in her hand.

She put them in the little serving well. "One fifty," she said.

"Thank you. And some matches. Matches?"

She frowned. I struck an invisible match on an invisible box and held it up, hoping she might recognize the invisible flame. We both stared at it for a moment. It wasn't until I shook the match to extinguish the flame that the penny dropped.

"Ah. Matches!"

She turned out to be quite a charades player herself. I'd be happy to have her on my team. I was just collecting my change when a man who had been waiting behind me stepped up with his request: "Twenty Marlboro and a Diet Coke, please, love." She reached for the items without hesitation.

Once outside, I struck a match to get my bearings and was just able to make out that one of the doors at the end of the alleyway was ajar, with an open padlock hanging from the hasp. Was it like that earlier, or had someone opened it while I was at the petrol station? I approached cautiously. Just in case the Silver Fox was in there, I decided to announce my presence with a tentative hello. There was no response. Probably just as well, I wouldn't have known what else to say.

It was even darker inside. I looked for a light switch, but there didn't seem to be one so I lit a couple of candles. A set of concrete steps turned back on themselves, leading straight down into blackness. Dare I venture further? I've never been especially scared of the dark, but no sensible person walks blindly into a strange basement alone. There could have been anything down there—rats, bats, a big snarling guard dog or a grotesque, homicidal dwarf in a red hooded coat, wielding a meat cleaver like the one at the end of *Don't Look Now*. Besides, it would be trespassing. Nevertheless, I somehow felt the need to investigate.

Once I'd gone down a few steps, the candles—enough, perhaps, to light up a two-year-old's birthday face, but not a dark cellar—seemed woefully inadequate. I could see my hand quite clearly, but anything beyond that fell away into the darkness. As my eyes adjusted, I began to get a dim sense of the space. The steps led down to a narrow brick-lined passageway with a concrete floor. At the end of it I could just make out a thin horizontal strip of pale orange light. I assumed it was some kind of underground tunnel connecting two buildings. I stepped down further and tried calling hello again, a little louder. But instead of a reply, there was a noise above and behind me, a slight scuffling. It took me a moment to realize that upstairs, someone was shutting the door to the alley. I leapt like a prancing springbok back up the steps, just as the door was rammed firmly into place. I shouted to whoever was outside, but all I could hear was the padlock being snapped shut and jiggled as if to make sure it was securely fastened. My candles had gone out; it was pitch black. I banged hard on the door with the heel of my hand and shouted loudly. Nothing. Was the person deliberately ignoring me, or merely unable to hear my cries? I kicked the door hard until my toe hurt. I realized then that I was still holding the damned Muesli I had bought at Mr Orhy's. Setting it down by my feet, I quickly struck a match and lit a handful of candles, comforted momentarily by the warm glow. I put my ear to the door and listened. Outside it was quiet. Whoever had been there seemed to have gone.

If there was an alternative way out, I would have to find it. I could feel a claustrophobic panic rising in my chest and it was that which forced me to go back down the steps and head for what I had taken to be light leaking from under a door at the other end of the corridor. The adrenaline was urging me to run for it, but I knew I had to stay calm or the candles would blow out. Their light threw looming shadows on the walls, cast by my cupped hand shielding the vulnerable flames. I passed a side door leading off to my right, and from behind it I could hear the low electrical hum of machinery. I wasn't going to look in there. The door at the other end was becoming clearer, the light from behind it promising salvation. I was just praying it wasn't locked.

There was a dark shape up ahead near the door that gave me pause. At first I thought it might have been a dog, but as the light caught its shiny surface, I could see that it was a black bin liner, its contents spilling from a split down the side—a pile of what looked like cheap, broken toys and grubby baby clothes. I thought I saw a card too, part of a board game or something, poking out from under the bag, but I wasn't sure and I wasn't stopping to find out. The door had one of those old-fashioned gate latches on it. I clicked the thumbpiece and the lever clacked open. I was out. Thank God, I was out.

I found myself in another basement, but this one had white walls and was properly lit. The unmistakable whiff of urinal cakes and the sound of a hand-drier emanated from behind the adjacent door marked 'Gents'. It swung open and a man emerged. He headed up the stairs two at a time, wiping his hands on the seat of his trousers. I had just blown out the candles, which were still smoking, but he didn't even look at me. Upstairs, the convivial hubbub of pub chatter, glasses clinking and **Bonnie Tyler** singing 'Total Eclipse of the Heart'. I was safe.

The door through which I had come had a sign on it: *Private*. I opened it again and saw an old metal light switch on the wall just inside. I flipped the toggle and the corridor lit up. It didn't look scary any more.

3

There *was* a card under the black bag.

It was last orders at the bar so I got myself a pint of Cider and some Crisps. I felt like I'd earned them. I laid the card in front of me on the table. It was obviously a Second World War recruitment advert, possibly originally designed as a poster. The War Office put out a lot of this kind of stuff at the start of the conflict. There was nothing to indicate that the card was part of a series, so perhaps these were handed out on the street or in cinemas and dance halls in an attempt to get young men to do their bit. **YOUR COUNTRY NEEDS YOU!**—the ultimate call to adventure. When I took a closer look at the soldier in the illustration, his face seemed remarkably familiar. Then I realized why. It was me. Not me exactly, obviously, but there was definitely more than a passing resemblance.

I was deep in contemplation about what this might mean when an older man in shirtsleeves clearing tables reminded me that it was closing time and asked me to finish my drink. He had

grey hair too, but it wasn't Jim Phelps. He waited while I drained my glass before taking it from me.

I had no idea which pub I was in—I didn't recognize the interior—but at that point I couldn't have cared less. When I got outside, I saw that it was the **Queen's Head**, the same pub I had passed that morning on my way to Hector Goodall's. The geographic proximity of the two locations had not occurred to me. The flag seller was long gone, but the block of polystyrene he had used to display his wares was still there, identifiable by the little holes that had been jabbed into it. One of the plastic **Union Jack** flags lay trodden into the ground. I bent down and picked it up.

I was exhausted, but when I got to bed I couldn't sleep. It had been an extraordinarily eventful day and I kept going over it in my mind. Understandable. How many people can say they've seen Jim Phelps off *Mission: Impossible*, given a **P**ork **P**ie to a member of the Royal Family and been locked in an underground passage—all on the same day? And at the end of it I had three cards, each one apparently left deliberately for me to find. The cards were all of a similar vintage, but from completely different series—yet I couldn't help thinking that they must somehow be connected to each other. It was too much of a coincidence otherwise. But what did they mean? What does the queen of hearts have to do with the May Queen or celebrating May Day? Perhaps it has more to do with the other kind of May Day, the *mayday* distress call to which Steve had referred. If the **queen of hearts** represents **Princess Diana**, then the **May Day** card could be telling me that she is in grave and imminent danger. And the third card? **Your Country Needs You!** If that's the next part of the message, then its meaning seems clear: Princess Diana is in grave and imminent danger and my country needs me. If that's true, then what is the danger, and what does my country need me to do about it? Why me, anyway? Why such an elaborately obscure way of delivering a message? And why, of all people, would Jim Phelps from *Mission: Impossible* be the appointed messenger? It made no sense. What possible connection could there be between Jim Phelps and **Diana, Princess of Wales**? I puzzled over it for some time and was almost drifting off to sleep when it suddenly occurred to me: Phelps had been wearing a jacket made from **Prince of Wales** check.

On a TV screen: a close-up of Prince of Wales check, the back of Jim Phelps's jacket. Jim moves away from camera; he is in a busy railway station heading towards a coin-operated passport-photo booth. A sign on the booth reads *Temporarily Out of Order*. Jim glances left and right before removing the sign and stepping inside. He draws the curtain and sits down. Taking a key from his pocket, he unlocks a small panel under the glass screen and a drawer slides out holding a miniature reel-to-reel tape recorder. Jim inserts a coin in the slot and the recorder plays its message.

Good morning, Mr Phelps. A flashbulb pops. A picture of an elegant man appears on the screen in front of him. *The man you are looking at is Prince Gadim, ruler of the tiny East European principality of Brashkinev.* Another flash. The picture changes: the prince in dress uniform with his pretty young bride. *Together with his American-born wife, Princess Maria, he is slowly converting their country to democracy, and has begun an alliance with the West. The union is much opposed by this man...* The picture changes. Phelps studies the wild-eyed extremist on the screen... *Gregor Karvos, head of an anti-American activist military group, the Hazad Revolutionary Army, dedicated to overthrowing the country's ruler. Karvos has hired an assassin to kill the princess in the first step in a campaign of terror against the monarchy. Your mission, Jim, should you decide to accept it, is to prevent the assassination and bring Karvos to justice. As always, should any of your IM Force be caught or killed, the Secretary will disavow any knowledge of your actions. This tape will self-destruct in five seconds. Good luck, Jim.*

Smoke begins to pour from the tape recorder.

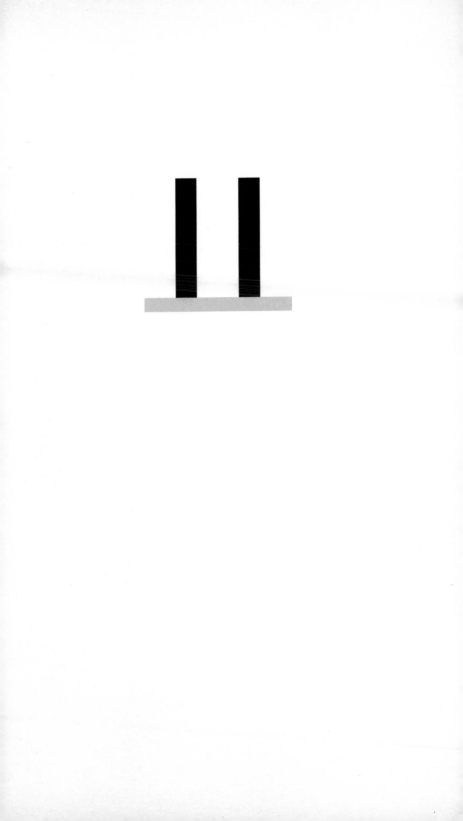

FOUR

1967. The printing works dance. A trio—drums, sax and piano—play a dismal rendition of Chris Farlowe's chart hit, 'Out of Time'. Two folding tables form a makeshift bar where lukewarm beer and soft drinks are served. Elvis stands nearby with a group of awkward-looking male co-workers, each of them clutching a pale ale bottle. All eyes are on the dance-floor, where the secretary is dressed to the nines in a short white chiffon dress decorated with a silvery sparkle bodice. Its skirt, buoyed by a flouncy petticoat, sways and swirls as she moves. She makes the best of the music with tugging hand gestures and chasséing side-steps in the modern groove. Her halo of sugar-frosted angel hair remains motionless. She glitters like a mirror ball, making all the other women in the room look frumpy and drab. Sporting a Manfred Mann-style polo neck and thick-rimmed glasses, her eager young partner from the accounts department jigs his arms, enthusiastically manoeuvring an invisible hobby horse round a series of tiny obstacles. He seems more interested in the swinging beat than in her. She occasionally glances coyly in Elvis's direction and fleetingly their eyes lock. While the other men are entirely focused on the secretary's shapely legs and how much more of them each twirl might reveal, Elvis seems transfixed by her very being. A colleague beckons his ear. Elvis listens, but is distracted by the secretary's dance moves.

"She's not half bad, is she?"

Elvis raises his eyebrows and nods.

"She keeps looking over here. You going to ask her to dance?"

He shakes his head regretfully. "Married man, me."

The colleague nods. "I might go over myself in a minute." He takes a swig of beer. "Hey, you know that job that got put on hold last week—the kids' bubble-gum cards? You know why they had to pull that card, don't you?"

"No. Why?"

He leans and whispers something in Elvis's ear.

"Don't be daft. Who's told you that?"

"It's true. One of the blokes from the artwork department at Chad told me."

"Did you see it?"

"No. Greenwood made us dump the plates and the proofs. I was delivering that day so I never saw it. Apparently one of the blokes put it in for a laugh and nobody spotted it."

"Are you sure? I checked the proof sheet and I didn't see any-thing like that."

"Yeah, but I bet you didn't look at every single card, did you?"

"Believe me, if there'd been a picture of anything like that, I'd have noticed it."

"Perhaps not, with you being a married man and all. You've probably become immune to that sort of thing."

"Nah. Someone's pulling your plonker."

"No, honestly. They were supposed to replace it with another card, but apparently there wasn't time so they're going to release the series with one missing, hoping nobody will ever find out."

"They can't do that."

"They can, you know."

"Isn't it illegal? Trade descriptions or something?"

"Probably. Still, it's only school kids. They'll just think it's a rare card, won't they? How are they going to know it doesn't exist?"

"So nobody can ever get the full set?"

"Just as well. Imagine the trouble old Greenwood would have been in if that one had got out. The press would have had a field day. I wish I'd got hold of one of those proof sheets before they got dumped. That card would be worth a mint."

Elvis nods, his smile a little strained. The colleague smoothes down his frizzy hair and checks the knot in his tie. "Right. Wish me luck."

Elvis watches as the man cuts in on the Manfred type, pulling the secretary close to him for his idea of a smoochy waltz. He gives Elvis the thumbs-up behind her back as he reverses her round the floor, ignoring the up-tempo beat. She steps nimbly, trying to keep her feet from under his. As the couple turn, the secretary catches Elvis watching them and pulls a little face to signal her distress. He laughs.

1,650

Of course, much of this part of the story is speculation now. I can only guess at the conversations that might have taken place, but everything here is based on facts I know to be true. I'm just filling in some of the gaps. I can't say exactly what the secretary looked like, but she must have been quite alluring. At 1,697 words I'm still within my editorial limit, but there's quite a way to go yet. Perhaps I should warn **M**ichael **M**allinsay that this is a story that can't be told in 2,000 words.

I had plenty of **M**ilk, but no **M**uesli, having left it on the cellar steps the previous night. I hadn't had any proper dinner either, so I went over to Nell's for breakfast. The café wasn't too busy, so she sat with me to drink her tea. I decided to tell her about the cards I had found and what I thought they meant, but was soon regretting it.

"So let me get this straight," she said. "A fictional character from a 1960s television series has left you a secret message: *Princess Diana is in mortal danger*, and the highly trained security specialists usually responsible for protecting her are not up to the task. So instead, they have decided to call upon the professional expertise of an unemployed man from north London."

Nell can be quite acerbic at times. I had actually chosen to take redundancy from my last job and was currently biding my time until the right career opportunity came along. Besides, she knew full well that I was now gainfully employed as a freelance features writer for **Card Collector Monthly**, which is a highly respected profession in anybody's book.

She continued: "—But instead of just asking you to do it, with a simple phone call or a letter, they have decided to recruit an actor from a TV programme to deliver coded instructions on a series of playing cards, which he will leave in various locations—places that he can be sure you will visit—in the hope that you will find the cards, decipher the message and carry out the special assignment."

"You're making it sound ridiculous."

"Why is that ridiculous? It sounds perfectly normal to me. You're the obvious choice to save her. Will she give you a knighthood as a reward?"

"She doesn't give out knighthoods. Only the Queen can do that."

"Oh. Pity."

"Look," I said. "The first card was the **queen of hearts**. Two hours later I am shaking hands with **Princess Diana**, who everyone refers to as the Queen of Hearts."

"Coincidence. It doesn't mean anything, love."

"Well, how do you explain this?" I said, pointing to the recruitment card. "Look at his face. That soldier looks exactly like me."

Nell took her reading glasses from the top of her head and squinted through them at the card. She snorted derisively and then quickly put her hand to her mouth as if to pardon herself.

"Oh. So you don't see any resemblance?" I said, a little testily.

She hunched her shoulders and gave a rueful grin. "They're just cards, Riley.—Random bits of litter you've picked up off the street. There's no secret message. I thought you didn't go in for all this fortune-telling stuff."

"It's not fortune-telling," I said. "It's a clear message. *Princess Diana in grave and imminent danger. Your country needs you.—*Meaning me."

"That's just your interpretation."

"What other interpretation is there?"

"Well, they could be saying anything, couldn't they?"

"Like?"

She studied the three cards that I had laid on the table.

"Well… Queen—that could be the rock group, Queen, couldn't it? And the second one—May. Now, what happens in May?" She thought it over for a minute. "Hey what's the name of Queen's guitarist, the one with the poodle hairdo?"

"I don't know." I did know, of course, but I could see where this was going.

"**B**rian **M**ay! Yes, that's it. There's your May connection."

"That's not it."

"Yes. It is." With a sharp intake of breath she covered her mouth—a gesture pantomiming a sudden moment of realization. "Riley."

"What?"

"**B**rian **M**ay from Queen wants you to join the Army."

I gathered the cards off the table and got up to leave.

"No, wait," she said. "That's not it. He wants you to join the group."

"Very funny."

"Yes. They want you to replace Freddie Mercury. He must have seen your new haircut. Oh, Riley, you must do it. Your country needs you!"

During the journey home I thought about what Nell had said. Random bits of litter? How could the cards be random? I'd actually seen Jim Phelps drop the queen of hearts in the alleyway. There was nothing random about that. Besides, all the cards were from a bygone era. How could she explain that? Even the playing card looked old. If I'd found these cards on the ground at a car boot sale or flea market, where people are dealing in antiques or vintage ephemera, or on the lawn of a stately home during the filming of *Antiques Roadshow*, there might have been a simpler explanation, but this was too much of a coincidence. After all, how often does the average person see a card lying on the street? Once a month? Once a year? Never? And I'd found three in one day. They were obviously placed there intentionally for me to discover, and the message they contained, now that I'd worked it out, was incontrovertible proof of their significance. However, what that message was specifically telling me to do was not yet clear.

I bumped into Steve on the stairs and he invited himself into my flat 'for a quick coffee', saying, "Only if you've got proper stuff, mind; I don't want any of that instant shit."

With his demands met—a new packet of **C**ustard **C**reams open on my kitchen table and hot water drizzling through the dusty remains of a long-forgotten packet of Douwe Egberts I found in the back of the cupboard—Steve prepared to give me his expert opinion. He sat with the three cards laid out before him and was straddling them with his elbows, his fingertips resting lightly on his temples as though he were picking up psychic messages. (It had been with some reservations that I'd told him about my latest card discovery in the cellar. I didn't want him involved, but since he'd figured out the true meaning of the May Day card, I thought he might be able throw some new light on the puzzle.)

He leaned back in his chair and placed his hands flat on the table either side of the cards, his long thumbs sticking out at right angles to create the lower corners of a makeshift frame. The device seemed to give him a clear overview of the picture. "*Princess Diana in grave and imminent danger. Your country needs you.*" He nodded sagely. "It sounds to me like you're being recruited by Special Forces."

"What special forces?"

"You'll probably never find out. If it's a covert operation, which I suspect this is, they won't want you to know who your contact is."

"Covert operation? You mean like *Mission: Impossible?*"

"No, Riley," he said, patronizingly. "Not like *Mission: Impossible. Mission: Impossible* is a television programme."

"You know what I mean.—MI5 or something."

"MI5, MI6.—Could be any one of a number of secret service organizations. No names; no pack-drill. All *Friends of the Family.*"

"Friends of the Family?"

"It's a code name used to refer to undercover agents without arousing suspicion." Steve took a sip of the coffee I'd poured him and pulled a sour face. "Jesus, he said, sniffing its surface. "How long have you had this?"

"Fresh open this morning," I said, innocently. —I'm not a big coffee drinker. Not like my dad was. "So you think a *Friend of the*

Family is leaving the cards? Why would MI5 be contacting me? I'm not a secret agent."

"Not in the way you're thinking, but civilians do sometimes get recruited. Certain delicate or sensitive espionage activities are best carried out by members of the general public. They're less conspicuous, and the connection between the recruited agent and the controller is harder to trace."

"Really? I thought secret agents had to go to spy school or something."

"Not necessarily. Depends what the job is."

"So you really think it's something to do with protecting **Princess Diana?**"

Steve raised his eyebrows. "It only takes one determined killer. He wouldn't even need to be a professional. Her security is practically non-existent these days. She goes shopping without a bodyguard—drives her own car. Anyone could take a pop at her. That's all it takes, just one nutter with a mission. A crazed fan. Look at **John Lennon**— here one minute, gone the next. Piece of piss. You don't need special training."

"You think someone's planning to kill her?"

"I wouldn't be surprised."

"A crazed fan?"

"Who knows? Could be an inside job."

"Really?"

"The Royal Family want her out of the picture. She's become a massive threat to royal protocol. Especially after doing that *Panorama* interview."

"You mean a plot from within? They'd never go that far, would they? How would they get away with it?"

Steve took a custard cream from the packet and bit into it, dropping crumbs on to the table and sweeping them to the floor with the flat of his hand. "Fake a suicide probably," he sniffed,

"—since she's already admitted trying to top herself. It's usually the first option. That's what they did with Marilyn Monroe. Or an accident. Nothing too sensational; it's got to look natural."

"How do you know about all this?"

"Ah. Inside information. Mum's the word." Steve had a whole kit bag full of such clichés.

"What do you mean, *inside information*?"

"Don't forget I work in security. I have certain connections."

"What kind of connections?"

He put his finger to his lips and spoke out of the corner of his mouth. "Official Secrets Act."

As far I understood it, Steve worked as a locksmith for a company in Streatham, a job that was not so much about espionage as it was about fitting new Yales and security chains on the doors and windows of the fearful and the vulnerable. Still, he seemed to know a lot about it; perhaps he was involved in extracurricular undercover work he was not at liberty to reveal.

"What happens if the civilian doesn't want to be a *Friend of the Family*?" I said.

"There are a number of ways to persuade people. These can be summed up by mice."

"Summed up by mice? How do they get them to do that?"

"Mice. M-I-C-E."

"Oh, you mean like an acronym?"

"Money, ideology, compromise, ego," he said, counting each word off on his fingers. "It's usually one of those. Money is a straightforward incentive, but if the recruit can't be bought, they'll dig up some dirty secret they can use to blackmail them."

"I don't have any dirty secrets, thank you."

"Well, if compromise isn't an option, and they haven't offered you any money, you're left with ideology: fighting for a political cause; or ego: the thrill and glamour of being a spy."

I didn't like to think of myself as fitting any of those categories, but if I'd had to choose, I suppose it would have been the latter. As a boy, espionage was a career path I had eventually hoped to take. *Danger Man, James Bond, The Man from U.N.C.L.E., Mission: Impossible*: there were many television shows that acted as recruitment adverts for the junior spy. It was the secret gadgets I liked. Napoleon Solo and Illya Kuryakin with shoulder holsters, and pens that doubled as radio transmitters. *Open Channel D.* Steed from *The Avengers* with his metal-lined bowler and sword-stick umbrella. There were numerous spy-themed toys on the market at the time. My favourite was the thrilling SECRET SAM attaché case, an innocent-looking piece of luggage that contained a gun with a silencer and a periscope, which fired long- and short-range bullets or secret message capsules out of the side of the case. It also had a hidden camera that could be operated by a lever near the handle. It was a toy I had longed for, but never owned.

"This bloke with the grey hair is obviously a courier," said Steve. "The intermediary between you, the agent, and your case officer."

"Who's my case officer?"

"You'll never know. That's the whole point of the courier."

"So what am I supposed to do next?"

"Sit tight. Await further instructions. They'll contact you."

"With another card?"

Steve shrugged. "It seems to be the established mode of communication. You'll probably be given an address, a secret rendezvous location where you will receive further instructions."

"But I still don't understand why they would choose me for such an important job."

"Beats me," said Steve. "You'd have been pretty far down on my list."

1967. Elvis stands at the counter of an off-licence attached to a pub. The warm babble of beery chit-chat wafts through from the other side, but in this section, where people can buy off-sales without going into the pub, the atmosphere is stark and cold. On the counter in front of him, a bottle of cider, a small bottle of red pop and three bags of crisps. He counts out coins to pay the woman serving. From the pub a voice calls him. He looks up to see the secretary from work. She detaches herself from a group of people and talks to him round the side of the decorative glass partition that divides them.

1,750

"Hello," she says, brightly.

"What are you doing here? I thought you lived over in…"

"My sister lives just up the road. Is this your local, then?"

"Yeah. I suppose so."

"You coming through for a drink?"

"No, not tonight. I've got to get back."

"We're going up the Beauchamp later for steak and chips. Have you been?"

"No, but I've heard it's very nice."

"I'm playing gooseberry to my sister and her husband."

Elvis nods.

"Where do you live then?" she says.

"Wingate Road. Just past the school."

"I'll have to stop by some time."

"Yes, one night my wife's not there."

She raises her eyebrows at the unexpected impropriety. "Oh? And what night would that be?"

He gathers the bottles and crisps to go. "No. I'm just kidding. She's always there.—Well, goodnight."

She nods, accepting the rebuttal with good grace, but as Elvis leaves the shop, stepping out on to the street, she notices that he is unable to close the door properly behind him.

I was just getting into the swing with my **card 19** article (1,986 words so far) when my buzzer went. The intercom handset still doesn't work so I went down. When I opened the door, there were two men standing on the doorstep. They were clearly on official business of some sort. Neat haircuts, broad-in-the-beam trousers and aftershave that smelled like toilet cleaner.

"Mr Riley Richardson?"

I nodded. They told me their names and that they were royal protection officers from the something-or-other constabulary.—I can't remember now what they said exactly. They asked if they might have a word with me and before I knew it, they were sitting on my sofa. Royal protection officers. On *my* sofa. I couldn't help smiling, imagining how Nell would be eating her words when I told her about it.

"Listen," I said. "I think I know why you're here. I've already worked it out."

"Oh, yes?"

"But I don't understand why I've been chosen."

"You have been chosen because of a potential threat."

"I thought so. To a certain royal personage?" I suggested coyly.

"Exactly."

"But what can I do about it?"

"We're here to tell you what you can do about it."

It appeared that Steve had been right. I was about to get my instructions.

The older one looked down at the sheaf of papers on his clipboard. "We understand that you were at St Leonard's Hospice yesterday."

"I was."

"—For the royal visit."

I nodded knowingly.

"And you gave something to the Princess."

He held up a photograph of me among the gawping crowd, with Princess Diana accepting my gift. I was squinting a bit and my hairstyle didn't have quite the look I was going for, but otherwise it wasn't a bad one of me.

"Oh. Excellent. Where did you get that? Do you have a spare copy?"

"Can you tell me what was in the bag?"

"A colour photocopy would do for now."

"Just answer the question." His tone had turned unfriendly. I was puzzled by the sudden swerve.

"Why do you want to know?" —He didn't answer so I told him.— "A **P**ork **P**ie."

"A pork pie. And wasn't there something else?"

"No."

"A note you wrote to the Princess?"

"No."

"You didn't write her a note?"

"No."

He held up an evidence bag—it actually said 'Evidence' on it. It looked like something that might have come in the Secret Sam attaché case. Through the transparent polythene I could see my writing pad. The cover was flipped back to reveal the letter I had started to write to the card dealer who had swindled me. I'd forgotten all about it; I must have left it in the carrier bag by mistake. The policeman read aloud:

"You are a liar and a cheat. I'm going to get you for this and I will stop at nothing so you'd better watch your back."

"I didn't write that."

"So this isn't your handwriting?"

"No. Yes. It is my writing, but…"

"What did you mean by 'I will stop at nothing'?"

"…I mean I didn't write it to her, I wrote it to somebody else."

"But you gave it to the Princess of Wales."

"By mistake. It was in the bag with the pie. I forgot it was there."

"Why would you give the Princess a pork pie?"

"I didn't know she was a vegetarian."

It was a barrage of questions, both of them chipping in. I thought they had come to give me my mission details and here they were interrogating me like some common criminal on *Taggart.*

"What was in the pie?"

"Pork," I said sarcastically.

"And what else? Rat poison? Broken glass? Razor blades?"

What were they talking about? It was a sick and twisted idea.

"Are you planning to harm the Princess of Wales?"

"Of course not. Why would I want to harm her?"

"Because she's *a liar and a cheat?*" suggested the younger one.

"I keep telling you, the letter was to someone else: a man who conned me out of a lot of money. I bought a bubble-gum card from him and it turned out to be a fake. He refused to give me my money back."

"A bubble-gum card?"

"It's extremely rare."

The younger man snorted and shook his head.

The older one said, "It's our job to investigate any potential threat to a member of the Royal Family and your letter was brought to our attention. Inadvertently or not, you've committed a very serious offence."

"It's an act of high treason to threaten a member of the monarchy," the younger one added.

"I haven't threatened anybody."

"Disloyalty to the sovereign. Plotting to cause injury to a member of the Royal Family. Not so long ago you would have been hanged, drawn and quartered for that. Offences against the Crown still carry the death penalty in this country."

"I don't think so," I scoffed. "'Capital punishment was abolished years ago."

"Well, that's where you're wrong, matey. It may not have been enforced recently, but the death penalty remains on the statute book for high treason. You could still be hanged for what you've done."

He didn't scare me. It was absurd. I remember my dad telling me that *defacing a coin of the realm* was an act of treason because it had the Queen's picture on it. He only said it because I'd used his hand drill to make a hole in a sixpenny piece to keep as a lucky charm. Mum said I was daft, but I didn't actually get into trouble for it. A couple of other boys at school copied what I'd done, including Jamie Wotton, whose dad was a policeman and would therefore have been obliged by law to report his son's crime. I don't remember seeing Jamie's dismembered head stuck on a pole outside the school gates or his quartered body parts on display in the playground.

"Ever been arrested for stalking?"

"Stalking? No. Of course not."

The first policeman flicked over some pages on his clipboard. "In March 1991 you were apprehended by security staff at London's Dorchester Hotel, attempting to gain entry to one of the rooms."

"I was not trying to *gain entry*. It was all a huge mistake. I was there visiting a friend and had been given the wrong room number."

"You weren't aware that the pop singer Kylie Minogue was staying there?"

"No. I had no idea whose room it was. I don't even like **Kylie Minogue**. I explained all this at the time. Ask your friends down at the station. All charges were dropped."

"And in 1981 you were caught climbing the fence at T.V.A.M's television studios wearing a monkey mask."

"I was not climbing over the fence. I was just trying to get a better look."

"Better look? Better look at who?"

"Nobody. Do we really have to go through all this again? It's sixteen years ago. There was no case."

"Why were you wearing a monkey mask, Mr Richardson?"

"Oh for heaven's sake. You're making this sound like something it wasn't." I made a point of emphasizing the tediousness of having to explain myself all over again. "Look, I'd been to a fancy-dress party. I was walking home. I was feeling a bit merry. I just wanted to see if there was anyone famous in the studios. Through the window. That's all."

"Why?"

"Why? No reason. Curiosity. I don't know why. Listen, you've got this all wrong. I'm not one of those crazed fans. I'm not going to jump out and stab **Princess Diana** or hit her on the head with a hammer."

They both looked up.

"Aren't you, Mr Richardson?" The main one stared hard into my eyes. "Are you quite sure about that?"

I don't know why I said that about the hammer. I realized it had made me sound a bit odd. Still, the whole idea was ridiculous. Harming Diana was the last thing on my mind. I could never hurt anyone or anything, least of all a member of the Royal Family. I had been all ready to go out of my way to answer the call of patriotic duty to act as her protector, and here I was being accused of malicious intent.

The younger policeman felt obliged to offer his opinion on the matter. "You sound like a bit of a nutter to me." He had stood up and was looming over me. He was just a thug and a bully.

How dare he talk to me like that?

"Do you have any weapons? Any guns or knives?" The older one was on his feet now too.

"No, of course not." I was furious. "And I am not a *nutter*, thank you very much." Actually I'd got a bit tongue-tied and might have told them that I was not an otter.

"You don't mind if we have a look round?" I did, but it wasn't a question; they'd decided they were going to anyway. I could hear them in the bedroom, opening cupboards and drawers. They came back to the living room still rooting round like truffle pigs. The young one pushed over a pile of magazines with his foot and kicked them apart to check the titles—no attempt to straighten them again. Disgruntled at finding nothing incriminating, they decided they'd had enough and made for the door. I didn't get up from my chair—I didn't even look up. The older one offered his parting shot:

"Right. My advice to you is to stay well away. If you're found anywhere near a member of the Royal Family again, you're going to be in serious trouble. Do you understand? We'll be watching you."

FIVE

1967. The clatter of typewriter keys. Slim fingers dance across a big old sit-up-and-beg Underwood. The pretty secretary with the Dusty Springfield hairdo is copy-typing from a sheet clipped to a little desk stand. The keys hammer the paper like machine-gun fire. She scoots the carriage across to start a new line as Elvis pops his head round the door. She smiles, waiting for him to speak.

"How was your steak?"

"Bloody."

"Bloody good or bloody bad?"

"Bloody awful, actually."

He looks around the office, taking in the details: carpet; the warm glow from her desk lamp; a coffee-making area with a kettle, cups and a jar of Nescafé (Continental Blend 37); her cardigan on the back of the chair. Cosy.

"Hey. Has that corrected artwork come in for the *Mission: Impossible* cards job?" he says, closing the door behind him.

She shakes her head.

"Jim Cole says they're not going to replace the withdrawn card. Is that true?"

"Apparently."

"So why are they sending new artwork? I don't get it. We could have used the plates we'd already made, then just dumped the withdrawn card once the sheets had been guillotined."

"Chad said the plates had to be scrapped along with the film. Strict orders. We even had to send the artwork back."

"Why?"

"I don't know. Some big deal about this particular card."

Elvis perches on the edge of her desk and begins to fiddle with an elastic band, stretching it between his fingers.

"So instead of forty-eight cards, there'll be forty-seven. Can they get away with that?"

She shrugs. "Who's going to find out?"

"But on the back of each card it says: a series of forty-eight. Bit of a cheat if there's one missing, isn't it? Not really fair to the collector. Are they trying to sell more bubble-gum or something?"

"No, I think they've missed their deadline and they have to get the series to the distributors."

"What was so special about this card, anyway?"

"I don't know. I never saw it."

"Me neither."

He looks up to find her staring at him. For a long moment she holds his gaze. He seems transfixed.

"I like your hair," he says quietly.

She flushes. "Thanks."

Suddenly aware of the intimacy between them, he gets up from her desk. He spots a bag of golf clubs leaning against the filing cabinet.

"I didn't know he played."

"Who?"

"The boss." He nods towards Mr Greenwood's office while selecting a club with a big chunky head from the golf bag.

"He doesn't. I do."

"You?"

"Yes. Why not?"

"No reason," he says.

"It's very good for the figure."

"Evidently."

He paddles his feet, perfecting his stance and adjusting his grip as though about to tee off. "I've never really got into golf," he says. "I always rather fancied it though. I imagined I'd be quite good."

"Your grip's all wrong."

Undeterred, he takes a practice swing.

She cowers, clutching her head protectively. "Mind that lamp!"

"Where?"

"Behind you. You nearly hit it."

He sees the lamp and repositions himself a little further away. "Which card is it they're going to remove—from the bubble-gum series—do you know?" he says.

"No idea."

"Could you find out?"

"You mean which number?"

"Yes."

"I suppose I could. I'd have to check the letter."

He takes another practice swing. "Well, then…?"

"Don't I look like I've got better things to do?"

"No, you don't actually."

She smiles, amused. "You'll be able to work it out for yourself when the new artwork comes in, won't you? Why do you want to know, anyway?"

"I don't. It's just that I had a bet with Jim. He says it's always card thirteen that gets withdrawn. He's bet me ten bob."

"He must already know then, if he's putting money on it."

"No, I don't think he does. He's got some daft theory about unlucky thirteen."

"And what did you bet the number was?"

"I guessed it was twenty-eight. Same as your age."

"Do you mind? I'm not twenty-eight."

"How old are you then? Thirty?"

She refuses to be baited.

"Go on," he says. "Just to settle a bet."

"All right, but if you win, you can buy me a drink after work."

"Ooh, I don't know if I can do that. I'm a married man."

She shrugs to show her indifference. "Please yourself. It's only a drink. I wasn't going to ask you to run away with me. I've got a date later anyway."

"Well, that's all right then, isn't it?" Elvis prods her upper arm with the shaft of the club, holding it like a snooker cue. "Go on. Have a look."

She tuts and gets up from her desk. "I shouldn't be doing this. No one's supposed to know there'll be a card missing."

Elvis watches as she flicks through folders in a filing cabinet. In spite of the professed inconvenience, her pose seems deliberately provocative. He averts his eyes, trying to keep himself in check. She takes out a folder marked *Chad—Mission: Impossible* and lays it across the open drawer to read through the various papers.

Just then, Mr Greenwood appears from his office. Elvis quickly slots the club back in the golf bag. Mr Greenwood seems puzzled by Elvis's presence and looks to the secretary for further clues as to why he is there. With nothing forthcoming, he resumes his original query. "Is this an old address I've got for Sterling Brookes?"

The secretary swiftly replaces the folder and turns to study the index card he is holding. "Yes, they've moved. I'll bring you the new one." —There is an awkward moment before Elvis makes for the door.— "Oh, I nearly forgot." The secretary's voice sounds a little theatrical. Her eyes flick towards Mr Greenwood who is looking down at the card in his hand. "You wanted to know that extension number?"

"Oh, yes. I did." Elvis also appears to have joined the amateur dramatic society.

"Nineteen," she says, rather overstressing the word.

"Nineteen. Right. Thanks. Well, I'd better get back."

Elvis winks and discreetly raises his thumb. Looking up, Mr Greenwood catches sight of this and, assuming it is aimed at him, tentatively mimics the gesture.

3,000

It's getting rather good now, my story. The printer has identified the withdrawn card and from this point on, the readers will be hooked. I wrote a short letter to Michael Mallinsay suggesting that my piece should probably be the main feature in next month's issue.

I was just checking the second post on my way out when I heard Steve coming down the stairs. He must listen out for me; I'm always getting caught. I was going to say something about the way he never sorts the mail, selfishly taking his own from the pile and leaving the rest for someone else to deal with, but halfway down he shouted, "Heads up," and threw something at me. Caught off guard and wary of what he might be throwing, I fumbled. It was his set of house keys. I had to dig them out from behind the hall radiator with a pencil. "Nice catch," said Steve.

"Well, why can't you just hand them to me?"

It was Steve's suggestion to swap spare sets in case either of us got locked out. It's quite a good idea really. I used to leave a key with Mrs Brooks in Flat 6, before she went into a nursing home; it had saved my bacon the night I lost my jacket at the Hammersmith Odeon. Still, I felt a little uncomfortable knowing that Steve had keys to my flat; I didn't even know him that well, but since he had entrusted me with his, I felt it would have been churlish not to reciprocate. Besides, I didn't know how to say no. It wasn't that I minded the idea of having a friend in the building. In *An American in Paris*, **Gene Kelly** is a struggling artist living in a small Paris studio apartment above a café frequented by ooh-la-la girls with names like Mimi and Yvette. Upstairs lives wisecracking would-be concert pianist **Oscar Levant** and together they have a high old time being starving artists. Steve wasn't Oscar Levant, and anyway that wasn't exactly the relationship I had in mind. When I first moved in, there was lovely Elaine downstairs on the ground floor and I had anticipated more of a *Breakfast at Tiffany's* kind of set-up with her. I think she was a textile designer or something; she seemed vibrant and extremely arty in all her choices. Her flat was full of reclaimed treasures and open-plan chic. I'd occasionally catch a glimpse through her open doorway as I was passing. There was an artist's drafting table and an old guitar hanging on the wall.

Once I had introduced myself to Elaine in the hallway, I naturally assumed that we'd be in and out of each other's flats (which we'd refer to as apartments), hanging out, sharing food and wine, being best of friends, and this, I imagined, would ultimately develop into something more romantic. It didn't happen, but not because she wasn't the social type. She'd frequently have her hip young friends round and in the summer they would sit out in the garden, taunting me with their easy laughter. I would watch in the darkness from my kitchen window. She only invited me in once, when she needed a hand to get her old washing machine into a skip. As we passed her bedroom, I noticed a large beefcake-style poster of **Jean-Claude Vandamme** in his underpants. It was signed in blue marker across his rippling midriff. I realized then that she wasn't my type.

I looked through all the newspapers in WH Smith's, hoping to find the picture of me with Diana that the royal protection officers had shown me. It was such a good shot, I figured it had to have been taken by a professional and would therefore be printed in one of the dailies, but it wasn't in any of them. In fact, there wasn't a single picture from her hospice visit. No one's interested in seeing her looking happy. Tomorrow maybe.

At the zebra crossing near to Hector Goodall's shop, I saw a man dressed as **Boy George** waiting to cross from the other side. His full-moon face was heavily made up with the over-saturated hues of a burlesque queen and he was wearing a large pink felt hat with a high crown and an asymmetrical brim that swooped down over one ear. The hat was studded with diamante swirls and looked quite authentic as a piece of costume, but the man was too hefty to carry it off and he had an Adam's apple the size of a teenager's fist. He was with a gaggle of overexcited friends, all dressed in similarly elaborate outfits, so I assumed they were on their way to a fancy-dress party. When the traffic stopped and he came towards me, I realized it wasn't, as I had first thought, just an ordinary fat bloke dressed up as Boy George—it really was Boy George. But then, I suppose that's who Boy George is these days: an ordinary fat bloke dressed up as Boy George.

I wanted to ask Hector about the cards I'd found and where they might have come from. Hector isn't a card specialist—I'm the locally recognized authority on gum cards from the 1960s—but he knows more than I do about cigarette cards so I thought he might suggest something that could offer some further clue to their meaning.

Hector was sitting in his usual place behind the counter, surrounded by the treasures of his trade. He sells all kinds of vintage printed ephemera: football programmes, scrapbooks, records, stamps, maps, newspapers, photographs, banknotes, magazines. Each item is carefully sealed in its own individual cellophane-fronted bag, dated, priced and organized into neat piles or displayed in specially labelled boxes. The more interesting examples adorn the walls and every available surface is occupied. Rescued from the scrap heaps of obscurity and lovingly conserved for posterity, Hector's ephemera is the very opposite of ephemeral. This stuff is here to stay.

There's something for everyone at Hector's Emporium. Whether you're looking for a birthday card for *a very special nephew* from the 1950s or a pocket diary for someone planning to keep a day-to-day account of the Apollo 11 space mission, you'll find it here. At Hector's, you can buy a 1958 *Radio Times*, a signed picture of *Liberace*, or an unused ticket for the 1966 World Cup quarter-final between England and Argentina. You might be tempted by a wartime ration book or a cinema lobby card for *Carry on Nurse*. Or perhaps you're after a Watney's beer bottle label or something to commemorate King Edward VIII's coronation? Whatever you need, Hector has just the thing. It's mostly printed stuff, but there are some small toys and games too: Dinky cars, action figures, particularly TV tie-ins, and there's a wealth of memorabilia relating to sci-fi films like *Battlestar Gallactica* and *Star Wars*.

Hector sits amongst it all in his hand-built nest of nostalgia. Old knitting patterns and saucy seaside postcards hang from a series of drooping strings above his head like home-made festive bunting. Crowded for leg room by the overloaded shelves and drawers behind him, he is forced to sit sideways in his chair, making him seem resolutely uninterested in his customers.

I have always thought Hector bears a passing resemblance to the actor **Michael Gambon**. His head looks big and heavy like a slab of something you might carry home from the butcher's to serve up at a large family gathering. On top there are thinning strands of long, wispy hair as a reminder of the hairstyle of which he was obviously once quite proud. Despite Hector's penchant for a natty shirt-and-bow-tie combination, invariably worn with a smart quilted body-warmer-style waistcoat, the overall effect is slightly crusty and dishevelled. He generally has a couple of days' beard growth, but it's pale and sparse, looking as though his jaw might have inadvertently picked up bits of stray hair and fluff from the shop.

I had already decided to keep quiet about my mission. Hector is inclined to ridicule the beliefs of others, so I told him that my finds were odds I'd picked up in a junk shop.

The May Day card was issued by Gallaher's, I knew that, but I was curious to know when. It wasn't a series that Hector recognized straight away, but he agreed that it was probably from the fifties. He got out his cigarette card collectors' catalogue to check.

"Gallaher's, Gallaher's," he mumbled, as he searched for the relevant page. He found it and ran a fingernail down a long list, resting his spectacles on his eyebrows as he squinted at the tiny print. "No. Can't see it. What's the series called again? *Great British Traditions?* Oh, here it is. *Gallaher Tobacco, 1955.*"

I was about to ask him about mayday being an emergency distress call when Hector's daughter came in, manoeuvring her baby-buggy-pushchair through the narrow doorway. I don't know why those things always seem like such an intrusion— their fat, clumsy wheels ramming their way into position. She's always popping in, fetching and carrying for Hector. His wife died last year so he has to manage on his own now. The daughter parked the infant in front of the counter while she took a bulging plastic carrier bag from a tray underneath the kid's seat.

"Here y'are, Dad." She handed over the bag with a receipt and some coins. "They had no chicken-and-mushroom so I got you chicken-and-leek."

"Oh, thanks, love," he said, peering inside the bag. "Did you get my Jaffa Cakes? Ooh lovely."

The kid was about a year old, I think; I'm not very good at guessing babies' ages. It was sleeping peacefully in the buggy, its mouth plugged with a big ugly dummy.

Hector raised himself up and leaned over the counter to look at him. "How's my little lad? Doesn't he want to say hello to his granddad?"

"I've just got him off, Dad. I don't want to wake him; he's been a right pain all morning. Can I have this; can I have that. I bought him some little soldiers to shut him up and by the time we'd got to Mirfield Park, he'd dropped half of them all over the street. Whatever you give him, he just chucks it down. The number of toys I've lost."

"Does he want some more of those cards I gave him?"

"No. It's all right, Dad."

"Doesn't he like them?"

"Oh, yeah. He loves them. Next time, perhaps."

When she'd gone I showed Hector the queen of hearts, explaining about the face being in profile. He didn't think it particularly unusual so I got him to compare it with the queen of hearts in a couple of old card packs he had. In each, the queen was facing forward, but Hector still wasn't convinced of its significance. "It's just a variation in the design, that's all," he said. "Probably made in a foreign country. I once had a pack of cards from Egypt where the printing colour was completely random: black hearts, red clubs, some cards missing, others duplicated.— Like they were made by someone who didn't understand what they were for."

I don't know what I was hoping for.—Something about the profile to link the card definitely to Princess Diana? Some clue to confirm that the cigarette card was about a mayday distress call rather than the May Day festival? Hector had no thoughts on that, but he agreed that the *Your Country Needs You* card looked like a miniature version of a recruitment poster.

"It's Second World War, isn't it?" I said.

"The poster is, but the card would have been much later. It's probably a nostalgia thing, perhaps a series on poster design or something. With nothing on the back there's no real way of finding out. It could be from anywhere, might not necessarily be British."

"Look at the soldier's face."

Hector peered closely at the card.

"Remind you of anybody?"

Hector shrugged his shoulders. "Gregory Peck?"

"You don't think it looks like me?"

Hector coughed up a little mocking chortle. "Er, no, not really," he said, handing back the card. "Why?"

"Nothing. Forget it."

So, no help from Hector.—A complete waste of time. I was just about to leave when he called me back.

"Hey, Riley. I nearly forgot. You collect the 1967 *Mission: Impossible* series, don't you?"

"Yes. Why?"

"I got a few odds in yesterday. I don't know if there's any you're looking for. Hang on; I wrote the numbers down somewhere. Oh, here we are." He picked up a scrap of card next to the till and read from it. "Forty-two, eleven, thirty-one, thirty five and…" he squinted at the card, shaking his head "…can't read me own writing." He put on his reading glasses and peered through them. "Oh, yes. Number nineteen. Any good?" He looked enquiringly over his glasses, holding the pose until he could no longer contain his laughter. "Oh, no, wait a minute," he chuckled. "I forgot. I sold them all this morning."

Every time I go in—the same hilarious joke.—Always pretending he's forgotten which card I'm looking for, even though it's the most sought-after card in the collecting world. He often gets me to rummage through his Odds-and-Sods box before 'remembering' that he sold the card or gave it away to a child, or that he chucked it in the bin because it was 'a bit scuffed'. I play along because he gets such a kick out of it. As far as the legend of **card 19** goes, Hector is a *non-believer*.

The library had quite a few books on playing cards, mostly on their use in fortune-telling. I don't go in for all that stuff, but I looked anyway. The queen of hearts apparently represents an affectionate, caring woman with water signs predominating. Water signs predominating? Does **Princess Diana** have water signs predominating? I've never noticed any.

There was one very good book on the history of playing cards. I would have taken it home to study, but it was really heavy so I decided to do my research there and then. That's the beauty of a good old-fashioned public library—nobody minds you taking your time. Unlike the mean woman in Sweeton's Bookshop earlier, with her fussy little handmade sign sellotaped to the shelf: *This is not a public library*. The word *not* underlined. So I thought, *Well then, I'll go to somewhere that is.*

It was fascinating stuff, all about what the different suits represent, spades originally being swords and what-have-you. Apparently, Catherine of Aragon, Henry VIII's first wife, was also affectionately nicknamed the **Queen of Hearts** because she was much loved by her contemporaries; rather less so by her husband, who was beating his brains out trying to find a way to have their marriage annulled so that he would be free to marry **Anne Boleyn**.

Now that he's divorced from 'Diana of Spencer', I wonder whether **Prince Charles** will marry **Camilla Parker Bowles**. And will he ever be king? The Queen seems to have the crown wedged on pretty tightly. All those years of him hanging around, playing polo and doing his royal visits, hoping one day to get a go at wearing his mother's hat. A man perpetually overlooked for promotion; how could his sons respect that? *What do you do, Dad? I'm a prince, son. Oh. Are you? So am I.* It would be like turning up on your first day at school to find your dad wedged into the desk next to you, no further along in his lessons than you are.

There was a chapter on the original designs for the court cards, showing how, through years of bad copying, certain details have been lost or misinterpreted. The king of diamonds has always been shown in profile, as have both the jack of spades and the jack of hearts, hence being known as one-eyed jacks. But, as I suspected, none of the queens in the book were in profile; they were all shown full face like on a passport picture.

Unsure what to do with that little nugget of knowledge, I wandered over to the Royalty section. Since I'd had the honour of talking to the *Princess of Wales*, I felt I should find out a bit more about her in case anybody asked about our meeting. To tell the truth, I felt like a bit of an outsider, knowing so little when the rest of the nation seemed so well informed. By reading all that stuff in the tabloids every day, the public have become Diana experts. Besides, if I was being assigned as her protector, I needed to know as much as possible about her so that I could identify the likely source of any threat to her well-being.

The books fell into two categories: insider kiss-and-tell exposés written by supposed lovers or former employees, or illustrated biographies venerating her as a glamorous role model, doting mother, altruistic do-gooder and saint. Princess Diana might not be a saint exactly, but that doesn't detract from her kind deeds. Who hasn't got up to no good in the past, making hoax phone calls or poking Kentucky Fried Chicken leftovers through people's letter-boxes? It's what makes us human. Diana's no different, I'm sure, and her public wouldn't want her to be.

"That's the one you want." A woman who had been lurking in my peripheral vision tapped one of the books with a sharp fingernail. Was she talking to me? Her eyebrows were pencilled in a high, surprised arch that might have been more appropriate on a circus clown. The book, a hardback, *Diana: The People's Princess*, was sticking out from the shelf. She tapped it again, saying, "That one. It's by far the best. Take it." Having made her recommendation, she walked away. I flicked through it and read the blurb on the back cover. It did look pretty interesting; perhaps she was right. I saw the woman watching me from the end of the aisle; she nodded and pointed at the book in my hand.

1967. A crowded pub. Elvis and the secretary stand huddled together, caught up in the midst of a boisterous but friendly crowd of revellers. She leans towards him to say something and they both laugh. When she gets nudged by a passing customer and spills some of her drink, Elvis instinctively provides a protective arm. The culprit, a jolly red-faced man, offers his effusive apologies, which they accept in good humour.

I was just setting off for the counter to check the book out when I caught sight of a playing card lying face down on the lino at the end of the Film Biographies aisle. I looked around to see who might have put it there. The clown-faced woman had gone. No other likely suspects nearby. No Jim Phelps. I sidled over to the card and bent down to pick it up. **THE FOUR OF CLUBS.**

Did it mean something, or was it just a card? I was pondering the possibilities as I waited to have my book stamped when I noticed various handbags and shoulder bags behind the counter. Each of them had a playing card attached to it by a clothes peg. I didn't get it at first, but then a man entered and the librarian asked him if he wouldn't mind leaving his bag—one of those rucksack jobs—behind the counter. There was no mention of theft, but that's what the library was guarding against. The man passed it over and the girl handed him the eight of clubs, tagging his bag with a duplicate card before stowing it on a shelf behind her. Then I understood: it was the library's quirky version of a cloakroom ticket. The card I'd picked up had nothing to do with Diana or Jim Phelps; one of the other visitors must have dropped it. I was going to hand it in while checking out my book, and explain that I had found it on the floor, but before I could say anything the librarian took the card from me and exchanged it for one of the bags behind her, unclipping the corresponding card before sliding it to me across the counter. It was a kind of satchel made from thick, richly aged black leather fastened by a sturdy brass clasp. I wasn't sure if it belonged to a woman or a man, but I did know that it didn't belong to me. I was about to say something when the librarian headed off towards Natural History, leaving me standing there with the bag in front of me. Well, what was I to do?

SIX

SITTING AT HOME with the bag and its contents set out on the coffee table made me feel bad about what I had done. What on earth had possessed me to take a stranger's bag? I went through the things one by one: a key ring with assorted keys; a packet of Polo mints; a wallet-style purse; a packet of paper tissues. In my head I could hear the announcer at the end of *The Generation Game*, calling out the prizes on the conveyor belt and, as if I were a contestant on the show, I felt compelled to try and commit each item to memory. A quilted make-up bag containing lipstick, powder compact and blusher; a nail file...

The most intriguing item was a pair of silver scissors in a black-velvet-covered case. It was the kind of case that might normally hold the precision instruments required to create elaborate geometric drawings or to carry out a delicate medical procedure on a hamster. The scissors had sharp points and the little stalk protruding from one of the handle loops told me that they were for *hairdressing*—I'd seen Mr Vann using a similar pair, but these seemed ultra-special, shiny and heavy, with a little knurled nugget of gold at the fulcrum. I took them out and snipped at the air. The blades met silently and effortlessly, as if they were slicing through double cream. They were like no other scissors I'd ever used. Yet there was something peculiar about them and I realized that they had been made for somebody who was left-handed. Using my left hand felt awkward so I tried them out right-handedly on the cover of the *TV Times*, cutting a fine fringe down the side of **Sean Connery's** arm.

When I opened the purse, I found various credit, debit and store cards, all bearing the same name, *Amy Truelove*, or variations on it: *A. Truelove, Ms. A. S. Truelove*. In the coin part of the purse, along with a dry-cleaning ticket and a few receipts, was a single twenty-pound note. None of the cards revealed her date of birth, but from her Travelcard picture I would have guessed that she was in her mid-twenties. She was pretty, with red lips and a head of thick amber hair in a tousled bob of curls that made her look a little like a Hollywood starlet from the 1930s. Despite the warmth in her eyes I felt her disapproval of me for interfering with her personal belongings. I wasn't supposed to be looking at this stuff. What was I doing with this woman's bag anyway? I had ruined her day, possibly her whole week. Thanks to me, she would now be unable get home because she had no Travelcard, no money and no means of withdrawing any from her bank. And even if she walked home, she wouldn't be able to get into her house because she didn't have her keys. She certainly couldn't give anyone a haircut without her special scissors, neither could she pick up her dry-cleaning, freshen her lipstick or suck on a peppermint. She couldn't even blow her nose and it was all my fault.

I was just putting everything back when I noticed that the bag had a little inside pocket which contained half a dozen stylishly designed business cards for **Amy Truelove**, *hairstylist*, located at 47 De Havilland Road in Islington. I remembered what Steve had said about a rendezvous location where I would be sent to receive further mission instructions. Maybe this was it.

1967. Elvis walks past a darkened room, its door slightly ajar. He gently pushes the door wider and peers inside. The bulb from the landing throws soft light on to the sleeping figure of a young boy. On his bedside table is a stack of cards. Elvis creeps in; the boy remains undisturbed. He carefully picks up the cards and begins to sort through them, turning them over to check the numbers on the back. Each one of the cards bears the boy's signature. Elvis holds them up to the light from the door until he comes to the card he is looking for, whereupon he removes it from the pack and holds it between his lips while he squares the remaining cards and replaces them on the nightstand. He creeps out of the room and pulls the door to, leaving the same gap as before. As he heads downstairs he slips the card into his shirt pocket. His wife is on her way from the kitchen carrying two cups on a small tray.

"Peurff. I can still smell the beer on you."

"I only had one."

"You smell like a brewery."

"I had to go. One of the lads at work is leaving."

He follows her into the living room and starts rummaging around in the bureau drawer. She sets down the tray and plonks herself on the sofa in front of the television.

"*Now* what are you doing?" she says. "Sit down."

"Just wondered where my passport was."

"What do you want your passport for? You're not going anywhere."

"I know. Just want to make sure it's up to date."

"Why?"

"Well, you never know. Oh, here it is."

She tuts, annoyed at the distraction. He checks that she is engrossed in the television and then slips the *Mission: Impossible* card between the passport's pages before returning it to the drawer.

"Don't let it go cold. It'll get a skin on it."

His heart sinks. "Do we *have* to have Horlicks every night?"

"You like Horlicks."

"Not really."

"You used to love it."

"Well, I don't now. I fancy something different for a change."

"Like what?"

"I don't know. Coffee. Why can't we have that?"

"Coffee? Eurgh, no. It's bitter." She pulls a face as if he has suggested eating dog shit.

"Well, I like it."

"You don't."

"I do. Lots of people at work drink it."

"Ooh, no. No thank you. We're not having that." She screws her eyes tight and shudders. He stares at her for a moment, speechless, but her eyes are now fixed on the TV screen so she fails to notice the resigned shaking of his head.

The following day. The boy has laid the *Mission: Impossible* cards face down in neat rows on his bedroom floor. There is a gap in the second row. One of the cards is missing. He checks his pockets; he checks behind his nightstand, under his bed, but he can't find it. He turns the neighbouring cards over to examine the numbers in the sequence: 16, 17, 18, 20.—All the cards appear to be there except for number 19. He stares at the gap where the missing card should be. Panic mounts. Did one of the other boys snatch it in the playground scuffle or did he himself accidentally drop it on his way home? Out on the street, he retraces his route from

3,600

school, scouring the pavements for the lost card, a search that will consume him for the next thirty years.

3,679

You see what I've done there? I've rather cleverly put myself into the story, strongly hinting to the reader that I was that boy, which of course will explain my specific interest in the missing card and why I am now writing this special feature about it. It's a pivotal moment in the article because from this point the reader knows that Elvis the printer—real name Brian—was my father. Michael Mallinsay is going to love this.

It didn't occur to me until quite recently that my dad might have confiscated the card as a way to protect himself. I had always imagined that it had been lost that day in the playground. No one owned up to having it, but I assumed that someone was lying. With the rapid swapping and trading that went on I had envisaged the culprit selling it to a boy from another school, and that boy trading it with his cousin in Ross-on-Wye or Bury St Edmunds or with a French boy he met during a field trip to Whipsnade Zoo. Within a week the card could have found its way out of the school, out of the city, even out of the country.

A couple of weeks later, the *Mission: Impossible* series was in the shops so I stopped looking for the original card and started buying packets of cards along with the other boys, in the hope of completing my series again. Of course it was not to be. Even under normal card-collecting circumstances, the odds were heavily stacked against me—only a one in forty-eight chance of getting the card I wanted (multiplied by the number of cards in each wax-pack wrapper). I couldn't do the maths, but after the purchase of several packets had left me with a disappointing handful of redundant swaps I began to realise the chances of buying a pack containing the last missing card were pretty slim. So, I gave up on that idea and decided to find someone who already had the coveted card and then devise a strategy—bribery, blackmail, torture, theft—to persuade whoever it was to part with it. But of course, it was all in vain; no one else had **card 19** either— not even the conscientious completists or the boys with pocketfuls of extra pocket money. They all found themselves one card short. Unbeknown to us, there was no replacement **card 19**. The only example of it had already slipped through my fingers, lost and seemingly gone for ever.

I still have the other forty-seven, the original ones I got as a proof sheet when I was a boy. The card edges are actually reasonably straight and accurate, considering they were cut by a ten-year-old with a pair of scissors—I must have taken great care—but technically they would be regarded as imperfect examples. I probably used my mum's dressmaking scissors for the job—the big heavy ones with blue handles, which she kept in her sewing box. She always insisted that they should never be used to cut paper or card, but I couldn't see why not; when I tried them, they seemed to work really well. What devalues the cards more—in collecting circles at least—is the fact that I signed my name, *R. Pincus*, in biro on the back of every card. How stupid of me. For a while—at least two card series—everyone at school did it. Perhaps, like the sixpence with the hole drilled in it, I was the one who started the craze. Throughout my childhood I felt compelled to write my name on all my possessions: books, cricket bat, satchel, comics, Action Man. Presumably I was worried that I might lose these things or have them taken from me, and believed that the R. Pincus branding would ensure that I would later be able to identify them as my own. I don't do that now, but lots of people do. They etch their names on their garden tools with special engraving pens, or use security UV markers to write their postcode on their video recorders and Playstation consoles in the hope that, should any of these items stray, and be recovered by the police from a burglar's haul, they will ultimately find their way home again. I can't recall whether I wrote my name on the *Mission: Impossible* cards before or after the disappearance of **card 19**, but as yet no helpful policeman has shown up to return that particular item to its rightful owner.

It was late when Nell rang. I'd been writing my article and had lost track of time.

"Did you watch it?"

"Watch what?"

"Don't tell me you didn't see it."

"What?"

"**Barry Manilow** on *The Des O'Connor Show*."

"Oh, no. I forgot."

"You were the one that told me about it."

"I know. I forgot. Was it good?"

"Brilliant. He did 'I Made It Through the Rain'. Don't worry. I taped it. I thought you'd be in at lunchtime."

"No, I had things to do."

"Do you want to come over and watch it?"

"Now?"

"We could have a nightcap."

"Maybe not tonight, Nell. I'm tired. Save it for me though."

"OK." There was a pause. "Any more secret messages from Lady Di?"

I didn't answer.

"Hey, you know she's going out with some rich Arab now. It was in the paper. He's the millionaire son of that bloke who owns Harrods. What's his name? Al Fayed? So you might be up against some stiff competition."

I was absent-mindedly studying Miss Truelove's Travelcard, which was still out on the table.

"So what have you been up to?" she said, deciding to change tack.

"Nothing really." I realized I was sounding rather distant. But what was I going to tell her? *Some policemen came round and accused me of trying to poison Princess Diana so I went to the library and stole a woman's handbag.* There was another pause before she spoke again.

"You're not upset because I teased you about the cards?"

"No. Course not."

"I was only having a laugh."

"I know."

"Who knows? Maybe there *is* some kind of message."

I knew she didn't really believe it.

I shouldn't have started thinking about memorizing the prizes at the end of *The* **G***eneration* **G***ame* because I lay awake in bed trying to remember the contents of Miss Truelove's handbag. I kept telling myself to stop and just go to sleep, but I couldn't. It reminded me of a party game we used to play at home: a memory test that involved twenty miscellaneous objects on a tea tray. You'd have sixty seconds to look at them and then they'd be covered with the tea towel while you recalled as many items as you could. While uncovered, the objects screamed their undeniable presence. The harder you stared, the more firmly embedded they became, their shapes pressing deep into the soft pastry of the brain. It seemed impossible to forget any of them, yet as soon as the tea towel was draped back over them, the objects began to disappear one by one, like fragments of a dream dissolving irretrievably to nothing. My mum was useless at it—out of sight, out of mind—but Dad had a winning technique. He said the trick was to make connections between the objects by creating a little story that incorporated them all. I think it's a recognized method—mnemonics or something. It wasn't working for me;

I had to get out of bed to check the handbag. I'd remembered everything except her Polo mints. So silly. What did it matter?

Sometimes when I can't get to sleep, my mind starts working itself into a fizz and I can't shut it down. If I start thinking about alliterated menus, I can be awake for hours. Coronation Chicken with Cucumber Chutney, Charred Celery, a Cream Cheese and Chopped Chestnut Crepe, Cranberry Coulis, and a Chiffonnade of Cabbage, Chicory, and Chard. I often work alphabetically, creating a different meal for each letter—which is pointless because I always get stuck at X. I can usually get something for all the other letters—even though Yam and Yoghurt Yakitori and Zucchini Zeppoles may not suit all palates—but what food begins with X?

At two thirty I was still awake because I was working on anagrams of people's names. Why? I don't know. It's hard to do them in your head so in the end I turned the light on and used pen and paper. Guess what I discovered: *Barry Manilow* is an anagram of *Library Woman*.

BARRYMANILOW
LIBRARYWOMAN

SEVEN

I COULDN'T WORK OUT where Amy Truelove fitted into all this—whether she was part of the MI5 mission or just an ordinary citizen. She didn't look like a secret agent, yet the playing card had led me to her bag. I was sure I'd seen something similar in a spy film, something to do with a left-luggage ticket and a suitcase, as a method enabling one agent to make contact covertly with another. I decided to pay her a visit—on the pretext of returning the bag—and see what happened.

Steve knocked on my door just as I was on my way out.

"Here's that book on **Oswald**. Check it out." He was wearing his usual camouflage trousers and an olive-green singlet. For some reason, his glasses were secured by an elastic strap that went round the back of his head, making them look like swimming goggles. He had brought a selection of reading material with him. On top of the pile, *The Search for Lee Harvey Oswald*. The cover bore the same mug-shot picture as the magazine I'd seen in Mr Orhy's.

"Oh, right. Thanks."

"And I've got that stuff on camouflage I was telling you about." He held up a thick book with a title in lettering so livid, it was hard to read the words. "This you are going to love," he said, handing it to me.

Despite my reluctance to let him in, he barged his way past me to dump the other books on my coffee table. Steve had become rather enamoured with the idea that I might be an MI5 recruit and, as my self-appointed technical adviser, he had promised to get me 'tooled up' for any covert activity that might be required of me. I remained standing by the open door, hoping to cut his visit short.

"It's the best book on SAS training and it's got tons about camouflage techniques. It gives you the seven rules."

I flicked through the pages of the book in my hand. "The seven rules?"

"**S**hape, **S**hine, **S**hadow, **S**ilhouette, **S**pacing, **S**urface and **M**ovement." Steve explained: "Number one—*shape*. You have to disguise your body-shape so that it's not recognizable."

"Do I? Why?"

"A camouflage print like this breaks up your outline."

I looked down at Steve's trousers—irregular blobby shapes of brown, green and black. He had enough pockets in them to carry the entire contents of the average person's home.

"What you really want is a ghillie suit," he said.

"What's a ghillie suit?"

"A ghillie suit, my friend, is the military sniper's secret weapon. It's an all-in-one suit on to which scraps of burlap or thread are attached in a range of earthy, natural colours."

"Why?"

"As camouflage, stupid. You wear a ghillie suit and you become invisible in the natural landscape. Half man; half shrubbery. Of course it's best to add vegetation from the specific terrain to make it blend in completely. Leaves, twigs, that sort of thing. You should make yourself one."

"I don't think so. Why would I need to become invisible?"

"You never know. Now. Rule number two—*Shadow*. In bright sunlight you can be detected by your shadow. Three— *Silhouette*. Avoid standing against plain backgrounds: water, a field and especially the sky. Keep below the horizon line."

"Right."

"*Shine*. Any shiny surface, belt buckle, watch, optical devices, must be dulled down with tape or cammo cream."

"*Cammo* cream?"

"It's what you put on your face. You usually get three different colours."

"Like eye shadow?"

Steve ignored my remark. "*Spacing*.—Very important. Nature never places objects in an evenly spaced uniform pattern. If you're in a group—spread out." Steve looked at his fingers. "Er, have I left out one of the **S**'s?" He counted his fingers again. "**S**hape, **S**hadow, **S**hine, **S**ilhouette, **S**pacing, **S**urface and **M**ovement."

"How come they all start with **S** except the last one?"

"Because movement starts with an **M**. And movement is the most critical of them all. Once the sniper moves, the enemy has all the proof he needs to summon the hounds of war upon you."

"Couldn't they find another word for movement that begins with S?"

He thought for a moment, annoyed at my interruption. "Nah. Movement is movement, isn't it?"

"What about *Shimmying*?" I suggested.

"*Shimmying?*"

I nodded and wiggled my hips. "That's movement."

"Shimmying is what poofs do at the disco. Nobody shimmies in the SAS." He looked disgusted at the very idea. "Of course, there's smell too." he said. "You need to watch that. There's a special cover scent you can get: No-Dor. It's an oil-based product that gives off the scent of decaying leaves and allows you to smell like part of the forest. You spray it on your inner clothing; it's one hundred per cent effective at masking the human odour."

"Are you serious?"

"Of course I'm serious."

"Really? So it's like a body spray fragrance designed specially for the SAS? I don't think I want to smell like decaying leaves."

"You do if you're deep in the forest, lying low in your sniper nest and you want to escape detection."

"What if I'm not *in* the forest? What if I'm in Tesco or sitting in the audience at my local cinema? The mouldy stench of decaying leaves might draw unwanted attention."

"Well, obviously you choose a camouflage and scent that mimics your environment, don't you?" said Steve. He tutted and shook his head.

I imagined myself at one of the multiplex cinemas, blending into my surroundings by wearing a suit made of red plush velvet and dousing my body in a popcorn-scented cologne. "So, is smell one of the rules then?" I said.

"Um. Not officially. It should be really."

"I would have thought so too.—Especially since it begins with **S**."

"Anyway. If you're going to be involved in espionage work, you need to get yourself properly kitted out."

"Well, thanks, Steve, but this is not really my kind of thing." I was glad he couldn't see exactly what my kind of thing was, that the leather bag slung over my shoulder actually belonged to a young female hairdresser and contained, not spare ammunition, cammo cream and scraps of burlap for my ghillie suit, but cosmetics, a purse and my library copy of *Diana: The People's Princess*, which I was planning to read on the bus. I tried to give him back the SAS book but he refused, pressing it firmly into my hands.

"You will be fascinated, my friend. There's all sorts of silent killing techniques: how to kill a man in the desert with your helmet—"

I decided not to tell Steve about the card I found in the library and the possible rendezvous address. I was having some misgivings about his involvement in the mission.

"There's a load of magazines here as well," he said. "Mostly on weaponry and stuff. Take them."

"Thanks, but I don't really…"

"Take them."

It was an order.

Number 47 De Havilland Road was an unremarkable-looking Georgian townhouse with steps leading up to the front door. Geraniums in pots on either side.—Quite cheerful. Not the kind of place you'd expect to find MI5, but I guessed that was the point. I stood across the road wondering what I was getting myself into. There were two cars parked nose-to-tail in a drive-way that had been designed to accommodate only one. In front was a haughty **R**ange **R**over jeep-type thing, hiked up high over its chunky wheels, and behind it, a blue sporty job with its perky posterior jutting out on to the pavement. I'm not very good on car makes; I can identify a **Mini** and a **Rolls-Royce** but I'm a bit hazy on everything in between.

A middle-aged man with sunglasses came out of the house, smoking a cigarette. His hair was slicked back neatly, a style pioneered by *Michael Douglas* and frequently adopted by the self-confident secret service officer type. He got into the sports car and reversed it quickly on to the road where he sat waiting by the kerbside with his engine running, cigarette smoke and light classical piano music wafting in equal measure through the open window. Next out of the house was a stockier man with thick dark hair. He wore sunglasses, too, and carried a blazer with gold buttons, which he laid carefully on the back seat of the Range Rover. He stood on the driveway surveying his surroundings for a few moments and then he touched his ear. I looked for one of those earpieces they wear with the little wiggly wires that poke down inside the collar, but I was too far away to see anything. The man climbed into the driver's seat and started the engine. Both cars waiting now. A minute later a young woman emerged carrying a raincoat. She trotted in high heels round to the passenger side of the Range Rover. I didn't get much of a look at her, but the unusual hair colour indicated that this was Amy Truelove. The Range Rover reversed out on to the main road and set off up the hill, the driver giving the thumbs-up to the first man as he passed. The sports car then zipped back into the driveway to occupy the space where the first car had been. The man got out and headed back indoors. He'd only driven ten yards but you could see he'd had special training. Who does forty miles an hour parking a car?

Perhaps I should have made my move then, gone over to knock on the door, but I decided to watch for a while longer to see if I could discover anything more about the operations being conducted from this address. There was a low wall bordering the front garden of one of the houses opposite so I perched on it, nonchalantly glancing at the pages of *Diana: The People's Princess*, as though I might be waiting for someone, and for a while all remained quiet. By then the sun was warm on my face, there was a light breeze and I was pleasantly mesmerized by the stillness and calm around me. It reminded me of the summers of my childhood. People quietly going about their daily business, and me just sitting on a street corner watching, with nothing I had to do, nowhere I had to be, and the long day stretching out before me.

A young girl, probably on her way to school, rode by on a new bike. She was gathering momentum as she sped down the incline and I could see that she was not yet mistress of her machine. There was a look of slight panic in her eyes as she clutched at the brakes and, to avoid a man walking his dog, veered off the pavement on to the grass verge. It reminded me of the bike I got for my seventh birthday.

In the run-up to birthdays and Christmases I had a tendency to snoop around the house in search of hidden gifts, but my parents must have been wise to it because on this occasion a certain amount of guile had been employed to keep the surprise secret.

Our garage was attached to the side of the house. Since we didn't have a car Dad would use it as a kind of workshop where he would mend and make things. He was quite good with his hands. It was cool and dark in there, smelling nicely of oil, turpentine and sweet, fresh sawdust. Neither the garage doors nor the back door of the house were ever locked so I would let myself in this way every day when I got home from school and enter the house through the kitchen.

One day I saw that the stepladders had been left out in the middle of the garage floor. If they hadn't been there, I'd probably never have looked up. What I saw puzzled me. Tied with washing-line to the rafters of the garage roof was Mandy Smith's bike. I knew it was hers straight away because I had ridden it many times when my mum was round at their house talking to her mum. What was Mandy's bike doing hoisted to our ceiling? I didn't ask, and neither my mum nor my dad mentioned it. It was probably a week later that I got a bike of my own for my birthday. It was royal blue and white. The blue was the same col-our as our back door and the paint looked sticky, with occasional lumps and runs. I was thrilled and, dumb though it sounds, didn't make the connection between Mandy's old bike and my new one, even when I noticed that it didn't have a crossbar, which suggested that I had been given **a girls' bike** by mistake. I asked Dad about that and he told me it was actually designed for both boys and girls. (He might have employed the word **unisex**, but the term had yet to come into common usage—and anyway my mother would never have permitted the utterance of anything so lewd-sounding.) This explanation satisfied me, but the other kids on the street were less easily convinced and decided to taunt me about its gender. Seeing that I was upset, my dad attached a length of broomstick between the saddle and the front upright, which he painted in a shade of blue that coincidentally matched the rest of the paintwork exactly. It broke off shortly afterwards when I caught it with my heel.

Mandy—whose birthday was only a few days after mine—turned up at the shops on a spanking new bike with professionally applied burgundy paintwork and shiny chrome spokes and handlebars. There was a smart white stripe running round the side of each tyre. I had never seen anything look so dazzlingly new. She was showing it off, parading slowly in wide loops, the sparkling spokes glinting in the sunlight as the wheels turned. The next time I checked the garage ceiling, Mandy's old bike had gone.

Nothing more happened at **47 De Havilland Road** until ten past nine when the first man came out again. This time he was wearing a striped tie and a sports jacket. Still smoking, he got into the sports car, reversed out and sped off up the road, clearly thinking he was James Bond or **Steve McQueen** in *Bullitt*.

It all went quiet again so I crossed the road to the house, mounted the steps to the front door and rang the doorbell. I had no idea what I was going to say if anyone answered, but I somehow sensed that all the occupants had gone out for the day and there'd be no one at home. It's funny how you can tell—or I can, anyway. It probably stems from my experience of door-to-door carol singing as a boy when I learned not to waste my 'Ding Dong Merrily' on any house that looked or felt unoccupied.

Deep inside the house a dog barked half-heartedly at the sound of the bell, but as I suspected, nobody came. I briefly heard doggy snuffling at the crack under the door and then the house fell back into silence. In Amy Truelove's bag, I had keys to the door but I was reluctant to use them, even though it was reasonable to assume that I had been given them so that I could let myself in. What if I'd got it wrong and this wasn't a secret MI5 rendezvous point but the normal domestic dwelling it appeared to be? I'd be breaking and entering. I noticed that the two locks on the door—a Yale night latch and a five-lever mortice—looked new and shiny, whereas I remembered the keys looking comparatively old and tarnished. Was that significant? I took them out of the bag and a quick check confirmed it: the keys didn't fit these locks at all.

Suddenly, there was a young woman behind me, walking up the steps. She wore an orange messenger bag across her shoulder and was carrying a handful of leaflets. She eyed me uncertainly, apparently unable to decide whether I lived there or was just visiting. I slipped the keys back into the bag and stood aside to offer her access to the letter-box. The woman lifted the flap and stuffed in a leaflet—something to do with pizza by the look of it. The letter-box sprang shut and inside the house, the dog barked once to acknowledge receipt.

I watched the woman go down the steps. At the gate she glanced back at me, presumably still trying to figure out what I was doing there on the doorstep. It was my cue to leave. I didn't want to arouse unnecessary suspicion.

At the top of the hill near the main junction my attention was drawn to a man on the other side of the road. He was looking in the opposite direction so I couldn't see his face, but he had grey hair and wore, if not a **Prince of Wales** check, then a similarly tweedy-looking jacket, in keeping with the Phelps style. I was sure it was the man I had seen the day before. I realized now that it was unlikely that he was really Jim Phelps—the *Mission: Impossible* connection was probably mere coincidence—but whoever he was, he was clearly related in some way to the mission. He was just standing there in the middle of the pavement doing nothing, like he had in the alley. Waiting? Waiting for what or for whom? As if sensing that I was about to approach him, he set off briskly towards the main road.

Following someone is not as easy as you might think, especially on a crowded street where the man became much harder to keep in my sights. His persistent resolve to keep his identity hidden had turned him into something of an enigma, like the man in a surrealist painting I once saw—looking into a fireplace mirror which reflects not his face, but the back of his head. The longer I pursued the grey-haired man, the more unsettling this *absence of face* had become and now I was a little afraid to see what he looked like.

It was strange how he seemed to sense my presence behind him. Steve had suggested that someone else could be following me, and then relaying ahead to him by radio to tell him when to drop a card. As I followed at a distance, I turned to look casually behind me as if I were looking for a bus or trying to locate a postbox.—A woman in dark glasses pulling a wheelie suitcase with a big yellow ribbon tied to the handle.—A man in his vest eating something out of a jar: pickled onions?—A businessman in a pinstriped suit wearing a crash helmet.—Everyone looks like an undercover agent when you put your mind to it.

Nell had formed a slightly different view of how it worked. When I'd tried to explain the system to her she had said:

"If this man is following you, then wouldn't you expect him to be behind you rather than in front of you? Isn't that the principal rule about following someone—not being the one in front?"

"He's sort of *leading* me"

"*Leading* you? Who is he, the Pied Piper?"

"I know it sounds odd, but…"

"*He's* leading *you?*"

"Yes."

"So really *you're* following *him?*"

Technically, I suppose I was.

At a pedestrian crossing he stood at the kerb edge with some other people, waiting for the green man. I was almost upon him when he suddenly darted out into the road, finding a gap in the traffic. It seemed an unnecessary risk to take and the driver of an oncoming car was forced to brake to avoid hitting him. The man held up his hand, signalling something between a thanks and an apology. I was determined not to lose sight of him so began to gauge how I might make the same move. I had my hand gesture ready, but the traffic had begun to pick up speed and no such opportunity presented itself. Phelps was heading further into the crowd at the entrance to the market. As I tried to maintain focus on him, I heard someone say "Hi," and turned to see a young woman standing next to me. Her hair was pulled tight into a skinny ponytail and she wore giant hooped earrings that looked like those Chinese linking rings that magicians use. I didn't recognize her but she seemed to know me. She was pushing a buggy-type pushchair. I nodded politely. Then I realized. It must be Hector's daughter who I had seen the day before. It was a momentary distraction, but I'd inadvertently taken my eye off my target. When the traffic did stop, a double-decker bus blocked my view and by the time I had weaved a path round it, the Silver Fox was nowhere in sight.

TOP TV STARS

25

Eamonn Andrews

EAMONN ANDREWS was born in Dublin, Dec 19, 1922. First radio job as a boxing commentator on Radio Eireann. Came to London in 1950 and became a quizmaster on the show *Ignorance is Bliss*. Chairman of *What's My Line* since 1951. Introduced *This Is Your Life* September 1955. Married, enjoys walking and talking; takes a keen and active interest in sport. Popular with children as compère of the BBC-TV series, *Crackerjack*.

Series 2. Issued by Niff LTD, MANCHESTER.

I didn't spot it at first, but as I headed back to the crossing, there it was, plain as porridge, lying face down in the gutter.—Jim Phelps had left another calling card.

I lingered at a bus stop nearby. Even though no one seemed to be taking much notice, somehow I felt shy about being seen bending down to claim the card. It probably stems from childhood. Most kids need to be discouraged from picking things up off the street. I was probably worse than most. Bottle tops, coins, discarded food; it was all the same to me. But however valuable the treasure I had found, my mum always said the same thing: *Put it down; you don't know where it's been.* I once found a chunky silver identity bracelet outside the launderette on Cooper's Road. It might have belonged to *Ringo Starr* or one of **The Dave Clark Five**, but even that was banished to the gutter because of its inadequate provenance.

My earliest memories of street-scavenging come from a time when I was out with my father who, on this subject at least, shared my mother's views. I was probably pre-school age, one hand holding on to his, while the other groped the pavements for leaves, old combs and soggy fag packets. At that time my father tended to underestimate my ability to comprehend simple instructions, and would talk to me as though trying to explain something to a dog. He would shake my wrist until the offending article was dislodged from my grasp, trying to inculcate negative associations with this unsavoury activity by bringing his face close to mine and saying the words: *Achh! Dutty!!* I can still hear him now—the tone guttural and harsh like a reprimand from a Gestapo officer.

I had to disregard those lessons he'd instilled in me if I was to discover what was on the card.

Perched on the bus-shelter seat nearby was a slovenly teen-age girl wearing stereo headphones over lank, straight hair. She flicked through a gossip magazine while distractedly blowing hard pink bubbles and snapping them loudly in her mouth. An old nylon shopping bag containing schoolbooks and papers sat between her scuffed shoes. Dangling from her wrist was a green vinyl Kermit the Frog coin purse that I assumed had been attached to her as a punishment for some misdemeanour. She glanced in my direction, but she was too engrossed in the celebrity lives of others to be distracted by me. What would she say, I wondered, if I were to tell her about my recent conversation with Princess Diana and my family connection to a certain Mr Manilow?

A 243 bus swung into the kerbside and folded back its doors with a hydraulic hiss. The girl picked up her bag and wandered on board. As the bus pulled away, I bent down and with one easy sweep of my hand, scooped up the card and fed it into my pocket.

The man in the picture is **Eamonn Andrews**, who hosted **This Is Your Life** for many years, ever-ready with his famous red book, waiting to surprise an unsuspecting showbiz personality or public figure. Each week, a different celebrity was caught and subsequently led out in front of a waiting TV studio audience to enjoy a retelling of his or her life story via sundry guests who would be called upon to pay tribute. It was like a surprise party—but instead of everyone jumping out at once to shout *Surprise!*, friends and relatives stepped forth one at a time from behind a screen to share an amusing or heart-rending anecdote that illustrated just what a wonderful person the special guest really was. Eamonn would stand formally, reading from the red book as though delivering a sermon, while the dumbstruck guest sat and nodded as if hearing these biographical details for the first time.

A few old, forgotten school friends and workmates would be trotted out—people who the celebrity had lost touch with or no longer cared about—each of them introducing themselves with a backstage vocal teaser, prompted by Eamonn saying, *And do you remember this voice?* Often the celebrity didn't, and didn't remember the face either, but all this was glossed over with the recalling of a shared memory and the suggestion that the two of them would get together after the show to catch up on old times. Little by little, the rows of empty seats on the stage would be filled. Fellow celebrities who were unable to appear in person due to 'work commitments', would send their greetings via a pre-recorded message on a television screen. It was interesting to find out who the star of the show's friends were.—There are some unlikely and incongruous connections in the world of showbiz. Who'd have thought that madcap TV funny man **Russ Abbott** would be pals with golfing legend **Jack Nicklaus**? The show always saved the best till last, either a big star or—less entertainingly to my mind—a long-lost or seriously ancient relative.

When **Eamonn Andrews** died, **Michael Aspel** took over as host. The show ran for donkey's years. Growing up watching the programme, I often imagined myself as the subject of the show and wondered who they would get to come on and surprise me. Miss Flavell, who recommended me for the school play because I could do a cartwheel and stand on my head? **Bob Monkhouse**, who would recount the story of how his leaky fountain pen had blotted my autograph book? Hector Goodall from the shop to talk about his amusing practical jokes relating to my lifelong pursuit of *Mission: Impossible* **card 19**? Nell—she would be there as a loyal and devoted friend. And more celebrities: **Lulu** perhaps—or **Dora Bryan**, who would apologize for making me wait in the rain outside the stage door of the Drury Lane Theatre in 1966.

This Is Your Life occasionally had slightly awkward moments: if there were skeletons in the family cupboard; if there had been a suicide in the family; or if the show's star had been married before or was secretly homosexual (in which case the 'wife' chair beside the star would invariably be occupied by the subject's mother)—but Eamonn smoothed over any biographical blemishes so as not to offend anyone concerned. It did make me wonder, though, how they'd handle my family situation. Who would they choose for the special surprise guest at the end of the show? No prizes for guessing that one. Eamonn would make the announcement:

"Yes, he's taken time out of a busy recording schedule and flown over four thousand miles from his home in Florida just to be here with you tonight: your cousin and close personal friend, international singing star, *Barry Manilow*!"

The screens would go back and Barry would be there with his white teeth and wrinkle-free smile. We'd embrace and speak into each other's ears about how great it was to meet again and pat one another on the back like men do. It would be a fitting finale. On the other hand, perhaps Eamonn would opt for a non-celebrity, family-themed reunion in a bid to bring a more heart-rending climax to the show. In which case, Barry would only be the penultimate guest; there would be one final surprise in store. Barry would take a seat alongside my other celebrity chums, clearing the stage for Eamonn's final revelation. I would adopt a quizzical look, pretending I had no idea what was coming.

"Well, **R**iley **R**ichardson, this is your life, and your incredible story is almost complete. But there's one special person who you haven't seen tonight, one person without whom your life might have taken quite a different turn. He walked out on you and your family without warning one Sunday morning back in 1967 and you haven't heard from him since that day thirty years ago, so you naturally presumed he was dead. Well, Riley, he's not dead, he's very much alive, and he's here tonight to say hello. Yes. Here he is, your long-lost father, Brian Pincus."

There wouldn't be a dry eye in the house as Dad stepped out from behind the screens, overwhelmed with emotion. Of course, there would be some awkwardness, neither of us knowing quite what to say to each other. On my part, understandably, there would be questions and a great deal of resentment, but I'd have to suppress that for the sake of the show. I suppose the tearful embrace would say it all: that though there were unresolved issues, we were still father and son and the strength of that bond would ultimately persuade me to let bygones be bygones. Then, at the after-show party, when the audience had gone home and the studio cameras had been packed away, I'd find a quiet moment alone with him so that I could punch his face in.

EIGHT

I WENT OVER TO NELL'S for a Salad Sandwich around lunchtime and settled in a seat by the window. There was a bit in the newspaper about a memorial service for fashion designer **Gianni Versace**, murdered the previous week by spree killer Andrew Cunanan—just like that; right out of the blue. The murderer used the same gun to commit suicide shortly afterwards. Police searched the houseboat where Cunanan died in order to try and piece together a motive but the only findings of any significance were multiple tubes of hydrocortisone cream and a fairly extensive collection of the fiction of C. S. Lewis.—Go figure.

The service was attended by various celebrity pals, among them, **Sting, Elton John** and **Princess Diana**. A memorial service is similar to an episode of *This Is Your Life*, except that the deceased doesn't get to find out which celebrities turned up to pay their respects. How thrilled Gianni would have been to know that Diana was present.

Elton and Diana sat next to each other during the service. They'd previously had some sort of falling-out apparently, but this was quickly forgotten when Diana offered a compassionate, comforting arm to the blubbering pop star. She gives so much to those in need, and perhaps that's her problem: her needs seem greater than anyone's, but who is there in times of trouble to hand *her* a Kleenex?

As Nell slid my **S**andwich towards me she noticed Amy Truelove's bag beside me on the bench seat.

"Ooh, that's a nice bag," she said. "Is it new?"

"Sort of."

"Where did you get it?"

"Um. I can't remember the name of the place…" I quickly changed the subject. "Nell, I have a question. On **This Is Your Life**, do you think the victims know in advance they're going to be on it?"

"Victims?"

"Well, you know, the stars?"

"No, absolutely not." Nell was adamant. "It's a closely guarded secret both to assure the star's spontaneous reaction and to build up audience anticipation. It's all genuine; I was reading about it in one of the magazines, *TV Times*, I think. It's pre-recorded now, but the subject never knows about it beforehand. Course, back in the fifties and sixties, when Eamonn Andrews hosted it, they did the whole programme live. They could never tell how the people were going to react. In the first series, the footballer **Danny Blanchflower** refused to do it."

"Really? Why?"

"I don't know. Something he didn't like. When Eamonn Andrews said 'Danny Blanchflower, this is your life,' Blanchflower said, 'Oh no it isn't,' and walked off the set."

Nell headed back to the kitchen and I was left pondering the significance of my recent card find, and contemplating whether, in the televisual coup of the century, the *Princess of Wales* was to be next week's candidate for the big red book.

My train of thought was interrupted when a man in white painter's overalls came into the café and made for the back. I thought he was probably there to see Nell about a bit of decorating work, but he had only stepped inside to use the toilet, something Nell discourages. **Toilets are for customer use only**; there's a sign on the door. She says she gets all sorts coming in off the streets just to use the bathroom facilities. On Wednesdays it's worse because of all the people from the market. She wouldn't mind if they bought something—a cup of tea or a cheese roll, but they don't, they just come in and treat it as if it were their own. She once went in there to find a man at the washbasin with his trousers rolled up, washing his feet. After that, she kept the toilet locked and only gave out the key if a customer requested it. People used to wander off with the key and she got tired of getting duplicates cut so she attached the key ring to a huge metal spoon—the kind you might see dolloping out the porridge in a prison canteen. When someone walked off with that, she gave up.

I had just figured out that an anagrammatical rearrangement of *Giani Versace* produces **Sincere Vagina** when my thoughts were jarred by a loud rapping on the window, right by my head. I turned to see Steve's smirking face through the glass and his finger-pointing jibe at having made me flinch. In a second he was inside, sliding into the seat opposite.

"Just been on a call-out to this bird's house. You should have seen her. Really fit, she was."

"Well, she probably exercises regularly and leads a healthy lifestyle," I suggested.

Steve didn't know whether I was joking or not so decided to let it go. "She was giving me the come-on, you know, all friendly chit-chat and making me a cup of coffee."

"Very come-hither. Did you ask her out?"

"Ooh, no. That's not the way to do it. Too sudden. You've got to be a bit more subtle than that, old son. I set it up though."

"Set it up? How?"

"My patented screwdriver ploy. Never fails. I leave one of my tools behind—accidentally on purpose. That way I've got a good excuse to call round in the evening. I'll give it a couple of days. —Don't want to appear too keen, do I?"

"Cunning."

Steve nodded, proud of his courtship strategy. "Is that leather?" Steve too had noticed Miss Truelove's bag.

"Yes, I believe so."

"A lot of them are fake, you know. You can check by putting a flame to it. If it's leather it won't burn; if it's plastic the surface will shrivel and melt." He'd already got his lighter out and was leaning over.

"No," I said, pulling the bag away from him. "It *is* leather and I *don't* want to test it, thank you."

"Is it yours?"

"Why wouldn't it be mine?"

"Well. It's a girl's bag, isn't it?"

"No. Actually it's **unisex**."

"Well, you'd know all about that."

I wasn't sure what Steve meant, but now he was on to something else.

"Here you are. Look at this," he said, removing a book from a candy-striped paper bag. He showed me the cover: *Espionage: The Spymasters' Casebook*. "I just found it in the remainder bookshop. Three quid." He turned and shouted across to Nell who was clearing plates from another table, "Tea please, love. And I'll have er..." he squinted at the menu board behind the counter, "...a bacon sandwich." Steve jabbed a dirty digit towards my chest, adding, "And he's paying." He seemed unable to make any gesture appear non-aggressive; I imagined that during his stint in the Territorial Army he must have had his rifle confiscated and been forced to carry out bayonet practice using nothing more than his right index finger.

Nell swung by our table on the way to the kitchen. "Ketchup on the sandwich?" she said.

Steve looked at her condescendingly. "Of course," he said. "—And no gristle if you don't mind."

Nell raised her eyebrows and looked at me. "Who's your friend?"

"He's not my friend; he's my neighbour. Steve."

Desipe the deprecatory tone in my voice, Steve failed to register the put-down. Nell had him pegged and understood that my remark was an apology for his conduct.

"Anything more for you, Riley love?" she said.

"No, I'm all right thanks, Nell."

Steve had already dog-eared one of the pages. The book fell open at a chapter entitled 'Dead Drops'.

"You know about dead drops, right?" he said, cracking the book's spine. I hesitated, so he filled me in, following the words with his finger as he read. "*A dead drop, or dead letter box, is a location used to secretly pass items or information between two spies, without requiring them to meet. The system uses a set of prearranged locations and signals that permit a case officer and his agent to exchange objects and information while maintaining operational security.*"

Steve had the book turned towards him so I couldn't follow the text, but there was a picture of a hollow metal spike with a screw cap for hiding a roll of 35-mm film. On the facing page there was a smaller black-and-white picture of a man in a deserted alley, dressed in hat and trench coat, crouching by the foot of a wall, as if tending to a weed. I couldn't work out whether the book was written for children or adults. Teenage boys, possibly. Steve continued:

"*The location of a dead drop could be a loose brick in a wall, a library book, a hole in a tree, or an empty cigarette packet left in a telephone box, et cetera. The signalling device to let an agent know that an item is ready for collection could be a common, everyday thing to which most people would not give a second glance: a chalk mark on a mail box or a vase of flowers left in a window.*"

Halfway through Steve's reading, Nell set down his tea in front of him. He didn't look up, so she craned her neck a little to glance at what he was reading.

"Are you the one who's been filling Riley's head with all this spy nonsense?" she said.

Steve looked at me sternly. "How much have you told her?"

"Nothing. She's my friend. I told her about the cards, that's all."

Steve tutted at this perceived lapse in security. He looked up at Nell and said, "It's not nonsense, love. This is the real deal. And the less you know about it the better."

Nell seemed faintly amused by his rudeness and set off back to the counter.

Steve called her back, saying, "And don't forget my bacon sandwich."

"It's on its way," she said, lightly. "We're just trying to find you some bacon with extra-gristly bits."

Unable to come up with a worthy riposte, Steve returned to the book. "Ah, here we go," he said. "Listen to this. *During the Cold War, operatives sometimes adopted other drop systems where the location was moveable and therefore less likely to be compromised. One such method, used by Soviet agents operating in West Germany, was known as the Card Drop.*"—He looked up to check my reaction before continuing.— "*Ordinary, inconspicuous playing cards could be left along a chosen route, say to and from the agent's place of business or from his home to the local market, without arousing suspicion. With a prearranged code where each card represented a particular word or phrase, a series of cards read in the correct order could* *spell out a secret message."*

"Wow. That's amazing." I said. "But they're talking about traditional playing cards, right? Not bubble-gum or cigarette cards?"

Steve looked back at the book. "It doesn't say, but it's the same principle. I don't imagine the Soviets had bubble-gum or cigarette cards."

"So these Cold War spies would have to remember fifty-two cards and what each of them meant?" I thought about my *Generation Game*-style attempts to recall the items in Miss Truelove's handbag, and the tea-tray memory tests of my youth.

"Maybe they didn't use all fifty-two. Who knows? The point is, it's an established method practised by spy organizations to pass on information." Steve hadn't finished reading. "*Cards would be left with their faces showing so that the agent, having memorized the code, could read the message without risk of drawing attention to himself by bending to pick them up.*"

"But my cards are always face down." I said.

"There must be a reason for that. Probably because you don't know the code, your message is encrypted in the form of a word puzzle. They need you to study the details more closely to work it out."

While Steve was tucking into his bacon sandwich I told him about the new card and how I thought it had something to do with Princess Diana being on *This Is Your Life*.

"She's not going to be on *This Is Your Life*, you div. They never do the royals."

"They do. I'm sure I saw **Princess Anne** on it once."

"No, you didn't."

"Yes. I think she came on at the end of someone else's life. A show-jumping sports personality or something."

"Sure you're not thinking of *A Question of Sport?*"—Perhaps I was.— "Anyway," he said, "they're never going to do Princess Di. Think about it. They'd have to have Charles on—and the Queen. And all those blokes she's been shagging."

He was right. The Queen would never consent to such a public airing of dirty royal laundry. **This Is Your Life** must mean something else. I wonder if it has anything to do with *Eamonn Andrews*.

NINE

DESPITE THE DISTRACTION of dropped cards and card drops, once Steve had gone, I spent much of the remaining lunchtime thinking about my piece for *Card Collector Monthly*. I wanted to incorporate something about the difference between a collector and a completist. It's quite an important distinction and highly relevant to the pursuit of **card 19**, but I couldn't figure out how to fit it in without seriously overloading my word count.

Just imagine. A ten-year-old budding secret agent and avid bubble-gum-card collector is suddenly given the entire set of *Mission: Impossible* cards—a series that isn't even in the shops yet. Did I feel like the luckiest boy in the world? In some ways, yes—but the real enjoyment for me has always been in the ritual of collecting: the searching, the waiting, the saving, the swapping. You embark on a journey, following a trail towards completion. Getting the whole lot at once makes you miss out on all of that. You may be the envy of your school friends, but the thrill of anticipation has been taken away. For you, the journey is already over. Losing **card 19** was naturally tragic because my series was no longer complete, yet in another way it was a blessing because at least I could continue searching—even though, because of its uniqueness, the void left by its disappearance might prove impossible to fill.

Some professional collectors will buy a whole series of cards at one time. Where's the joy in that? It's like getting a jigsaw that's already been done or a crossword puzzle with all the answers filled in. When I was young, the amount of pocket money I was given determined the collecting pace, and it was always just right. I could never afford more than a couple of packets each week and this invariably left me wanting more. It allowed me to familiarize myself with each new acquisition before it became assimilated into the collection. Of course, there were spoilt boys at school, those with too much pocket money who preferred to take the short cut. Mark Flatlace—*Fatface*, we called him—once bought ten packs of **Man from U.N.C.L.E.** cards in one go. Ten packs! That was half a crown, which was considered an enormous sum of money. There were six cards in a pack, if I remember correctly, and only fifty-five in the series, so in theory he could have got the entire set with one purchase. Unsurprisingly, he didn't, but what if he had?—No swapping interaction with other boys, none of the delight in coveting the rarer cards—just buy the whole lot and have done with it. As it happened, Fate dealt Mark Flatlace an unusually high proportion of repeats; his ostentatiously extravagant gesture brought him no nearer to completion than the rest of us. He didn't realize how lucky he was.

When footballer cards were all the rage, some members of our card-collecting fraternity would demonstrate their unconditional allegiance to their favourite team by purposely excluding any cards from their collection that featured their rivals. Such loyalty, or discrimination, left them with a number of omissions, but the Chelsea-ites and the Arsenal fans were steadfast in their refusal to show any kind of support to the enemy. To me, this partisan devotion seemed insane. I mean, as a boy I wasn't terribly keen on **Val Doonican**, but I'd never have eliminated him from my *World of Pop* series (A&BC Ltd, 1966). With his cosy charm and his 'Bright Elusive Butterfly of Love', he tended to appeal more to mums and grannies. His easy-listening style was at odds with my penchant for the rowdy and raucous—**The Kinks, The Small Faces, The Move**—yet I recognized Val as a valid member of the collection. Does that make me a completist? I suppose it does, but who wants gaping holes in their collection? Better to have the full complement of chart toppers, even if it does mean including cardigan crooners and ruffle-chested balladeers. If you want to get the whole series, you have to be prepared to take the smooth with the rough.

After lunch I did a bit of window-shopping. I suppose it was partly an excuse to wander the streets in search of my next card, but I found nothing. When I'm out walking now, I'm aware that I rarely look up in case I miss something on the ground. My eyes are constantly scanning the pavements and gutters for the next piece of the puzzle.

On my way home, I cut through Mirfield Park for a change of scenery. It's not quite the oasis of unspoiled calm that it once was, frequented more commonly now by marauding youths on BMX bikes and young mums in tight jeans, their stilettos clacking the asphalt paths as they roll their kids out for a rare breath of fresh air. Where once you might have found picnicking families, now there are clusters of drunks and addicts arguing among themselves or lolling back in a hazy stupor. But still, today the sun was shining and the air felt good. I passed impressive trees with lush foliage and wide, grassy areas for Frisbee-catching dogs to run around on. If I filter out some of the less savoury aspects, I can see the park as largely unchanged from when I was a kid, when to me it seemed like a boundless garden of earthly delights.

In those days, my friends and I would go there to hang around by the swings in the hope of meeting girls; or to smoke cigarettes that we had clubbed together to buy from the machine across the road. On sunny days we would play kick-about football until our throats rasped dry, then quench our thirsts at the water fountain or with bottles of pop we'd pinch from the park café. The café was an easy target for nicking pop and sweets and I gradually became more daring, in a boastful display of boyhood bravado. (Interestingly, though, I never stole bubble-gum cards.)

By the time I was twelve I'd advanced to shoplifting Airfix aeroplane kits from a model shop on Albery Road and was ultimately caught with a **Messerschmitt 109E** shoved up the front of my anorak. It was a five-shilling kit that came in a box the size of a telephone directory. The police were summoned and after a stern talking-to, I was driven home in a police car so that my mum could be informed of my crime. She was deeply ashamed of me—*thoroughly disgusted*—and so angry that she slapped my face and sent me to my room. I could hear her talking to the policemen so I lingered at the top of the stairs hoping to discover what was to be my fate. My mum was telling them that I'd never done anything like it before and suggested that, having recently been abandoned by my father, I was probably emotionally traumatized—she actually used those words,

emotionally traumatized.

—I guessed it was something she'd read in a magazine. It had never occurred to me to use this as an excuse. Nearly two years had passed since my father left and by then, though I hadn't exactly forgotten about him, I'd learned to put him out of my mind and get on with my life. To me, it seemed absurd to suggest that his disappearance might be the catalyst for my lawlessness, yet the policemen must have accepted the explanation because no further action was taken. The warning and the humiliating slap were the only punishments I had to endure, but I never stole anything again.

The park may have seen better days, yet there wasn't much litter on the ground. The only rubbish that had escaped the park keepers' attention was that which had collected under shrubbery, in ditches and behind railings—difficult places for them to reach. Litter had also accumulated in the no man's land area between the park perimeter fence and the pavement, where the demarcation of refuse-collecting responsibility was unclear. These are the places I'm now drawn to in the hope of finding a card amongst the detritus. Today I came across something that at first looked like a card—it was the right size and shape, it even had the right kind of pattern on the back—but when I turned it over, I found it was just a handout for a nightclub.

Beyond the trees, I noticed that the old **mini-golf** course was still there, but I couldn't see anybody playing so I wasn't sure if it was operating or not. I was taking my usual route through the wooded area by the lake when a voice startled me.

"Halt! Who goes there?" It was Steve, lurking in the bushes.

"Jesus. What are you doing there?"

Steve was now dressed in full camouflage gear so he must have been home to change.

"I thought you had to go back to work?" I said.

"Nah. Took the afternoon off. Just came for a little target practice. Get a load of that." He held out a handgun.

"Christ. Is that thing real?"

"Certainly is. Walther CP88."

It was black, compact and stylish, like something **Danger Man** or one of the *Mission: Impossible* team might wear in a shoulder holster.

"Does it fire real bullets?"

"Pellets. One seven sevens."

"Oh, so it's like an airgun. I thought it was real."

"It is real. CO_2-powered. It's got a muzzle velocity of four twenty-five FPS. Feel the weight of it."

I had to admit that it was rather impressive-looking. It was like the grown-up version of the gun that came in the Secret Sam attaché case. As a boy I would have sold my soul for such a weapon.

"What if it goes off?"

"It's not going to *go off*. It's not a fucking firework. The safety catch is on. Look."

He pointed the weapon at my chest and snatched at the trigger. I winced and tried to get into the foetal position.

"Don't! Don't point it at me, you maniac."

"It's not going to fire; that's what the safety is for."

"Yes, well, point it somewhere else. Didn't they teach you that in the Army— never point a loaded gun at anybody?"

He looked at me like I was an idiot. "Er... No—funnily enough," he said sardonically. "Here. Hold it."

He thrust it into my hand. I studied it. It was lighter than I'd thought—some kind of hard plastic casing. Still—it looked like a proper weapon.

"It is loaded," said Steve. "Here. I'll take the safety off."

"No. Don't do that."

"Go on. Fire it. —There's hardly any recoil."

"I don't like guns."

"Oh, just fire it, you wimp."

He wasn't going to let it lie so I relented. Besides, it wasn't strictly true. I actually found guns quite thrilling; I just hated what they did.

"What shall I aim at?"

"There's a glove puppet on the end of that branch," he said, pointing to a tree some distance away.

I couldn't see it clearly—a pink blob and a splash of colour for the body—so I just aimed for that. I clicked the trigger and the gun spat out a pellet. I don't know where it went, but the puppet remained on the end of the branch, shimmying tauntingly in the breeze.

"Go on. Keep going. There's eight in the magazine."

I aimed again and kept firing, the gun clacking repeatedly as more shots were discharged. When it was empty, I handed it back.

"It's dangerous. You could really hurt someone with that."

"No kidding."

"What do you shoot with it? Poor defenceless animals?"

He seemed insulted. "No. I would never do that. I'm a vegetarian."

"You? Vegetarian?"

"Why is that so hard to believe?"

"I don't know. Maybe because I saw you eat a bacon sandwich in the café yesterday?"

"Bacon's different. I very rarely eat meat. And I would never kill an animal. I respect all living creatures. Except you, of course."

"Princess Diana's a vegetarian," I said.

Steve rolled his eyes.

He packed his gun into a special carrying case. The weapon sank comfortably into the corresponding gun-shaped hole that had been cut into its foam-rubber lining. It was not unlike the **SECRET SAM** case, except Steve's had fewer gadgets. "Come on," he said, snapping it shut. "I'll walk back with you."

He set off towards the tree where he had stuck the glove puppet. The body was a simple shapeless turquoise cotton shroud with wiggly gold braid glued on as decoration. Grotesquely exaggerated cartoon features grinned inanely as if it were thrilled to see him, its tiny arms outstretched in welcome. Steve snatched it from the branch and inspected the face. There was a pellet lodged in the soft pink plastic. As he squeezed, the puppet's features distorted as if wincing in discomfort. He dug the pellet out with his thumbnail, saying, "Cor. Look at that. Right in the kisser."

"Did I do that?"

"Nah. You were fucking miles away."

"Isn't the puppet at a bit of an unfair disadvantage, being so brightly coloured? You should make a little camouflage outfit for it to wear. A ghillie suit, perhaps. Even up the odds."

Steve held the puppet by its short, flaccid arms as though considering this. Its unsupported head lolled back in surrender. Steve responded by tossing it before him and booting it with an almighty drop kick. The hapless puppet sailed through the air and landed in the bushes.

The track between the trees up to the road narrowed and Steve took the lead. He had a strap hanging down from the back of his jacket; there were straps all over it, but I couldn't imagine what this one was for. I was watching it dangle and sway as he walked, when out of the corner of my eye I spotted a card in the undergrowth, not far from where the glove puppet had landed. It's like I have special radar now that detects them. Maybe it's a collector thing. Hector Goodall has described having a similar gift when he's at flea markets or car boot sales, on the lookout for *Star Wars* figures—his special area of collector interest. He's become so highly attuned that he can spot a Luke Skywalker or an Obi-Wan Kenobi amongst a pile of worthless tat from fifty yards away. It's akin to a superhero power, like Superman's X-ray vision or Daredevil's sonar-like ability to perceive objects around him. I suppose I've always had a special gift for seeking out cards. Perhaps that's why they have chosen it as the modus operandi to deliver my instructions.

ACE ADVENTURES

30. SPACE MISSION ZERO

EXPLORING LAVA CAVES on the newly discovered planet, Magadden 654, Captain Reece heard a sudden cry over his intercom. It was his first officer, Bob Vera, calling from the flight deck of the XR2 space rocket: "We're in trouble, skipper. One of the combustion heads on level 3 is overheating, the atmosphere pressure's nudging 300lbs and there are fractures in the safety chamber. I think she's going to blow, sir." The Captain was quick with his response: "Shut down section 12 immediately and disconnect all K6 booster pods. Hold tight, Vera, I'm coming back to get you."

COLLECT ALL 30 CARDS IN THE SE

Presented by Kane Kards ©1956

Steve had gone quite a way ahead before he realized I was no longer behind him. He stopped and turned. "What're you doing?"

"Another card," I said.

I studied the card's futuristic illustration as Steve headed back towards me. It looked like it was from a bubble-gum series, but not one that I remembered. A&BC did a space cards series and there was a set that came with Brooke Bond Tea, *Out Into Space*, but it wasn't from either of those. When I looked at the back, I saw that it was from a series issued by Kane Kards in 1956. A bit before my time.

"Where did you find it?"

I indicated the spot by the path.

"Let's see it," he said.

I held it up and Steve read the words out loud:

"Space Mission Zero."

It didn't take me long to decipher the message; I'm quite good at word-based puzzles. *Space Mission Zero*. *Space* is an area that is unoccupied, an empty gap between two points, an interval of nothingness, a void. *Space* means nothing and *Zero* means nothing. Nil, none, nought. So, if **Space** and **Zero** don't mean anything, I'm left with the word in the middle: **Mission**. And that means a great deal in my new line of work. **This Is Your Life Mission**. A mission related to Princess Diana appearing on *This Is Your Life*? Maybe there was a plan to kidnap her on her way to or from the TV studio, or someone in the audience was going to jump up and attack her? Steve didn't see it the same way.

"I told you, it's got nothing to do with the stupid TV programme. It's telling you that this is the most important mission of your life. **Princess Diana is in grave and imminent danger. Your country needs you. This is your life mission.**"

It sounded so serious. It was flattering to have been chosen, but I wasn't sure I wanted to shoulder such an enormous burden of responsibility. "Why can't I just tell the police? Surely they'd be better at protecting her?"

"Ah, but who can you trust?"

"Well, you have to trust the police, don't you?"

Steve spluttered and shook his head, apparently amused by my naivety. "In this game, you trust no one."

"What about the royal protection officers? I could tell them. It's their job."

Steve shook his head again. According to him, everyone was either corrupt or part of some huge conspiracy. Or both.

"Why is it *my* life mission?" I said. "That's what I don't get. Why isn't it *yours* or someone else's?"

Steve shrugged his shoulders. "*You're* the card collector."

I had to spell it out for Nell. "*Princess Diana in grave and imminent danger. Your country needs you. This is your life mission.* How could it be saying anything else?"

Nell seemed to think it all rather amusing. "I don't know. It just seems funny to think that MI5 would be contacting you. How do you know you're not picking up someone else's messages? There might be a real secret agent out there awaiting instructions, searching the streets, looking for his cards. You might have ruined the whole plan."

"You don't believe they're contacting me, do you?"

"No, frankly, Riley, I don't. Do you realize how crazy you're sounding?"

"Yes. But that doesn't mean it's not real."

"So what do you think they want you to do?"

"I don't know yet. I expect the next cards will give further instructions." I decided not to mention the De Havilland Road meeting-place address; I didn't want to admit how I'd got it.

"But can't you see that you might be forcing your own hypothesis on to these cards, seeing messages that aren't there? No matter what's on your next card, you'll turn it into something about saving Princess Diana."

"I'm not *seeing messages*. It's there in black-and-white... and colour."

"Not really, love. This doesn't say Princess Diana; it says the queen of hearts."

"Same thing."

"So you've decided. And this doesn't say *in grave and imminent danger*, it says May Day."

"That's what *mayday* means. It's a distress signal like S.O.S."

"Yes, and it also means May Day, when children dance round the maypole."

"It's a word puzzle; it has to be decoded."

"Oh, so this one has to be decoded, but this one, *This Is Your Life*, doesn't? It seems to me they're only in code if they don't say what you want them to say."

"I don't want them to say anything. I didn't ask to be involved in this. I'm just following instructions."

"Why?"

"Why what?"

"Why are you following instructions?"

"I don't know."

I suppose she had a point. What if I wasn't specifically targeted for the mission but had made myself a candidate and by taking the initial bait, the queen of hearts, I had inadvertently volunteered for the job? What if they were simply waiting for someone—anyone—to respond?

1967. Elvis is smartly dressed in sports jacket and pink button-down-collar shirt. He carries a maroon vinyl golfing bag. He pauses at the kitchen doorway to speak to his wife, who stands with her back to him, ironing.

"Right. I'm off"

"You're a bit dressed up to play golf, aren't you?" she says, glancing at him over her shoulder. "Why aren't you wearing your golf cardigan?"

"It's in my bag. I'll change when I get there."

"You haven't just shoved it in that bag?"

"It's fine. I've got to go."

She looks up at the kitchen clock. "Well, you've missed the twenty past," she says.

"One of the lads is picking me up in his car."

"Where?"

"The corner."

"Why doesn't he knock at the door?"

"I don't know," he says dismissively.

"Has Mrs Whittaker *given* you those clubs or is it just a loan?"

"She didn't say. They were her husband's. She couldn't bring herself to get rid of them. Said she felt better knowing that someone was using them."

"Well, mind you don't break them."

"*Break* them? How would I *break* them?"

"I don't know. You broke my food mixer."

Elvis sighs. "I didn't *break* it; the motor burned out." It's an old argument and he wants to avoid a revival. "Anyway, I've got to go."

As Elvis heads for the front door, the boy thunders down the stairs, leaping the last six to land at the bottom. Mother's stern voice from the kitchen: *You'll go through that floor!*

"Dad. Don't forget to bring your scorecard home this time."

"What?"

"Your scorecard from the game. For my scrapbook."

"Oh. I'll see, son."

"Go on. You always used to let me have it."

"It's difficult now, son."

"Why?"

"We have to hand them in at the end."

"Why? Have the rules changed?"

He touches the boy's shoulder. "'Fraid so, son. See you later."

The boy calls him back. "Dad?"

"What, son?"

"Have you ever got a hole in one?"

"No. That hardly ever happens. You've got to be really good to do that."

"But you're good, Dad, aren't you?"

His father looks into his eyes and then shakes his head wistfully. "No, son," he says. "Not good enough." With that, he turns to leave, closing the door behind him.

On the corner, Elvis is looking anxious. He stands with the golf bag between his feet as he checks each approaching car.

Back in the house: "Mum, can I go round to Robert's?"

"Go on, then. But just for an hour. And mind how you cross that road."

A red Mini pulls up at the street corner. Elvis opens the door and tips the passenger seat forward so that he can deposit the golf clubs on the back seat. He then flips the seat back and quickly slides in. As the car draws away from the kerb it becomes clear that the driver is the young secretary. Waiting at a zebra crossing at the end of his street, the boy watches for a break in the traffic. The Mini pulls up again to let him cross. Distractedly, he takes in the woman driving. They've never met before, yet she smiles at the boy warmly and he smiles back. In doing so, he fails to recognize his father in the passenger seat, head bowed and with his hands to his brow as if deep in thought.

4,200

TEN

I HAVE HAD TO FILL IN a lot of the gaps in my **card 19**
magazine article through guesswork based on the information to
hand. I know that my dad went off to play golf once a week—
so that part's right. I can't be certain the secretary was a golfer
but it would be a good excuse for them to meet, and she seems
like the kind of modern Miss who would be comfortable behind
the wheel of a Mini. It's funny—when I first started writing the
story I pictured the secretary as more of a **Dusty Springfield**
type, but I realize that in my mind she's changed. Now she looks
more like Jeannie, the pretty young blonde widow from *Randall
and Hopkirk (Deceased)* played by the actress **A**nnette **A**ndré—
sophisticated, independent, but with a touch of vulnerability. In
the series, Annette André drove a Mini— that's probably where
I got the idea from.

It was about seven when I went back to 47 De Havilland
Road. The same two cars were in the driveway, though now they
had switched places: the sports car was in front and the **R**ange
Rover behind. At that point I still wasn't entirely convinced that
this was an undercover meeting-place; it looked so authentically

normal. I decided I was going to play it casually—return the bag as if I had come across it by chance and wait and see what happened.

When the door opened I recognized Amy Truelove from the picture on her Travelcard and from my glimpse of her running to the car that morning. She was even more attractive up close.—Flawless skin and perfect make-up, like a face one might see in a magazine advertising lipstick or toothpaste.

"Are you Amy Truelove?"

"Yes?"

"I have your bag."

"Oh. Great. Where did you…?"

"I found it. In the park. It was dumped in some bushes."

"Oh thank you so much," she said, taking it from me. "Someone stole it yesterday. It was so nice of you to bring it round. Come in."

Very trusting. For all she knew I might have been the one who stole it.—Which I suppose I was. Still—at least I was there to make amends. I stepped inside and she closed the door. She led me into a room off the hallway. The décor was slightly old-fashioned, yet comfortable and welcoming.

"Sit down. I suppose all my stuff's gone?" she said, opening the bag.

"No, everything's there.—Well, at least I think so. I wouldn't really know." In truth, I could have listed the contents from memory, but that might have seemed strange—like I'd spent too long studying them. "I had to look inside to see who it belonged to. Your name and address was on one of the cards. *Is* there anything missing?"

I sank into a plump armchair as Miss Truelove began to open her bag. It was then that I noticed the open book straddling the arm of the sofa: ***Diana: The People's Princess***. Just at that moment, Amy pulled my library copy of the same book from her bag. I could see she was confused.

"Oh, that's mine. Sorry. I was carrying it in your bag to keep the rain off. I walked here—through Mirfied Park—and it was spitting a bit earlier."

"No, that's OK. It's just that…" She lifted her copy of the book from the sofa and held them up together. "Snap!" she said.

I didn't say anything about the 'coincidence'. I decided to wait and find out what I was there for.

"Are you enjoying it—the book?" she said.

"I've only just started it. Do you think she's in grave and imminent danger?"

"**Princess Diana**? Yes, actually. I do."

"Me too. What do you think is going to happen to her?"

"Well, she's an embarrassment to the Royal Family now, isn't she? She's told everyone about Charles's long-standing relationship with **Camilla Parker Bowles** and talked of her own affairs: **James Hewitt** and the rest of them. There is strong royal disapproval about her choice of lovers. She's been seeing that Hasnat Khan heart surgeon chap for years and now she's going out with **Dodi Al Fayed**. And she's far too popular with the public. Buckingham Palace don't like that. She's always on the front page of every newspaper. The Queen and Charles don't get a look-in."

"But she's divorced from Charles now. Can't they just wash their hands of her like they've done with Fergie?"

"No, because she's still the mother of the heir to the throne. That's their problem. They want the offspring, but they don't want Diana. They can't have someone like her upsetting the apple cart and destroying centuries of royal protocol. She's dabbling in politics—speaking out about the use of landmines, embarrassing government ministers. Once she started acting up, they were never going to let Diana be queen. Mind you, I don't see how Camilla Parker Bowles would be any better. Given the choice between the two of them, Princess Diana is the one I'd queen."

"I'm sorry. What?"

Amy repeated the last part, thinking I hadn't heard. "Princess Diana is the one I'd queen."

"Princess Diana is the one-eyed queen?"

Amy looked puzzled. "Yes," she said. "Why? Do you disagree?"

"No, no. I'm with you." Amy paused and I took a moment to think about what she had just said.

"They're bound to do their best to get rid of her," she added. "How?"

"Who knows? But they're a very powerful organization."

"Who?"

"The Firm."

"The Firm?"

"It's what they call the Royal Family. She's claimed several times that they're plotting against her."

"What do you think they're going to do to her?"

Before we could go any further, the first secret service chap came in, the one in the sports car—except that without the sunglasses he didn't look much like an MI5 agent.

"I *thought* I heard voices."

Amy attempted an introduction. "Uncle Derek, this is… sorry, what's your name?"

"Riley."

"Riley?" said Uncle Derek, shaking my hand. "Ooh. Were you named after the car?"

"I don't think so…"

"Lovely cars, Rileys. I sold one a few years ago. Two-tone RME saloon, the '55 model, it was."

"Riley found my bag and brought it over. Wasn't that nice? Whoever stole it dumped it in the park. Nothing's been taken, though; everything's still here. Cash and everything."

"Well, that's strange. Credit cards?"

"All there."

"I bet you wish you hadn't cancelled them now."

"Oh well. It was my scissors I was worried about."

"Scissors?" I said, pretending to know less than I did.

"Yes, I'm a *hairdresser* and my scissors were in my bag. They cost nearly four hundred pounds."

I was shocked. "Really? Why?"

"They're special. They're left-handed scissors, for one thing, and they can only be used for cutting hair. I was imagining someone finding them and not realizing, cutting paper or something with them and turning them into a cheap pair of office scissors."

Oops.

"So we needn't have changed those bloody locks either?" Uncle Derek laughed resignedly.

"Sorry," I said.

"It's not your fault, Riley." Uncle Derek insisted that I should banish the thought.

"Well," said Amy, "I couldn't get hold of you or Daddy that day so I just called a locksmith. It seemed like the safest thing to do at the time."

"No, you did the right thing, love. You can't be too careful." Uncle Derek leaned towards me with a little jocular aside. "I tell you though, Riley, it was a bit of a shock coming home to find all the locks changed. I thought the family were trying to tell me something."

I chuckled amiably at his little joke.

"It was very kind of you to return the bag," he said. "Not many people honest enough to do that these days." He reached into his pocket and peeled some notes off a thick wad. "Please."

"No. Really. I couldn't."

He looked to Amy for guidance. Her tiny frown and a barely perceptible head-wobble were enough to suggest that a cash reward might seem insulting. I wasn't insulted; I just felt bad about all the trouble I'd caused. By rights I should have offered to recompense them for the new locks.

"Well, let's at least give you a drink," said Uncle Derek.

I looked at Amy for similar guidance. She smiled and nodded.

"OK. Thanks very much."

Uncle Derek went off to fetch some wine.

"I can't believe we're reading the same book," said Amy. "Isn't that an amazing coincidence?"

"I don't know. Is it?" Amy looked slightly puzzled. Then I said: "Are you a friend of the **Princess**?"

"You mean like a proper friend?"

"I though perhaps you were her *hairdresser* or something."

"Her hairdresser? Me? God, no. Why would you think that?"

"I don't know, really. Silly idea, I suppose."

"Why? Are *you* a friend of the **Princess**?"

"Well, no, not really." I decided to be modest about our relationship. "I only met her briefly the other day."

"Wow. You actually met her? Was this at the hospice?"

"Yes. Were you there?"

"No, I was at work all day. Do you work at the hospice, or something?"

"No, I just happened to be passing so I was in the crowd."

"Did she speak to you?"

"Yes, we had a little chat."

"Really? That's amazing. What about?"

"Oh, I gave her a gift so we talked about that."

"What did you give her?"

"Oh it was just something … something for her boys."

"Well? What was it?"

"It was…"

"Yes?"

"It was… a kitten."

Uncle Derek was pushing the door open with his foot. "Knock, knock," he said. The tray he was carrying had big glasses of wine on it and there were little glass bowls of crisps and nuts. "I'll leave you two alone," he said, winking at me surreptitiously. What was that about? I wondered.

Amy chatted away. She had beautiful teeth, white and even, and I found I was becoming fixated on her mouth and the way her lips moved over them as she spoke. The thick mop of hair I had noticed in the photograph was even more remarkable in real life; it was an incredible colour, not like a hair colour but more like the rich golden-yellow of honeycomb toffee.— Cinder toffee, my mum used to call it. I asked her if she cut her own hair.

"No, someone at the salon does it."

"It's nice. I thought you worked from home. Your card…"

"I do, sometimes, but I'm at the salon most of the time."

This is how it went on. There was no mention of playing cards or secret trails; there wasn't even a hint of any connection to MI5. Was Amy part of a secret mission to protect the Princess, or was she just a fan like everyone else? She seemed oblivious to the whole plan, yet there was clearly something significant about the book we were both reading and her reference to the **one-eyed queen**, though what that had to do with **Princess Diana**, I wasn't sure.

Uncle Derek came back in with the bottle of wine. He had a tea towel over his shoulder. "Who's for a top-up?" He didn't wait for an answer. "Dinner in five minutes, Amy."

I stood up, thinking it was my cue to leave.

"Will you stay for dinner, Riley? Nothing special, but you'd be very welcome," he said.

I faltered. I didn't want to outstay my welcome, but I didn't want to leave either.

"Stay," she said.

I was quite tipsy by the time I left. Buses were still running, but Uncle Derek insisted on driving me home in the **R**ange **R**over and Amy came along for the ride. I could have walked, but the park closes at night, which adds quite a bit to the journey. So, Amy and I sat in the back together and Uncle Derek made jokes about being our chauffeur. I don't know how many whisky-and-ginger ales he'd had, but it didn't seem to affect his driving. Amy must have been a bit light-headed like me because she leaned over and kissed me on the cheek.

It was nice to have been made so welcome. I felt like part of the family. Amy's mum was charming and kind; I gathered that she spends most of her time in bed. I don't know why; she didn't look poorly. She and Uncle Derek smoke constantly and light each other's cigarettes. Mr Truelove, the man I had seen driving the Range Rover, seemed a bit more 'old school'. They all call him Daddy. He's a keen Rotarian and goes to a lot of meetings, apparently. Amy has a married older sister called Charlotte and a brother doing archaeological anthropology or something—they both live away from home—and there's an overweight black labrador called Winkle.

During dinner I mentioned my new job as a freelance magazine writer and told them about *Barry Manilow* being my cousin. I can't remember how the subject came up, but they were all really impressed. Uncle Derek and Mrs Truelove (Mummy) are quite big fans and have one or two of his records. I'm not sure he's Amy's perfect cup of tea, but the celebrity connection impressed her I think. We all agreed that 'Could It Be Magic?' was his best song ever.

"He's doing something at the Albert Hall in October, isn't he?" said Uncle Derek.

"Yes, the twenty-second."

"Do you get together when he's over here?"

"We try, though he's often really busy."

Mrs Truelove nodded understandingly. "We saw him do something on the telly, didn't we, Derek? *The Des O'Connor Show*. Did you go to that, Riley?"

"No. Stupidly, I forgot all about it."

"He was very good, wasn't he, Derek?"

"Oh yes," said Uncle Derek "The consummate professional. He's a very polished performer."

"He's amazing live," I said. "Most of his fans are women. They go crazy when they see him. Grown women swooning and jumping up and down. I just go for the music.—And because he's family."

"Will you be going to the Albert Hall?" said Amy.

"Oh, yes. I expect so."

"I'd quite like to see him live," she said.

"Oh. Well. I'll get you a ticket, shall I?"

"Really?"

"Yes, Barry always puts a few aside for me."

Mummy and Uncle Derek looked down at the table. Like Winkle, they have learned that you don't get treats if you jump up and beg. I threw them the titbit they were waiting for:

"I can get tickets for everyone if you like."

"Well, that would be marvellous," said Uncle Derek. "We don't mind paying."

"Barry wouldn't hear of it."

"Are you up to an evening at the Albert Hall, Mummy?" said Uncle Derek.

"I'll have to be, won't I? Can't miss a chance like this. It'll be a nice family outing. Daddy, you'll want to come, too, won't you?"

"Rather!" said Daddy excitedly.

"Can you get five, Riley?" she said.

"Shouldn't be a problem."

I couldn't think how I was going to get hold of five tickets, but what better way to join forces with Amy than through a family-shared experience involving the greatest solo entertainer of all time?

"Will we be able to go backstage afterwards?" Mrs Truelove was getting excited.

"I'll have to check about that."

Amy told them about me meeting **Princess Diana** and the kitten I had given her and naturally, they wanted to know everything. I described her dress. I told them about her clear blue eyes, her perfect pink complexion, and I recounted our conversation almost verbatim, remembering to substitute the word *kitten* for pie.

"Well I'm quite certain none of us have met anyone nearly as famous as Princess Diana," said Daddy.

Mummy said, "You've sold cars to one or two famous faces, haven't you, Uncle Derek?"

"One or two, yes," he said, modestly. "**Mica Paris, Gordon Banks?**" He offered the names for me to acknowledge.

"Uncle Derek deals in classic cars," said Amy.

"You must remember **Gordon Banks**, Riley?" said Uncle Derek.

"Oh, yes. Absolutely. The England goalkeeper." I nodded enthusiastically.

"Some say the greatest goalkeeper the world has ever seen."

"Yes, he was very good," I said.

"That is, until his car accident in 1972 when he lost the sight of his right eye. He was no good after that. Without binocular vision you can't judge distances so well, and of course only having one eye narrows your field of view. Tragic, because he had so much to give. If it hadn't been for the accident he'd definitely have beaten Shilton's record for England caps."

"Oh, definitely," I said, trying to sound knowledgeable.

"And do you know, Riley," said Mrs Truelove, "the car he crashed in was the actual car that Uncle Derek sold him."

Uncle Derek folded his arms and nodded, quietly proud of his part in the sporting tragedy. "Of course, there was nothing mechanically wrong with the car, he just lost control of it and drove into a ditch. Silly bugger. But in those days nobody wore seat belts, did they?"

Dinner turned out to be Chicken Casserole so that was enormously pleasing. When I'm a guest in someone's house I rarely get food that fits within my rules. I was enjoying myself so much that I was prepared to accept any dessert that was offered, whatever letter it began with. When we'd all finished and were sitting back in our seats Uncle Derek clapped his hands together and said, "Right. Who's for a piece of Mummy's Chocolate Cake?"

Halfway through the evening I excused myself and made a trip to the bathroom. I hadn't expected this to be a social visit so, apart from the business in hand, I checked my appearance in the mirror. My eyes were pink and floating gently as if at zero gravity. My hair didn't look quite right either. I wasn't sure Mr Vann had captured the essence of what I was after. I tried to tease it into a better shape, wondering what Amy's professional opinion of it was. Then I took a Kleenex and wiped my nose—I like to keep my fire engine clean. When I went to throw the tissue in the bin, a little flash of silver caught my eye. There among the discarded tissues I saw a ***ten-pound note***, its silver security strip glinting in the light. The note was quite worn and had been folded in half. It must have been thrown away by accident.

Downstairs, Uncle Derek said, "Ten quid. Blimey, how did that get there? Mummy, have you been throwing my money away again?"

They laughed.

"It must have been when I was emptying pockets on laundry day. Well, it's not mine. Is it yours, Daddy?"

"No, not mine. Always carry notes in my wallet."

"Amy?"

"Not mine. I'd have noticed."

I offered the note to Uncle Derek and then to Daddy, but neither would take it. "Well, it's definitely not mine," I said.

"You have it, Riley. It's not ours," said Mummy.

"It must be. I can't take it."

"Go on," she said. "You deserve it. For being so honest."

"Yes, a lot of young men would have pocketed that and kept quiet," said Uncle Derek.

Daddy went one further: "A lot of young men would not have gone to the trouble of returning Amy's handbag. We're all very grateful for that." Everyone agreed.

"But it's yours. I don't want it."

"Take it."

I refused again, unfolding the note and laying it on the table. There was a felt-pen scrawl on the Queen's face in the shape of an **R**. Uncle Derek spotted it. "Look, it's even got your initial on it, Riley."

Mummy picked it up and pressed it into my hand. "Give it to charity if you must."

"Yes, you take it, Riley, and give it to a good cause," said Daddy.

They all smiled warmly at me as I finally yielded. It seemed rude to argue with them.

After dinner, we went into the sitting room and Uncle Derek played 'Could It Be Magic?' on the piano. The tune got a bit lost among his Liberace-style frills and flurries up and down the keyboard, but Mrs Truelove helped to pin down the melody with a mumbled vocal accompaniment. Uncle Derek saw any gap between the words as an excuse to show off. By the time he'd reached the final chorus he was bouncing chords off the lower keys to punctuate his fluttering embellishments up at the other end. Amy seemed to be in the groove too now; she was singing a little and swaying gently to the rhythm. I felt too shy to sing so I played more of a supportive role, silently mouthing the lyrics while offering bright facial expressions of encouragement. Amy sniggered at what I was doing and I realised I must have looked like one of those overreaching moms prompting her daughter from the wings at a child beauty pageant. Sing out, Brittany, and for God's sake SMILE!

1967. The red Mini pulls up in a deserted car park behind a church. The engine is cut and the lights are switched off, leaving the car in darkness. The wind rustles the leaves of a nearby tree, but otherwise it is quiet and peaceful. Inside the car, the couple sit side by side, staring ahead. On the seat behind them—the maroon vinyl golf bag. For a moment they enjoy the stillness of their surroundings, but the urgency of their need for each other overwhelms them. Leaning over in their seats, they kiss passionately. The secretary tries to slide across, but the handbrake is in the way. He releases it so that it lies flat. The car shifts a little, but then comes to rest. Unimpeded, she falls backwards into his waiting arms.

m
ọ̃

4,325

ELEVEN

When entertainers such as Johnny Mathis or Lulu sing love songs, they tell us that falling in love can make the heart turn cartwheels. The heart can also go 'boom-bang-a-bang', 'oops' or 'giddy-up', depending on the speed and depth of the emotional attachment. And you think to yourself, well, surely all this is just romantic Eurovision-style nonsense (or possibly the early warning symptoms of a serious heart condition). But when I saw Amy again my heart did all of these things, lurching hard against my ribcage like an overexcited young goat keen to escape the confines of a flimsy cardboard box.

"I wasn't sure if I'd got the right flat," she said. "You left your book last night." She handed me *Diana: The People's Princess*.

"Oh yes, thanks." She paused on the doorstep. Neither of us knew what to say. I looked down at the book and then back at her. We both laughed nervously.

Steve appeared on the stairs behind me. I tried to ignore him. He called out: "Did you find him all right?"

"Yes, thanks," said Amy, peering over my shoulder into the hallway to answer.

"Oh," said Steve, wiggling a pointed finger. "I know you, don't I?"

"Do you?" said Amy.

"Yes. I changed your locks the other day. Tuesday it was."

"Oh that's right. Dave, wasn't it?"

"Steve."

Amy nodded, not knowing what else to say. I tried to block Steve with my shoulder.

"As a matter of fact, I think I might have left my screwdriver behind," said Steve.

"You did. We found it."

"Great. I could call round one evening on my way home from work. How about tonight?"

"No, don't trouble yourself. I'll just give it to Riley and he can pass it on to you."

Ha! Steve's dastardly plan had been thwarted. I was particularly pleased because Steve was not in my good books. I'd arrived home last night to find a scrawled note on my door, stuck with a drawing pin straight into my fresh paintwork: *Fancy a pint? I'm in the grapes. Steve.* When I had seen him earlier that morning, on my way to take out the rubbish, I'd said to him, "Thanks for the note and the big pinhole in my door. Have you never heard of Blu-Tack?" He'd said he hadn't, and suggested that I should be less of a *big fucking girl*.

He looked a little deflated at Amy's rebuttal, but seemed determined to keep things going. "I don't suppose your handbag ever turned up?" he said.

"It did actually. Riley found it." She touched my arm proudly.

"Riley found it?" Steve turned to me, trying to get it straight in his head. "You found her bag?"

"Yes—in the park," said Amy. "Whoever stole it must have dumped it there."

"Huh. Minus all your stuff, I suppose?" said Steve knowingly, intent on belittling my heroic deed.

"No—actually everything was still there," she said. "Including my house keys, would you believe? So there was no need to change the locks after all."

"Well, that's what the thief wants you to think, doesn't he? A lot of bag thieves get a set of keys cut and then put the originals back."

"Why would they do that?" I said. "Why not just take the originals?"

"Cos if your keys have gone missing, you're bound to change the locks, aren't you? But if they're still there, you don't bother. The thief waits 'till you go out—then lets himself in with the spare set and helps himself to all your lovely goodies." Steve's eyes momentarily strayed to take in Amy's breasts. "So you did the right thing, love. Trust me."

Steve was still lingering, trying to push his nose in, like an uninvited guest sniffing round the vol-au-vents.

"Isn't that your phone, Steve?" I said.

He cocked an ear towards the stairs. "I can't hear anything."

"Yes. I'm sure that's your phone. Might be important." —You can play a similar trick on dogs. Pretend to throw the ball, and the dog will go chasing off to fetch it, but the ball is actually still in your hand. I checked that he was scampering back up the stairs and then asked Amy if she'd like to come inside for a minute.

She shook her head. "I've got to go to work," she said. "Daddy's giving me a lift."

I saw Mr Truelove waiting in the **R**ange **R**over. He thrust his thumb in the air and saluted. I waved back. "I'd better go," she said.

I nodded. There was another pause. The Range Rover's engine ticked over.

"Amy? If you're not doing anything tonight…"

She came quickly to my aid. "No. I was going to ask…"

"What?"

"I wanted to ask you more about the book—" she said, "—what you thought of it."

"Yes, great." We sounded like inexperienced teenagers, but it didn't matter.

"Do you want to come over later? What time do you get off work?"

"I'm freelance at the moment. Writing."

"Oh, that's right. About seven then?"

She hurried back to the Range Rover and Daddy set off, tooting his horn.

As I turned to go back inside, guess what I saw?—A card on the path. Now, I'd been out less than twenty minutes earlier to put the rubbish on the street—the Council has a strict timetable for refuse collection—and I'm certain the card was not there then. Even if I'd overlooked it on my way out, surely I'd have spotted it on my way back? The obvious conclusion to draw was that the card had been left by Amy; that she had simply placed it there before knocking at the door, knowing that I would see it as I watched her return to the car.

The previous night I had decided that she was not connected to the Diana mission and that my finding the card in the library—which had led me to claim her shoulder bag and subsequently enabled me to trace her to her home—might have been more about **romantic** *fate* (if such a thing exists) than anything to do with my assignment. I was even prepared to regard the fact that we were reading the same book about Diana as a fluke. Looked at objectively this morning, it seemed so obviously more than mere coincidence and I felt foolish for not having realized it. Amy had to be part of the whole thing; she might even be

MODERN DANCE
MOVEMENTS

14. CHA-CHA-CHA

In 1952, dance teacher, Monsieur Pierre, travelled to Havana to find out what the Cubans were dancing at that time. He noted that the dance craze there, the Cha-cha-cha, had a split fourth beat and to dance it one started on the second beat, not the first. He brought this new dance idea to England and eventually created what is now known as Ballroom Cha-cha-cha. The Cha-cha-cha remains as quite possibly the most popular Latin-based dance in the world today. Its syncopated rhythm is adaptable to many favourite songs such as the popular hit, Tea for Two from the 1925 musical No, No Nanette. The Cha-cha-cha is exciting to dance, and to watch, featuring slick footwork and exciting patterns. At professional level it has tremendous speed, sharp leg actions and a playful, flirtatious personality.

my case officer. Why, then, had she not mentioned it? Even if she couldn't say anything in front of her family, there had been an opportunity earlier in the evening to speak to me in confidence. Perhaps she was just getting round to it when Uncle Derek interrupted us. I remembered something she asked: *Are you a friend of the Princess?* The way she said it sounded like she was using the word *friend* to mean someone who acts in support of a cause, or one who holds an affiliation with a closed or secret fellowship. Steve had referred to an MI5 agent as *a Friend of the Family.* 'A friend of' is often used as a kind of code: *A Friend of Dorothy*, referencing the character played by **Judy Garland** in *The Wizard of Oz*, is a euphemism for a gay man. And don't the Mafia use a similar expression when making an introduction? I'm sure I saw it in a mobster film. *A friend of mine* indicates that the friend is not connected, whereas *a friend of ours* refers to someone who is a member of another Mafia family. Perhaps that was all Amy needed to ask to be sure of my commitment to the cause. *Are you 'a friend of Diana'?* I hoped I had given the right response.

The card itself was a puzzle. I had not expected my life mission to be to dance the cha-cha-cha: a ballroom dance with small, mincing steps and swaying hip movements, performed to a Latin American rhythm. Surely this could not be my ultimate goal? The card looked like it was printed in the 1960s—from a series of trade cards called **Modern Dance Movements**—so in that sense it was consistent with the others, but its meaning eluded me. I went back inside and sat with a cup of tea, trying to work it out.—In fact, it was the tea that made me think of it. *Cha*, the informal English word for tea, as in *Do you fancy a cup of cha?* is taken from the Cantonese word for tea: *chá*. So, *cha-cha-cha* would translate as *tea-tea-tea.* **T-T-T**? I tried all kinds

of interpretations, but **T T T** didn't mean anything to me. **Tyne-Tees Television?** No, that couldn't be it.

I wanted to check whether the cha-cha-cha card was in some way unique or unusual in the world of card collecting. Hector Goodall was able to confirm by telephone that *Modern Dance Movements* was a series given free with Whitbread Ales in 1964. Dad didn't drink much—when he did, it was Bulmer's Cider, not beer, so I never saw the dance cards.

"I haven't got a full set," he said, "but they do show up from time to time. I've got a few odds, not in terribly good condition. I sold one the other day, as a matter of fact."

"Really? Could it have been number fourteen, 'Do the Cha-cha-cha'?"

"I don't know. It was in the Odds-and-Sods box."

"Do you remember who bought it?"

"A woman, I think."

"Could she have been a young woman with golden hair?"

"*Golden hair?*" He seemed amused by my choice of words. "I don't know, Riley. We get a lot of people coming into the shop, you know. I don't write down the hair colour of every customer."

"But it was a woman?"

"I think so. Why?"

"And she just bought that one card?"

"I don't know. What *is* this, Riley, the Spanish Inquisition?"

One thing that concerned me about this new development was the possibility that Amy's interest in me might be purely professional, and that what I had taken to be a budding romance was merely a cover for espionage work. Maybe true love had been too much to hope for. Either way, I couldn't understand why she felt the need to communicate my instructions via the cards instead of whispering them to me when we were alone—which, frankly, I would have enjoyed more. If Amy *was* my case officer, then perhaps she was not really a *hairdresser* and the Trueloves were not her real family. On reflection, it seemed un-likely that an MI5 secret agent would be living with her mum, dad and Uncle Derek. Perhaps they would all now reveal them-selves to be undercover agents working for MI5 as I had first suspected, or even royal protection officers on a campaign to eradicate potential threats to the Crown. Was the happy family all just a clever subterfuge or was Amy working alone? Uncle Derek had spoken of **Gordon Banks** losing his sight in one eye. Was this a coincidence or was it a coded reference to the one-eyed queen of hearts?

The ⊤⊤⊤ thing was still bothering me so I went back to the library to look it up in the hefty encyclopaedias they have in the reference section. There was something about Time-Temperature

Transformation, a diagram used in materials engineering to determine isothermal transformation properties, but I instinctively knew it wasn't that because I had no idea what it was all about. When I turned the page, however, I was amazed to discover that TTT is also the standard Morse code prefix for a safety warning. This made perfect sense. The encyclopaedia further informed me that on 20 January 1914, the International Convention on Safety of Life at Sea adopted the Morse code signal TTT

dash   dash   dash

three letter T's, spaced correctly so as not to be confused with the letter O (- - -), as a signal to precede warnings of impending danger. The spoken radiotelephone equivalent for TTT is *security*. This corresponds to the French pronunciation for *sécurité*, which means 'safety'. So, the cha-cha-cha card meant that a safety warning was to follow, and this, I imagined, would alert me to the specific threat to our future queen. (Actually—technically—Diana was no longer our future queen. Amy informed me that following the divorce from Charles she had been demoted from *Her Royal Highness* to *Diana, Princess of Wales*. Nevertheless.)

Was I supposed to let Amy know that I had received and successfully deciphered the message? I wasn't sure, but I felt rather proud of how quickly I had solved the puzzle and wanted her to be impressed. I decided I would drop a hint that evening.

Whatever the nature of our relationship, I planned to look my best on our date. I had in mind a smart, yet stylishly casual jacket with a youthful edge that might blur the age gap between us a little. I tried several shops in Islington High Street but nothing looked right, so I gave up and set off to Nell's for a cup of tea, tea, tea.

As I passed the shoe repair place by the station I saw two men in their socks sitting on high stools at the 'heel bar'. I assumed they were having their shoes re-heeled while they waited, but who knows, perhaps they were from a religious cult which had shunned footwear and were taking advantage of the shop's key-cutting facilities—key cutting and shoe repair, two seemingly unrelated services frequently brought together in one establishment.

Seeing the man working at the buffing wheel made me think of the unfortunate coincidence that it should have been Steve who had been called out to change Amy's locks. Now he was trying his luck with her and it was actually because of me. By stealing her bag, I had inadvertently brought her to his attention. If the Trueloves hadn't been so security-conscious, they would not have required the services of someone like Steve.

It wasn't like that when I was young; no one in our neighbourhood worried too much about locking their doors. People didn't seem to get burgled in those days—it just didn't happen. Except one time—it did. Maybe. An intruder let himself in through our back door—which of course was open as usual. It was a particularly scary incident for me because by chance I was off sick from school that day so I was in my bedroom the whole time, listening to him moving about downstairs. I thought he was going to find me and strangle me, but luckily he didn't come upstairs. When my mum got back from the shops I told her what had happened and insisted that we should call the police. She wouldn't have it, telling me that I was imagining things. If there had been a burglar, she said, then why hadn't anything been stolen? The TV was still there; the insurance money on the hall table was still there. "It was probably just Mrs Charlesworth from next door or the window cleaner come to fill his bucket." In the end I began to accept that she might have been right.

Once upon a time, afternoon tea at around four o'clock would have been a café's busiest time, but nowadays it seems that everybody drinks coffee and they choose to frequent the little American-style coffee shops instead. I suppose in that sense I'm something of a traditionalist.

Nell was standing in front of the counter; I could see her through the window, watching me approach from across the road. As I came through the door she turned and pointed the remote control at the stereo that sits on a shelf above the microwave. Setting the remote down on the counter, she raised her hands above her head with a dramatic flourish, striking a pose as though in readiness for something. I wondered what on earth she was doing. There was some tape hiss and then the music started up—much louder than she normally plays it, and I immediately recognized the classic Latin dance favourite. One or two of the diners, startled by the sudden percussive intro, looked round. Nell began stepping back and forth with a little *chassée* in between—gradually building more elaborately expressive movements into her routine. I had to admit she was quite an accomplished dancer. Then, just to add an extra layer of icing to her carefully prepared teatime surprise, she began singing the words:

Picture you—upon my knee
With tea for two—and two for tea.
Just me for you—and you for me. Alone !
(Hoy, cha-cha-cha, three-four, cha-cha-cha)

Back home, I was still feeling bad about how I had reacted. What had made it worse was that some of the older patrons, particularly the pensioners who go there most afternoons to play cards, thought Nell was putting on a floor show and had joined in with the singing and clapping. It was as if the whole café were mocking me. Now, I'm no stuffed shirt when it comes to humour; I'm always prepared to see the funny side of things—even with a custard pie in my face. So yes, I could see that suggesting doing the cha-cha-cha as part of my assignment was droll, witty, comical and hilarious—and yes, it was clever of her to visit Hector Goodall to find a card from the right period, but at the time I was angry that she had diverted me away from my true mission, sending me on a pointless and time-wasting detour. And if I'm honest, I was embarrassed at how easily I had made the new card fit. With huge, trampolining leaps from a Latin American dance, my analysis had landed me squarely on the seemingly pertinent Morse code safety warning. It made me wonder if, by playing her little practical joke, Nell had proved her point: that I was making the cards say what I wanted them to say.

I'd even laughed along with her at the joke, but for the sake of my assignment I'd felt it necessary to explain how her playful prank had kept me from important business. And because I was annoyed that she had undermined the seriousness of my quest, it was with a bitter sarcasm, which I now regret, that I suggested she might want to amuse herself further by making hoax 999 calls: perhaps sending a fire engine on a wild goose chase, or waylaying some paramedics on their way to save a child's life. She looked hurt and said it wasn't the same thing.

"I don't think you quite appreciate the importance of my mission," I said.

"There *is* no mission, you stupid thing. That's what I'm trying to tell you. Can't you see what you're doing? You're making it all up." There were tears in her eyes.

TWELVE

"AMY! THERE'S A HANDSOME young man here to see you." Uncle Derek winked at me as he called upstairs. Mr and Mrs Truelove had both come into the hallway to welcome me as if I were a cherished family member. With the discovery that cha-cha-cha was a prank, I'd had to retrace the path I had taken—all the way back to **Space Mission Zero**. Since it had been Nell, not Amy, who had left the card on the front path, I knew now that Amy was not an undercover agent and that Mummy, Daddy and Uncle Derek were almost certainly not spies working for MI5; they were just an ordinary happy family.

A drink was offered and we all chatted in their big, warm kitchen. Daddy put his hand on my back, absent-mindedly stroking and patting me as he talked. The previous night, he had done the same with Winkle, their black labrador, who had rested his shiny head on Daddy's thigh and stared up at him adoringly.

Amy was radiant. I could tell she'd made a lot of extra effort, which suggested that she considered this a proper date. But the delicious excitement of possibilities spreading inside me was curdling with the nagging guilt I still felt about how I had spoken to Nell. I tried to put those feelings aside, resolving to make amends with her the following day.—We'd never fallen out before. On a practical level, Nell's piece of mischief had made me re-examine the cards and question my analysis of them—though the point she was making was more fundamental. She was saying that the cards were meaningless, random finds and therefore my interpretation of them was irrelevant. So, before I got ready for my date with Amy, I had set them out on the table. Although I tried to see them through Nell's eyes, I just couldn't accept that a series of mere coincidences had brought these cards to me.

Amy and I bade farewell to the proud family, who saw us off at the door, waving as if we were about to embark on a transatlantic voyage. In fact, we were heading to a restaurant nearby that Amy had suggested.

The next card turned up on our way to the restaurant, right on cue. It was in the gutter outside Budgen's, lying face down as usual, and it had a traditional playing-card back. It was almost too obvious. Was it another of Nell's hilarious practical jokes? I was sure she wouldn't play the same trick twice, especially after the way I had reacted. Besides, I was a long way from home and she couldn't have anticipated my current location. This had to be the real thing. Nell's sabotage attempt had briefly derailed me, but now I was back on track.

I hadn't yet told Amy anything about my mission—and seeing me bending down to gather a grubby playing card from the pavement might not be a first-date sort of thing to do. *Achh! Dutty!!* Had I picked it up there and then, the spontaneity of the gesture might have made it seem more acceptable, but before I had time to think, we'd gone past it. I glanced back at the card and she caught me.

"What are you looking at?"

"Nothing."

"Did you drop something?"

"No. I thought I saw… a mouse."

"A mouse?" She turned to look.

"It was just a leaf."

We were moving further away from the card and I was trying to think of an excuse to go back and retrieve it. The street cleaners round there are pretty conscientious and I didn't want to risk leaving it lying on the pavement until morning. We were practically at the corner when I said, "Do you want to just wait here while I pop back to Budgen's for some mints?"

The homophone had confused her. "*Mince?* Like beef mince?"

"No, *peppermints.*"

"Oh." She nodded. "I've got some Polos."

"No, not mints. I mean toothpaste."

"Toothpaste?"

"Yes, I've run out. Best get some while I think about it."

She looked a little nonplussed, perhaps thinking I meant something else, but said, "OK. I'll come with you."

"You don't have to—I'll just nip back."

"I'm not standing here on my own." She was already heading us back to the shop.

Had there been time to weigh up which made me look more peculiar—picking litter up off the street or taking a tube of toothpaste with me on a dinner date—I might have recognized that, like an overbearing perfume designed to mask an unpleasant odour, my diversionary tactic was in danger of drawing more adverse attention than the original deed. Misdirection is a technique used by magicians to make the audience look one way while the real business goes on elsewhere. I've done a bit of

sleight-of-hand, so I know how it works. The skill is in ensuring that the misdirection is not so heavy-handed as to arouse suspicion. There's a scene in *The Great Escape* (or was it *Albert R.N.?*) where **Steve McQueen**, or someone like that, is making a midnight run for it under the perimeter fence. The POW camp is quiet and still. The guards are probably half asleep or thinking about their loved ones: ideal escape conditions. Yet once the British escape committee hear of the young American's daring dash for freedom they say, *Come on, lads, we'll create a diversion.* They love creating diversions. They start whooping and singing with jingoistic gusto and dance about the hut like fools; they think they're so clever, outwitting *the goons* with what they see as an ingenious distraction. Now, if I were a German guard, disturbed in my quiet reverie by such a sudden and deliberate cacophony, the first thing I'd think is, *Hello? Diversion? Somebody must be trying to escape—I'll get my gun.* And if I was **Steve McQueen**, snipping away with my home-made wire cutters, I'd be thinking, *What the hell are those idiots doing?* The German guards would by now be wondering why every prisoner in the camp had suddenly decided to burst spontaneously into 'What Shall We Do with the Drunken Sailor?' and bang a saucepan with a spoon. Consequently, they'd all be on the lookout for any untoward activity. In the film, the guards are successfully thrown off the scent, but in real life, I suspect **Steve McQueen** would be dangling from the barbed-wire fence, riddled with bullet holes. *Yeah, thanks for the diversion, guys. Really helpful.*

The card was still there; I tried not to look at it as we passed. We went into Budgen's, selected a tube of Colgate with cavity protection formula and approached the counter. A woman buying a lottery ticket was dithering over her numbers. I handed Amy the toothpaste and a five-pound note, saying, "Can you pay for this? I'm just going outside."

She showed concern and asked me if I was all right. I told her I was fine. She looked puzzled, but agreed. By the time she came out, clutching my change and the toothpaste, the card was already in my pocket.

The restaurant was a French-bistro type of place, Chez Jules. Candlelit, small and romantic. With her being younger than me, I'd imagined Amy would choose somewhere modern with loud music, but I was beginning to realize that wasn't really her thing. She'd be more likely to have **Cary Grant** or **Gregory Peck** on her bedroom wall than **Claude van Damme**.

With wine in our glasses and our food ordered, Amy rested her folded arms on the table and leaned forward, smiling. The skin on her shoulders glowed in the candlelight.

"Can I ask you a question?" she said. There was mischief in her eyes.

"Yes, of course."

"What did you pick up?"

"Pick up? What do you mean?"

"Just now, outside the shop, while I was paying for your toothpaste. You picked something up off the pavement."

I gave her my quizzical look, as if questioning her line of enquiry. "No, I didn't pick anything up."

"Didn't you? Oh." She seemed to accept my barefaced denial, which surprised me. Much practised at school, this technique of contesting any accusation, no matter how irrefutable the evidence against you, had seldom worked for me in the past.

Amy hung her handbag over the back of her chair, but suddenly thought better of it, tucking it securely under the table between her feet. "I'm paranoid about getting my bag stolen now."

I nodded, feeling guilty.

There was **L**eg of **L**amb with **L**entils on the menu, so that was good, but I couldn't find an **L** starter. Amy had ordered two courses and I didn't want to make her feel left out, so I asked for a green salad. Well, that's just Lettuce, isn't it?

When we were eating I asked her if she had gone to public school.

"No," she said. "Why? Did you?"

"No. I just thought… because you call your parents Mummy and Daddy."

"What do you call yours?"

"Mum and Dad. Well, I *did*. My dad's no longer with us."

"Do you think *Mummy and Daddy* sounds silly and posh?"

"No, not at all," I said, and as an afterthought added, "Well, yes, a bit."

"It's funny because we're not posh really. I don't know where it comes from; we've always used… those names."

"And who's Uncle Derek? Is he your mum's brother?"

"No, he's not my real uncle. He's just a friend of the family."

"A friend of the family?"

She took a sip of wine. "Yes."

"And what does that mean—*a friend of the family?*"

She looked at me, somewhat bemused, and set down her glass. "What do you mean, what does it mean? He's a friend of the family."

"And he lives with your mum and dad?"

"Yes."

"That's quite odd."

"Odd?"

"Well, unusual."

"Is it? I've never really thought about it. He's always lived with us, since I was little."

"And your dad doesn't mind?"

Amy shrugged. It had never occurred to her that he might. I was going to make some remark about her having two dads and me not having any, but thought it might sound fatuous so I decided to let it drop.

"Have you always lived at home?" I said.

"No, of course not. I was married for two years. I'm only living there temporarily while I look for a flat."

"Married? Really? But you're not any more?"

"Separated. I still see him from time to time. We had a flat together so there's always stuff to sort out. What about you? You're not married, are you?"

"No. I was with someone for a long time, but she went away to work and the whole thing just fizzled out."

"So you're single now?"

"Yes."

"Me too." She widened her eyes with mock flirtation.

We concentrated on our food for a while.

"Amy?" I said. I'd started, but didn't know how to continue.

"Yes?" she said. "What is it?" She sounded slightly apprehensive about what I was going to say.

"About the Albert Hall. I may have misled everyone last night about **Barry Manilow**. People always assume that I see more of him than I do. He really is my cousin—my family tree proves it—so we're obviously close because we're family, but that doesn't necessarily mean I can get free tickets. I don't know why I offered."

"That's OK. We're happy to pay."

"Well, the fact is—there aren't any tickets. They're completely sold out. I checked."

"Oh, well. Not to worry."

"I know—but I said I could get them."

"It doesn't matter, Riley. They'll understand." She rubbed the back of my hand. "We'll get tickets to see something else. A West End musical, perhaps. Mummy would like that."

"What about you? Do you like musicals?"

She wrinkled her nose. "Sometimes," she said.

"I'm not that keen either. Unless it's a really good one."

"So, how often do you meet up with Barry Manilow?"

"Well, not as often as you might imagine. The truth is—and this is strange really—we've never actually met. I've written to him a few times to let him know of the family connection, but he hasn't got back to me—not yet anyway. I don't want to keep bothering him—he's always so busy."

"Oh, well. I'm sure you'll get together one day."

Amy seemed to like it when I told her stories about my childhood. She would listen intently, like a psychiatrist analysing a patient, seeming to glean valuable insights into my personality that other conversation failed to reveal. I was flattered that she was taking such an interest, and since each story seemed to draw her closer to me, I was happy to keep them coming. I told her the one about getting Mandy Smith's bike for my birthday.— Because I'd recently thought about it, I suppose it was still fresh in my mind. Amy laughed at the bit about the broomstick cross-bar. I told her about some of the famous people I'd met, but she somehow turned the conversation around to my family.

"When did your father die?"

I didn't know how to answer. "Well, I presume he's dead. I'm not actually sure. He left home when I was little and we never heard from him again."

"Where did he go?"

"I don't know. He just walked out one day without saying a word."

"Why?"

"There was another woman."

"Oh, that's awful. You must have been very upset."

I shrugged. "I got used to it."

"So you've never tried to find him?"

"No. What for?"

"And he's never tried to contact you?"

"Nope."

Amy's eyes searched mine for the emotion behind my nonchalance.

"What about your mother? Is she alive?"

"Yes. She remarried and moved to Devon. I see her a couple of times a year. Christmas and that."

"What makes you think your father's dead?"

I shrugged again. "A feeling."

"So your mum doesn't know what happened to him either?"

Just then, the waitress came to check that everything was all right with our food, and thankfully the interruption ricocheted the conversation in another direction. We talked about this and that, and from time to time Amy would gaze into my eyes, as if she were weighing up something in her mind. I couldn't tell what she was thinking, but the look seemed filled with tenderness, so I gazed back, hoping that she meant something by it. At one point she reached out. I thought she was going to take my jacket lapel and pull me towards her to kiss me like **Grace Kelly** does to **Cary Grant** in *To Catch a Thief*—but instead she dipped her fingers into my breast pocket and took out the card. When she turned it over I saw that it had a completely blank front.

"What's this?" she asked.

"Nothing, just a card,"

"You *did* pick it up, didn't you?"

I nodded. "I collect cards—cards I find on the street."

"Playing cards?"

"Yes, or bubble-gum cards, cigarette cards. That sort of thing."

"Why were you being so secretive about it?"

"I thought you might think I was a bit peculiar, picking things up off the pavement."

"Well, you are, aren't you?"

"You think I'm peculiar?"

Amy laughed, choosing not to answer. Instead she said, "So why do you collect cards?"

I decided to tell her the truth, more or less, and see where that got me—*laying my cards on the table*, so to speak. I told her about my bubble-gum card collection and my lifelong pursuit of *Mission: Impossible* **card 19** and how at first I thought the silver-haired Jim Phelps might somehow be leading me to it. (I had to explain who Jim Phelps was.) I told her about how the queen of hearts he had dropped led me to **Princess Diana**, I told her about mayday, the recruitment card, *This Is Your Life* and the recently acquired **Space Mission** card, and I explained the message that the cards were spelling out. I thought it best to withhold certain details: the visit from the royal protection officers, Nell's hoax card and the fact that I had accidentally borrowed Amy's bag from the library.

"That's incredible," she said. "Like pieces of a jigsaw. So how does this card fit in if it's blank?"

"I'm not sure yet."

"But who is the man with grey hair? Is it really the actor from the TV series?"

"Probably not, though I've never seen his face. I call him the Silver Fox—it's a nickname for people with grey hair."

"But he's definitely the one leaving the cards?"

I nodded.

"So he's sending you on a kind of treasure trail?"

"Kind of."

"That sounds like fun. I wonder where it's leading you. Uncle Derek used to lay treasure trails for us in the garden when we were young—hiding little messages with clues we had to work out to lead us to the next message. There'd be a prize at the end, a toy or some sweets. We loved it. He never let on that it was him; we always thought the fairies had left them."

She had made my mission sound like a silly children's game.

"I think this is a bit more serious than that, Amy.—More a set of coded instructions. My neighbour, the one who changed your locks, knows quite a bit about security. I probably shouldn't be telling you this, but he's pretty sure I'm being recruited as a secret service agent for MI5 or MI6 and that the message is from them."

"Really?" Amy pulled her cardigan over her shoulders and sat a little further back in her chair.

"My mission is to protect **Princess Diana**.—That's what the cards are telling me. You said yourself she's in grave and imminent danger—that she believes others are conspiring against her."

"And you think you've been chosen to protect her?"

"Well, yes." Hadn't I just explained what the message meant? Amy was still smiling, but the sparkle had left her eyes.

"I know it sounds crazy," I said.

"You don't think your neighbour might be having you on?" she suggested.

"Having me on?"

"Yes. Playing a joke on you. —Leaving the cards for you to find."

"Steve? No, he doesn't have grey hair. Anyway, he'd never go to all that trouble."

There was a long pause while we ate. Eventually she said, "Did your father have grey hair?" Her voice was light, casual.

The question made me uneasy. Not only because she'd mentioned my father again like he was common currency, but also because she was talking about him in the present tense. I had grown to think of him as someone from the past. "How do *I* know?" I said. "I don't even know if he's alive—which he probably isn't. He didn't have grey hair when I last saw him, but that was thirty years ago, so I couldn't tell you."

Amy looked at me. I realized I had sounded rather peevish.

"But he was a young man then," she said gently. "How old was he, thirty?"

"About that."

"So he'd be sixty now. Stands to reason that if he were alive he'd have grey hair. Doesn't it?"

"Maybe. But that doesn't make him the one who's leaving me the cards. Lots of sixty-year-olds have grey hair."

"Still. Don't you think it could be him?"

"My father?"

"Yes."

"Working for MI5?"

"No, not working for MI5. Just leaving cards, like calling cards. Trying to make contact, maybe?"

"After all these years? Why now, all of a sudden? He's never bothered before. And why wouldn't he just talk to me, or write or telephone like a normal person?"

"I don't know, Riley—I'm just saying it could be him. He might feel guilty, afraid to confront you face to face."

I shook my head. "I don't think so, Amy. Anyway, why would my father be leaving cards telling me to protect Princess Diana?"

"*If* that's what the cards are really saying." She'd put huge emphasis on the *if*.

"They are." I was quite firm. I'd had enough with Nell undermining my interpretation.

"Is it someone else then? A friend playing an elaborate practical joke?"

"My friends wouldn't do that," I said haughtily. I thought about Nell and her cha-cha-cha mischief and Hector Goodall wheezing with laughter at his regular **card 19** routines, but to tell her about them would have weakened my argument. I shook my head. "No, it's not a joke, Amy. I've been specially commissioned. **This is my life mission**."

Earlier in the evening I had imagined that on the walk back to her house I might have held Amy's hand or even kissed her, before being invited in for coffee and a nightcap, but my candour about the card trail had rather put the kibosh on all that. When we arrived at her house she thanked me for a lovely evening and closed the door gently in my face.

THIRTEEN

STEVE WAS COMING OUT of Hector Goodall's as I was going in.

"Guess who I'm fitting home security window grilles for tomorrow," he said.

"**Mike Tyson**."

"No."

"**Bugs Bunny**."

"No. Shut up. Minnie Driver."

"Who's Minnie Driver?"

"*Minn-ie Dri-ver*," he said, saying the syllables phonetically, as though that would explain.

I shook my head.

"**Minnie Driver**," he said, "is an actress and a singer and a babe. Not necessarily in that order"

A babe? Was Steve serious about using that expression?

"You must have seen *Good Will Hunting*?"

I hadn't.

"You've *never* seen Minnie Driver? She was in *Goldeneye*. I've got all the Bond films on video. I'll lend it to you. I've also got a video of her swimming at her local health club, but you're not borrowing that."

I winced. I didn't want to think about how he might have come by such a thing.

"So you're going round to her house?" I said. "Where does she live? Hollywood?"

"Nah, she's English, you div. She lives off Rosebery Avenue."

"How do you know that?"

"I've got a friend who works in the post office. He can get the address of anyone famous in London. He's got a list he prints out on the computer, sells them for twenty-five pounds."

"Who to? Stalkers?"

Steve nodded frankly. "Sometimes," he said.

"Are you sure you've got the right Driver? It might be **Betty Driver**."

"Who's Betty Driver?"

"She plays Betty Turpin in *Coronation Street*. She works in the **R**over's **R**eturn.—Makes the hotpot. Betty's hotpot is famous."

Steve looked irritated and confused. "Why would I want to fit her window grilles?"

I shrugged. "I don't know.—Just a thought."

"Anyway, she hasn't actually put an order in yet, but I'm going to go round to do a sales job on her—point out how easily her present security system could be breached, particularly at the rear of the house. I'll recommend security grilles on all the rear windows, fitted internally rather than externally, which is the most effective way to achieve a maximum level of security. It's also the most effective way to get me inside her house so I can chat her up."

"Are you going to try your screwdriver ploy?"

He didn't like me teasing him. "I might try a bit more than that," he said. "She is red hot and she's gagging for it."

I didn't know who **Minnie Driver** was, but I suspected that Steve was exactly the kind of person the proposed window grilles were designed to keep out.

"*Gagging* for it?" The words stuck uncomfortably in my throat. "With you?"

Steve was indignant. "Why not?"

I shrugged. "You'd have been pretty far down on my list."

Hector Goodall said that you can buy decks of blank cards. Arts and Crafts types use them to design their own playing cards or tarot cards. Sometimes people make up new games. He figured that my latest find was probably from one of those. "They're quite common," he said.

I'd been unable to find any hidden message. What could a blank card be saying? Nothing? Then why was it there for me to find? The best explanation I could come up with was that there was nothing more to follow: *Princess Diana in grave and imminent danger… Your country needs you… This is your life mission… End of message… Over and out.*

Terry Burnside was also in the shop. He never buys anything, but he likes to hang out there. He's all right as long as you don't get him talking about *Star Trek*. I showed Hector the *This Is Your Life* card; I thought he might be able to tell me something more about it. I was aware of the series, but had never collected them. It was issued in 1960—just a bit before my time.

"Oh yes, I know them," he said. "*Top TV Stars*—I've got a full set. One card's not worth much as an odd—a pound or two at most." Hector thought he was there to offer an *Antiques Roadshow*-style valuation; I wasn't interested in that.

"But it *is* from that series?" I said.

"Have a look if you want." He took one of the thick ring-binder albums from a shelf behind him and opened it up on the counter. Each of the plastic pages was divided into six gum-card-sized pockets. He quickly found the *Top TV Stars* set and turned the book towards me. As I leafed through it, I saw TV shows and personalities of yesteryear, some of whom I didn't recognize, but most I did: **Harry Secombe**; *Sunday Night at the London Palladium*; play-in-a-day guitarist, **Bert Weedon**; **Roger Moore** in *Ivanhoe*—his impressively broad shoulders making his head look like a tennis ball on top of a wardrobe; **Acker Bilk, Pat Boone, Bruce Forsyth**—they were all there. *Rawhide*—I remember that. *Dial 999* was before my time, but I did watch *Sea Hunt* and *The Lone Ranger*. I'd expected to see *This Is Your Life* among them, but there was no sign of it. I checked the number on the back: 28. Number 28 in Hector's series was a picture of nurse June Browne from *Emergency Ward 10*.

"Was there a second series of these, Hector?" I said.

"Yes, I believe there was. Why?"

"Your number twenty-eight is different from mine."

Hector looked at the two cards. "Yes. Look. Yours is from series two—different-colour back. I think I've got a few odds from this series if you want any more. I'm sure I've seen this **Eamonn Andrews** one recently. Have a look in the box."

"No, I don't want any more. I just wondered.—What about this one?" I said, showing him *Space Mission Zero*. "Do you know this series? I've never seen it before. *Ace Adventures*."

"There were a lot of Space series. Who issued them?"

"Kane Kards. Copyright 1956. It's not in any of my books."

"No. Never heard of them."

Terry Burnside, reading the sleeve notes from an LP cover, turned and shook his head to indicate that he hadn't heard of the series either.

"Could be one of those that came with breakfast cereal. Or it could be foreign. Holland produced loads of series in the sixties.

In English. They can all speak it over there, you know. I think there was even a Dutch *Mission: Impossible* series. Ooh, wait a minute." There was a sudden note of urgency in Hector's voice. "I know what I was going to tell you—"

"What?"

"I found a box of mixed cards at the car boot sale on Sunday. —Mostly sixties stuff, I think. I bought them as a job lot. The bloke only wanted a quid for them. I haven't had a chance to go through them properly yet, but I did see there was one *Mission: Impossible* card in there. I couldn't remember which number it was you're after."

I smirked dutifully. Same old routine.

"No, seriously," he said. "Is it seventeen or nineteen? I honestly can't remember."

I nodded, acknowledging the familiar set-up, but this time there wasn't the usual trace of suppressed laughter—no devilish twinkle in the eye. Terry Burnside wore a similarly deadpan expression.

"Honestly, Riley," said Hector. "I'm not messing about."

Terry Burnside concurred: "It's true. He was asking me which number it was. I didn't know."

"Take a look, because I did see one in there. It's probably not it, since the bloody thing doesn't exist, but I thought you'd want to check."

He handed me a battered old chocolate box. I slid off the lid, waiting for the custard pie in the face, but it didn't come. Still no laughter. There was a bundle of tea cards, *Wild Flowers*, held together with the remains of a crusty rubber band. (Rubber bands are the card collector's enemy because the rubber perishes over time and the first and last cards in a set are often stained or damaged.) Next to the tea cards was a loose pile of about a dozen odds. I looked up warily. Hector was watching with what looked like genuine interest; Terry was still distractedly flicking through the record albums. I sorted through the gum cards one by one. The first three or four were from the second *Batman* series. There was **Billy Bremner** from the A&BC 'blue back' footballers, a couple from the James Bond *Thunderball* series (very poor condition) and a cartoon cowboy with a big head and tiny body from a children's card game called **Cheeky** Chappies.

Then, there it was: a square of cardboard that had once been the back of a cigarette packet. On its plain side, carefully but inexpertly drawn in blue felt-tip pen, was a portrait of the *Mission: Impossible* team copied from their familiar publicity pose. Underneath it, in neat, spidery writing: *No. 19. Mission: Impossible.* I assumed from the extent to which Terry Burnside was now doubled over, that he was the artist responsible. I also guessed that he had not been to art school.—Cinammon's neck was wider than her head, and the figure I assumed was supposed to be Willie, the strongman, was so small compared to the rest of them that he looked like a puppet sitting on **Martin Landau's** knee. The only other identifiable character was Jim Phelps because of the grey hair, but his features looked squashed and uncomfortable. If Terry had been to school at all, it was not to learn how to spell the word *impossible*, which he had written as *impossable*. Hector was laughing so much that he was fighting for breath. What a couple of **Cheeky** Chappies.

My kettle had conked out the day before so I went to John Lewis to get a new one. It was hot and crowded on the tube ride home. I sat trying to read my Diana book but I was finding it hard to stay awake. My head intermittently lolled forward and then jerked itself upright as I slipped in and out of the land of Nod.

At one point I woke up to find that the carriage had cleared of passengers except for three men sitting opposite me, who were

staring blankly ahead. They all looked to be in late middle age—
I presumed they were mutual friends or colleagues—and all of
them, I noticed, had a full head of grey hair. It occurred to me
that most men over a certain age have grey hair—if by then they
have any hair left at all. I have a few grey hairs myself. Some
men, like **Paul McCartney**, deny the presence of grey by using
off-the-shelf Just For Men products that '*restore* grey hair to its
natural colour'. It's not *dyeing*, but *restoring*, apparently—somehow turning back the clock to reverse the 'unnatural' greying
process.

My mum periodically used a product called **No Gray**, which
must have originated in America because of the *g-r-a-y* spelling.
The **No Gray** secret was an acrid-smelling cream that came
in a plastic bottle with a long nozzle, polythene gloves and a
little applicator brush with which she'd stab what looked like
HP sauce into the roots of her silvery parting. She would stand
before the bathroom mirror, a towel draped across her shoulders,
swabbing the trickling stains from her forehead with cotton
wool as though tending to a head injury.

I hadn't seen the Silver Fox in a while. I wondered if I had
got a little too close that day when he had been forced to step out
into the traffic to escape me. Perhaps since then he had found a
way to continue leaving me the cards without jeopardizing his
anonymity. I'd only ever seen him from the back so I didn't know
exactly what he looked like. Any one of the men on the train
could have been him, but without the characteristic check sports
jacket and classic brogues as confirmation, I had to assume they
were not. Of the three, the closest to him in style was wearing
a grey tweed jacket over a white open-necked shirt. It wasn't
the Silver Fox or Jim Phelps—just another stylishly dressed
man with grey hair. (Neither was it, as Amy had suggested,
my father leaving me a treasure trail of cards in the hope of a

family reunion. Absurd.) The man in the tweed jacket stood up
to study the tube map above my head. He clutched the steel pole
as he absent-mindedly tapped out a chinking rhythm with his
wedding ring. I assumed he had a tune running through his head
to which this was the percussive accompaniment, though to me
the pattern of beats seemed irregular and non-musical. Had he
been my MI5 courier, he might have been tapping out an entire
set of instructions in Morse code, unaware that it would all be
lost on me because I only knew SOS and TTT.

   Between Pizza Hut and the bank there is one of those funny
religious organizations with a shop front. I've walked past it many
times, but never really known what it was. I guessed it was probably
the Church of Scientology—the one founded by L. Ron Hubbard
(not to be confused, as can so easily happen, with film director
Ron Howard, who in his youth played Ritchie Cunningham in
Happy Days). It's an old stone building and the architecture is
quite impressive. Looking up, I saw that carved into the stone
above the door was a crucifix. Underneath it, the word *MISSION*.
Was this a coincidence, or could it have something to do with my
Space Mission Zero message? Further investigation revealed that
the Mission is the Catholic Church's official instrument for the
spreading of the Gospel, *especially in countries where the Church is
new, young or poor, raising awareness and funds for its missionary
and pastoral work worldwide.* Leaflets on a rack outside the door
showed African men shouldering a crude wooden crucifix, and
the cover of *Mission Today* featured a group photo of beaming
young African men in long white **Demis Roussos**-style robes
with a vertical amber stripe running down (or up) the front. The
Mission didn't look like a secret meeting-point to me, but then
The Man from U.N.C.L.E. agents frequently entered U.N.C.L.E.
headquarters in New York City through a secret entrance in the
back room of an inconspicuous-looking tailor's shop.

I must have been lingering too long outside.

"Hello. Do come in. We have to keep the door closed, otherwise rubbish blows in off the street." The woman looked me up and down. "Are you looking for bric-a-brac?" She must have surmised that I was not looking for spiritual guidance.

"Bric-a-brac? Er. Possibly."

"I'm sure you'll find exactly what you're looking for."

"I'm not looking for anything in particular."

"Well, you won't know what it is until you see it, will you?"

I found myself in a church-hall-type of room with parquet flooring. Trestle tables were aligned in neat rows and several men and women of retirement age had set out their wares, despite the absence of customers. They tried not to appear too keen, but when they saw me walk in, the sellers perked up noticeably. One man couldn't help himself. "Everything's half-price today." I nodded appreciatively, taking in the tabletop arrangement of pointless knick-knacks.

The room was overheated and stuffy, with a whiff of mildew and furniture polish. I moved on past a pink lady with baby-doll hair and a sparkly tiger on her sweater. I wasn't sure exactly what she was selling. Fussy ruched poodle pomander covers and crinoline-wearing table-lamps with glittering waterfall-effect shimmer. Their combined light cast a rosy glow on the lady's face. She didn't look up, instead making a note of something in a little book, her bejewelled spectacles chain swinging against her face. I could only guess at what she had written: *Dear Diary. It has now been three long years since I sold anything…*

Another woman was selling vintage clothes and seemed to have some quality stuff—mostly women's, but there were a few men's things too. I don't go in for the full vintage look like some people you see—dressed head to toe as if they're time travellers from another era or overenthusiastic extras on some period BBC drama. There's a bloke near where I live that does all that—demob suits, plus fours, spats. The other day I saw him in the post office wearing a pith helmet. It can look contrived, but there are some classic designs and beautifully tailored garments to be found—and these can be imaginatively integrated into your everyday wardrobe. **Suggs** out of Madness, **Noddy Holder** from Slade, **Johnny Depp**, and that annoying bloke with the monocle off *Antiques Roadshow* have all demonstrated intelligent use of vintage wear.

The item that caught my eye was an elegantly tailored black jacket. I lifted the hanger from the rail to take a closer look. It had a slight military styling without looking too much like a fancy-dress costume. The tailoring was exquisite, with crisp epaulettes, the edges of which were piped in black silk, and it had a high tunic collar. Single-breasted, with five black buttons that the woman said she thought could be vulcanite. I nodded. *Vulcanite?* Was she seriously suggesting that the buttons might have been manufactured on a distant planet by highly logical people with pointy ears? The embossed design on them was of a sheep's head, which seemed pretty down to earth.

"Beautiful, isn't it? Probably 1930s. It's in perfect condition. Look at the lining."

I nodded in agreement. "Is it from a uniform?" I said.

"Yes, it's Swedish, I think. A dress uniform. I'm not sure if it's army, navy or what. It could be for the police or the fire brigade. That would have cost a fortune in its day. Very fashionable now. One of the Oasis brothers wears something like it, doesn't he? Of course, his is just a cheap copy; you can't buy these any more. My nephew wanted it, but he was too broad in the shoulders. It fits you perfectly though. You two were made for each other."

She was right. It was the most beautiful jacket I had ever seen. I could just picture **David Bowie** wearing it at a gallery opening or an informal concert for a select group of friends. Amy would love it. Some of her clothes looked like vintage classics. It would show her that I too could be quirkily creative in my attire. The minute I put it on, I knew I had to have it. She showed me to a full-length mirror. It was exactly how I had always wanted to look.

"You look really handsome in it."

I was too modest to agree, but she was right. "How much is it?" I said.

She fished around for the tag hanging off the collar. "I've got fifty-five on it, but I can do it for fifty."

Bargain. She folded it nicely and slipped it into a plain white carrier bag. As I handed over the money, I noticed one or two of the other stallholders looking on enviously.

I was feeling rather good about my purchase so was perhaps more inclined now to browse. A bit further round the room, a man and woman sat side by side behind a table of neatly arranged miscellanea. They were sharing home-made sandwiches and tomato soup from a tartan thermos. They stood up as I approached, moving the Tupperware sandwich container from view and quickly swallowing their food. Their thing was books, magazines and other printed ephemera: a bit of sheet music, old letters, theatre programmes, postcards, that sort of thing—much like Hector's but on a smaller scale. I noticed they also had some cigarette and tea cards—always worth a look. The tea cards were from the late sixties and early seventies: *Butterflies of the World*, *Vintage Cars* and a set of cigarette-card cricketers from the forties. I picked up some cards that looked like reproductions of nineteenth-century political history engravings. Not my cup of tea at all. I was only trying to see what was underneath them.

"Eight pounds. There's a full set there. Twenty-five. Count them."

"I'm sure you're right."

"Count them. It's always best to check."

I didn't want to, but he was insistent, so I flicked through them. There was one missing. "There's only twenty-four here," I said.

"Are you sure? There was a full set this morning."

I counted them again and put the pile back on their table.

"Is there one on the floor?" asked the woman helpfully.

It seemed unlikely, but I had a quick look, just to show willing. And there it was—face down on the floor with its corner poking out from under the tablecloth.

"Ah. Here it is," I said.

"Someone must have dropped it," she said.

I paused for a moment, taking in what she'd said. Was she trying to tell me something?

The man held out his hand. I hadn't even seen what was on the front of the card, but I was reluctant now to hand it over, thinking that it might be meant for me. I drew the card towards me possessively. "You wouldn't consider selling this one card on its own, would you?"

"Oh, no. It's part of the set."—He was right. Silly question.— "I could do them for seven," he said.

I knew I hadn't got any more cash; the jacket had taken care of the fifty I'd just got out of the machine. All I had was a handful of loose change.

"I haven't got any cash. Do you have credit card facilities?" They shook their heads glumly. I might as well have asked them if they had an MRI scanner. I fished in my pockets for change and discovered the *ten-pound note* I'd found in the bin at Amy's. I'd put it in the little coin pocket of my jeans to keep it separate from my own money and forgotten all about it. I wasn't comfortable spending it, since I'd promised to donate it

to charity, but I needed it there and then—so I handed it to the
stallholders to secure the next card in the sequence.

Prepare to Execute!

It was quite a shock when I turned the card over. *Prepare to
execute?* No thank you. Had I known it was going to say that, I'd
have left it on the floor. If that's what this mission's about, they
can count me out; I no longer want to be a secret agent. A bit
of covert surveillance or code-breaking is one thing; executing
someone is quite another. Even if this person—a psychopath of
some kind, presumably—is planning to harm the Princess, that's
definitely not for me. Out of the question—I just couldn't do it.
I would have been happy to do what I could, alert the appropriate authorities or whatever, but I am not prepared to execute
anybody and that is final.

It's hard to imagine MI5 going to such extremes, but I expect these decisions have to be made. If the CIA had been aware of **Lee Harvey Oswald's** agenda, would they have recruited someone to 'take him out' before he could kill the President? Of course, if, like Steve, you subscribe to the popularly held conspiracy theory, you might believe that the CIA were the ones who recruited Oswald to carry out the assassination in the first place—in which case the idea may have been to hire someone to eliminate Oswald *after*, not before, he'd carried out his plan.

On the way home I stopped and joined the short queue at the cash machine. A man wearing a sleeping bag as a cape sat on the pavement nearby, making everyone feel awkward. "Can you spare any change, please?" He delivered the line with renewed cheery optimism as each customer stepped forward. When refused or ignored—people had different techniques for saying no—he'd tell them to have a lovely evening. As I approached the machine to make my transaction, I pretended I hadn't really noticed him sitting there. When the money came out of the slot I dealt off a ten-pound note and slipped it to him. He looked up, surprised. "You're a diamond," he said.

"Not really," I said. "Just keeping a promise."

I stood on the corner, tucking the remaining notes into my wallet. I had fulfilled my moral obligation to donate to charity the ten pounds I had found in the Trueloves' bathroom waste-bin. It wasn't the exact same note, but that wasn't important, surely? Then I started to worry that the banknote I'd spent at the bric-a-brac market, with its distinctive letter R scrawled on the Queen's face, might somehow fall into the wrong hands. What if Amy or Mrs Truelove went to the Catholic Mission to buy some old postcards or a vintage knitting pattern from the same stallholders, or if Uncle Derek should happen to stop by to pick up some 1940s sheet music? What if they paid with a twenty and by chance received that very same *ten-pound note* in their change? They'd recognize the letter **R** and assume that instead of giving the money to charity, I had spent it on something for myself. How could I prove that I had later made a charitable donation of an equal amount from my own pocket to a homeless person? Who would believe me?—I was being silly, I realized that, but it was a niggling worry and I couldn't let go of it. In the end, I went back to the beggar by the cash machine. At least he remembered me as his recent benefactor. He offered his hand in friendship, which I took in mine as I lowered my head to speak to him.

"Sorry. That ten pounds I gave you. Do you think I could have a receipt?"

FOURTEEN

BEEF, BROCCOLI AND BORLOTTI BEANS for dinner last night. Again, a bit dry. It could have done with some gravy. I really like gravy, but unless you're having goose, which to me can only be at Christmas, there's no meat that begins with G to put it on. **G**uinea fowl?—You can't get that in my local Sainsbury's. There's **G**ammon—but, ironically, that's the one meat that comes *without* gravy. **P**ineapple or **P**arsley sauce—that's what you have with **G**ammon. And neither of those really goes with **P**ork or **P**astrami. It can be very frustrating.

All this began with shopping lists. If I was popping to Mr Orhy's for a few things, I would keep the list in my head rather than write things down. I found it easier to remember those items that happened to begin with the same letter. *Milk, corn-flakes, Melon, Mr Sheen, jam.* Well, three of the five begin with M, which gives you a clue if you forget something. Three **M**'s, a C and a J. Then I realized that if I adjusted my list slightly—**M**uesli instead of cornflakes, **M**armalade instead of jam—all five items would begin with **M**. This is how my mind works. I'm not sure it's always a good thing.

I hadn't telephoned Amy since we'd had dinner at Chez Jules, the night I had *drawn a blank*. I rather thought I'd blown it altogether, but it was actually she who made the first move to get things rolling again.

Someone must have let her into the building because she knocked directly on the door to my flat. I had just finished breakfast. I assumed it would be Steve so it was quite a shock to see her standing there. She said she was on her way to play tennis— it was Sunday—and wondered if I'd like to go for a drink later. She suggested a mews pub near her house and we agreed to meet there. With that settled, there was a pause. I suspected that she wanted me to invite her in, but I couldn't, not with all Steve's SAS stuff piled up in there—she already had her doubts about me. The book he had most recently foisted upon my reading list, *The A–Z of Torture Techniques*, was not the kind of title a girl wants to see lying on the coffee table of her new suitor.

"So what have you been up to?" she said, glancing over my shoulder into the flat.

"Oh, nothing much."

She nodded; I smiled.

"Have I come at a bad time?"

I could tell by the way she said it that she was wondering if I had someone in there with me. "No, I'm just… busy. Doing a bit of cleaning. Everything's in a real mess." I'd made myself sound fussy and effeminate.

She smiled and nodded. "I'll see you later then. Have fun. Don't wear out your polishing mitt."

I got there before her and stood at the bar trying to look manly. Amy arrived looking like a **Cecil Beaton** fashion plate. She wore a chestnut-brown 1950s party dress: delicate brown lace over rustling rust-coloured taffeta (or chiffon—something like that), with a chocolate velvet ribbon accentuating her slim waist. It was perfect, like a dress **Grace Kelly** might have worn. The colour looked incredible with her Crunchie-Bar-yellow hair. She had gone the whole hog, stylishly accessorizing the look with short gloves and a perky little hat. Some might have considered her slightly overdressed for the local pub, but she seemed completely at ease. Sitting beside her on a low bench outside, I felt drab, unimaginative, unworthy. In my new jacket I might have been able to hold my own, but I had taken it to the dry cleaner's and it wouldn't be ready until the following day.

"That man you were talking about," said Amy, "he's been watching our house from across the road." She absent-mindedly stirred the ice in her drink.

"What did he look like? Did he have grey hair?"

"I don't know. Uncle Derek was the one who saw him, but whoever he is, he's obviously the person who stole my bag. He must have had a set of keys cut, like your neighbour said—and he's waiting for an opportunity to burgle us. Luckily we changed all the locks so he won't be able to get in, but it's still really creepy to think of him skulking about. Uncle Derek called the police but by the time they came, he'd gone. So that's why he's been hanging around—nothing to do with your MI5 thing."

"Well, actually it's more complicated than that."

"What do you mean?"

"He's not going to burgle you."

"How do you know?"

Amy listened while I explained how I hadn't actually found her bag in the park; that I had sort of taken it from the library.

"Hang on. So you're saying you're the one who stole my bag?"

"No. I'm the one who gave it back to you."

"—Having stolen it in the first place. You took a bag that didn't belong to you—my bag—rifled through my personal belongings to find my address, came to my house and inveigled me into inviting you into my home by pretending to be doing a good deed."

It didn't sound so good when she put it like that.

"Isn't that a classic ploy used by serial killers to gain the confidence of their victims?" she said.

"I don't know." I said. "Is it?"

"Yes, yes. It's quite a commonly used con trick, I think."

"Ah, I didn't know that because I'm not a serial killer."

"Well, that's what all serial killers say, isn't it?"

I shrugged. "How would I know that?"

She stared at me, trying to weigh me up. I detected the faintest trace of a smile.

"It's perfectly innocent," I said.

"Is it?"

"Yes. You must have dropped the playing card they gave you when you handed in your bag at the library. —What were you doing at the library, anyway?" Amy pulled a face so I decided not to pursue it. "You see, *I* thought the card had been left for *me* so that I'd find your bag and track you down. It's a method used to introduce one secret service agent to another. I saw it once in a film.—Quite clever, really. That's why I thought you were in on the whole Diana operation.—The mission to save her from harm. When I saw that we were reading the same book, I assumed it was some kind of sign."

"Very clever. Except I'm not a secret agent."

"No. I realize that now. Perhaps it was some other kind of sign. Another kind of connection."

She held my gaze for a few seconds before looking down at her drink. With her straw she began to prod the lemon slice that was floating amongst the ice on the surface.

"I don't get it," she said. "So who's the man watching our house?"

"I presume it's the Silver Fox, the MI5 man I was telling you about. He's what's known as a courier; his job is to pass messages between the case officer and the agent. They never meet each other, so the courier is the only link between them. Steve, my neighbour, has explained how it works.

"So he's not trying to burgle us, this man?"

"No. He's waiting for *me*. He has another message to pass on. But this time, I don't want it."

"Why not?"

I showed Amy the latest card and explained how things had taken a dark turn.

"*Prepare to execute?* Prepare to execute who?" she said.

"I don't know. I expect the next card will tell me, but I don't want to know. I can only assume it's someone who poses a threat to **Princess Diana**. A stalker, or an obsessed fan probably. —Like the man who shot **John Lennon**."

"And you think someone's telling you to kill this person?"

"That's what it looks like. The picture is quite clear and the words spell it out."

"Jesus, Riley. Who's leaving these cards?"

"I don't know. Steve thinks it's probably MI5."

"—Government secret services recruiting innocent civilians to carry out assassinations? You really think they would do that?"

I shrugged.

"You're crazy. MI5 would never sanction anything like that."

"Steve says a lot goes on that we don't get to hear about."

"Steve…" Amy tutted and rolled her eyes—instantly dismissing my primary source of insider information. "Why would MI5 choose you anyway? You couldn't execute anybody. Could you?"

"Of course not."

"You're supposed to chop someone's head off?"

"Well, I don't suppose it's that literal. In espionage, the method of execution tends to be a bit more subtle: a whiff of poisoned gas squirted from a contraption hidden in a newspaper, a poisoned dart shot from the tip of an umbrella.—That's how they do it when they want to assassinate someone. They have some amazing stuff: propelling pencils that fire bullets, a cigarette packet that contains a gas-firing device… There's even a thing called a stinger—a reloadable .22-calibre firing device concealed inside a tube of paint."

"What are you on about? Are we talking about James Bond now?"

"No, it's real. The CIA used them after World War Two."—I knew it was true because *The Spy Handbook* that Steve had lent me devoted a whole chapter to concealed weapons and there was a picture of it. I did wonder, though, if I'd got the propelling pencil confused with something that came in the **SECRET SAM** attaché case.

"You can't get involved in something like this. It's absurd."

"I know that, Amy."

"It must be someone playing a joke on you. A pretty sick joke if you ask me."

"No, it's not a joke."

"Why wouldn't MI5 just get the police to arrest the suspect?"

"I don't know."

"Well, you're just going to have to walk away from it. That's all there is to it. Whoever it is, just tell them you're not going to do it; you don't want to play their little game any more."

"Yes, but what if they won't let me walk away?"

"Don't be daft. What are they going to do to stop you?"

"I don't know. Apply pressure? They can be very persuasive, these people."

"*These people*, whoever you think they are, no longer seem like the good guys, Riley. You need to get yourself out of this."

"How?"

"I don't know. If you believe this is real—go to the police."

"And tell them what?"

"Tell them there's a plot to assassinate Princess Diana. That's what you think, isn't it?"

I imagined myself at the police station—an old *Dixon of Dock Green* sergeant at the desk studying my cards. *Ah, yes. Now let's have a look at what we've got here. Queen Mayday—preparing to execute Eamonn Andrews during his next space mission. Ooh. Yes, I see what you mean, sir. This is a very serious offence. Right, just you leave it with us. We'll get a couple of men on to it right away.*

"I can't go to the police. They'd never believe me."

"No, and I don't know why you expect me to believe you either."

"The man with grey hair, the Silver Fox. Uncle Derek saw him."

"But we don't know for sure it was him. And anyway, the man with grey hair could be anybody. Why don't you have it out with him? Ask him why he's doing this with the cards."

"I can't."

"Why not?"

"He runs away."

"*He runs away*," she echoed, mockingly. "How old are you? Five?"

"I'm scared to confront him."

She turned, suddenly more tender. "Scared? Why?"

"I don't know."

She squeezed my arm. "I don't think you're cut out to be a spy."

"Too late. I've already been selected."

"You're looking at this all wrong. Nobody *chose* you; *you* chose you. You're the one picking up the cards—putting yourself forward as a candidate."

"Well, I've committed myself now. They've seen me pick up the first seven." I wasn't counting the card in the library or the cha-cha-cha.

"So what? Just don't pick up the next one. You said the cards are always face down? If you see another card—any card—just ignore it. Then you'll never know who you were supposed to execute. If you don't receive any further instructions, how can they expect you to act on them?"

Amy was right. I had to take control.

We stopped back at her house and I waited in the kitchen while Amy popped upstairs to use the bathroom. Uncle Derek was busy at the sink with the dinner dishes so I sat and chatted with Mrs Truelove. When the phone rang, she went out to the hall to answer it. "Oh, hello, Joan… Have you?… Oh dear." She caught sight of me through the doorway and rolled her eyes, mouthing the word *sorry* as she turned away to continue the call. "…And when was this? Today?"

Left on my own, I picked up the newspaper that lay folded on the table. Another bit of Diana tittle-tattle had found its way on to one of the inside pages: an editorial piece with side-by-side comparison photographs of young **Prince Harry** and **Princess Diana's** former lover, **James Hewitt**—speculating on the dubiety of the child's paternity.

Amy appeared and sat down beside me, glancing at the paper to see what had captured my interest. "That's ridiculous," she said. "All that stuff about James Hewitt being Prince Harry's father. Just because they've both got red hair. Diana didn't even meet Hewitt until after Harry was born so he couldn't possibly be the father."

"The press making something out of nothing as usual," said Daddy, who had wandered into the kitchen holding a pair of black slip-ons. "Have we got any black shoe polish, Mummy?"

Mrs Truelove was still on the phone, hovering in the doorway. "I have to go, Joan. I'll call in the morning, Yes, all right. Bye." Then, to Mr Truelove: "In the cupboard with the polishes. Use your eyes."

I turned the newspaper towards Amy. "Well, they do look rather alike," I said.

"Not really," said Amy.

The sink gurgled noisily. Uncle Derek turned the washing-up bowl upside-down to drain and came to sit next to Mrs Truelove at the table, wiping his hands on a tea towel. I decided to fill everyone in on what I'd read:

"The newspaper makes a big deal out of the fact that **Prince Charles** and **Prince William** are both left-handed, whereas Harry is right-handed."

"Is left-handedness necessarily hereditary?" said Amy.

"According to the *Daily Mail.*"

"I don't think it is, is it?" she said. "I'm left-handed, but Mummy and Daddy are both right-handed. It could be just a coincidence. Lots of people are left-handed; Uncle Derek's left-handed. It doesn't prove anything."

Uncle Derek and Mummy looked down at the table. Daddy suddenly remembered that he needed to water the hanging baskets, leaving his slip-ons and shoe-polishing paraphernalia on the kitchen floor. I was amazed. Here it was, practically out in the open, and Amy seemed totally oblivious, almost wilfully failing to make the connection. A huge, stampeding Nellie the Elephant had found its way into the room and she didn't even look up.

Uncle Derek cleared his throat lightly and shifted in his chair. He reached for his cigarettes and offered one to Mrs Truelove. She declined with a tight little shake of her head, preferring to lie low until she felt the storm had passed. Uncle Derek glanced sheepishly in my direction as he touched the cigarette's tip with the flame from his lighter. I averted my eyes, pretending I hadn't noticed anything untoward, and the three of us sat in silence staring fixedly at the table while Amy lazily flicked through the pages of the newspaper, glancing at one or two of the articles as she went.

"Hmm," she said nonchalantly, "It looks like it's going to get warmer at the weekend."

Back at home I discovered another pile of magazines on my coffee table. Steve had actually used my spare key to let himself in. The cheek of it. Despite my instinct to dump all of his warmongering literature in a skip, I found that my chosen *Book at Bedtime* reading had me engrossed in sniper techniques of concealment. It turns out Steve was right about cover scents such as the spray-on decaying forest fragrance. The book said that snipers are forbidden to use deodorant in case the enemy smells it. Since the distance between a sniper and his target is likely to be well over 100 metres, that would have to be some pretty powerful underarm protection.

FIFTEEN

SOMETHING ODD HAD BEEN happening with my phone at home. When I picked up the receiver the next day to ring Amy at the salon I could hear voices. No dial tone, just two men talking. I listened for a minute.

—*It doesn't give us very long.*

—*No, it's only… what is it today? The nineteenth?*

—*Er. Twentieth.*

— *That's like… a week and a bit. I don't think it's possible.*

I should have kept listening, but at the time I just assumed it was a crossed line. "Hello?" The voices stopped, but I could still hear breathing. I spoke again: "Hello?" There was a click and the dial tone returned. I put the receiver down and picked it up again—dial tone as normal. Was it a crossed line, or was it something else? With digital technology, was there even still such a thing as a crossed line? I hadn't heard one for years. I started to dial Amy, but thought better of it.

The phone box by the church had that distinctive fragrance combination that can also be found in multistorey car parks: Kentucky Fried Chicken with underlying base notes of urine, disinfectant and old cigarettes. (In its proper setting, I'm rather partial to KFC. It's practically impossible to order anything there that doesn't begin with **C**. Their standard meal deal is **C**hicken and **C**hips, **C**oleslaw and **C**orn-on-the-**C**ob with a **C**oke. And if you don't like fizzy drinks, you can substitute the **C**oke for **C**offee.) The cigarette smell was thanks largely to the previous occupant who had been there when I arrived. I'd recognized her as Hector's daughter, but she was too busy smoking and yakking loudly on the phone to notice me. There was a missing window panel at her shoulder so I could hear her quite clearly, going on about a nightclub she'd been to. I pictured her there on the dance-floor with the pushchair, forcing its wheels between people's dancing feet as she cut a path to the bar.

While waiting for her to finish, I tried not to stare. I kept wishing that instead of blowing her cigarette smoke directly into the phone receiver I was about to use, she might think to turn her head and exhale through the gap—but she didn't. The pushchair had been parked outside with a nine-roll pack of Andrex toilet rolls dangling from the handle, while its usual occupant could be seen inside the phone box, playing between his mother's legs. The confined space enabled him to gain some valuable experience in passive smoking. When my turn came to use it, I found that the receiver was still warm, the mouthpiece dotted with tiny beads of condensation from her excited breath. I held it slightly away from my face as I spoke.

"Amy, I think they might be bugging my phone. I could hear men talking on the line."

"Do you think someone's listening now?"

"No, I'm in a phone box."

"What did they say?"

"I don't know. Nothing really. Something about not having enough time."

"Enough time for what?"

"I don't know."

"No one's bugging your phone, Riley. It's probably just a crossed line."

"Yeah. I suppose so." —I wasn't entirely convinced.

"Hey. I saw your neighbour—the locksmith—today."

"Steve?"

"He was waiting for me outside the salon when I went out at lunchtime."

"How does he know where you work?"

"I don't know, but he was there."

"What did he want?"

"He said he was just passing and suggested we get a coffee together."

"And did you?"

"No. I told him I had to get back—that I had a client. I find him kind of creepy. He's a bit too keen—you know what I mean?"

"Yes, I know exactly what you mean."

"He said, where are you going now, and I said, to get a sandwich, and he said, well, I'll come with you—so I had to go and buy a chicken salad sandwich I didn't really want while he stood there with me in the queue, going on about how battery chickens have their beaks cut off with a hot blade to stop them pecking each others' eyes out and how the meat was blasted off the bone so I was really eating skin and eyelashes."

"Charming."

"The funny thing is—later on, there was a van parked over the road from the salon: *Goldie Locks*. I'm sure it's the company he works for; I remember seeing the van when he came to our house."

"Goldie Locks—such a stupid name."

"It might not have been his van; I couldn't see anybody inside, but I got the feeling he was watching me."

"I'll have a word with him."

"No, don't say anything. It might not have been him."

"You need to be careful. You might come home one day to find all your porridge eaten and Goldie Locks Steve asleep in your bed."

Amy chuckled.

"Seriously, Amy. You don't want him hanging around you. He's a bit weird. He told me his last girlfriend had a restraining order put on him."

"Really? What for?"

"I don't know.—Some domestic thing. He says she was crazy, but it makes you wonder."

I was treading on something sticky and happened to look down at my feet to see what it was. On the floor in the corner of the phone box was a card.

It was obvious they weren't going to leave it like that, with the message hanging in midair. *Prepare to execute...* Prepare to execute who? The card was the size and shape of a cigarette card and had the characteristic typographic design on the back that carries the information. I could just about make out the series title: *Speed Kings.* It made me nervous to be standing so close to it, thinking what might be on the other side.

"Riley? Are you there?"

"Er. Yes." I was too distracted to talk and had to consciously avert my eyes from the card. "Listen, Amy—I've got to go."

"OK. Come to my house tonight. No, not tonight, I've got someone coming over. Tomorrow night."

"OK."

"And Riley—"

"Yes?"

"—Don't forget: if you see a card, whatever you do, don't pick it up."

It felt good to walk away from it. Taking control. Amy would have been proud of me. While I'd been in the phone box I was worried that the card might somehow flip itself over and reveal a vital clue to the intended victim's identity, thereby forcing me to accept the commission.

Back home, I tried to put the card out of my mind by continuing work on my feature for **Card Collector Monthly**. The last word count I did was 4,372. It's way over, but I don't think **M**ichael **M**allinsay will care when he reads it. He may suggest that I'm veering slightly away from the point, but by following the journey of the central characters, we're also following the journey of the card—which at this stage is still tucked between the pages of the passport in the bureau drawer of Elvis's home.

1967. The Supper Club. Elvis and the secretary—a slow, sauntering foxtrot on a tiny dance-floor. Her cheek is pressed to his and her fingers caress the back of his neck. Elvis looks awkward—less committed to the dance. His eyes discreetly scan the room to see if any other diners are watching. She turns her face towards him—perhaps inviting a kiss, but he pretends not to notice. The tune finishes and couples on the dance-floor clap politely. Elvis and the secretary return to their table. Elvis looks relieved to be out of the spotlight's glare.

"Does it make you uncomfortable, being here with me?"

"I'm just worried that someone will see us."

"Who do you think is going to see us here?—Your wife?—Someone from work? Nobody knows us here."

"I know. I just feel..."

"Is this how it's going to be?"

"Sorry. I'm not used to this. I'll get better at it."

SPEED KINGS

A SERIES OF 50

28

S. PRINCE

Stuart Prince became a professional driver in 1948. His early career was meteoric. 1955 was a seminal year; he was signed by Mercedes-Benz, to partner legendary World Champion Juan Manuel Fangio. That year saw Prince shadow the great Argentine in most Grands Prix, famously beating him to win the British Grand Prix at Aintree racing the Mercedes-Benz W196 Monoposto. In that same year, he also won the epic 1,000 mile Mille Miglia road race in the Mercedes-Benz 300 SLR, at an astonishing average speed of 97.9mph on public roads, the Targa Florio road race, again in the 300 SLR, and the Tourist Trophy at Dundrod.

D.B. ALBEMARLE & SONS
BRANCH OF THE IMPERIAL TOBACCO
CO. (OF GREAT BRITAIN & IRELAND)

"I don't want you to get better at it. I'm not interested in a casual affair."

"I know. Neither am I. I want us to be together, it's just..."

"You don't know how to leave your wife?"

"It's really difficult. My son—What would I say? How could I explain?"

"I know. It *is* difficult. But I'm not prepared to be the other woman."

He looks miserable—racked with guilt and indecision. She puts her hand on his—speaking more tenderly now: "You said you wanted to be with me."

He clasps her hand tightly between his own. She looks into his eyes and he melts. They seem about to kiss when a waitress approaches with a tray of candles flickering in amber glass bowls and sets one down on their table. As she heads to the next table, Elvis quickly leans in and blows out the flame.

4,650

It was about midnight when I went back to the phone box. I wasn't going to pick up the card; I just wanted to see if it was still there. The street seemed unusually still. It reminded me of that film with **Michael Caine**, or someone like that, as a Cold War spy. What was it? *The Quiller Memorandum? The Ipcress File?*— one of those—where the agent is in a phone box on a wide, deserted street—somewhere in East Berlin. It had occurred to me that I might have been under surveillance, but there didn't seem to be anyone about. I didn't want to start getting paranoid. Further down the street, a young couple parked their car and went into one of the buildings. There were lights on in the flats opposite, though I saw no one at the windows.

I pretended I was waiting for someone—wandering casually up and down, glancing nonchalantly into the phone box. At first I thought the card had gone—it had moved slightly—but it was still there, still lying face down. I was curious to know what was on the other side, but I knew I couldn't pick it up without committing myself to further involvement.—Then what was I doing there?

I opened the door and stepped inside. I was fairly sure there was nobody watching me—but even if anyone was, I might legitimately have been there to make a phone call. There were some telephone directories clamped into a swivelling metal contraption so I opened one as if I were looking up a number, but my eyes were actually fixed on the card in the corner. I slid the tip of my toe towards it, thinking I might manage to flip it over briefly to take a peek.—Just a peek, that was all. Suddenly the phone jangled. It made me jump. Then it rang a second time. I'm not sure why I picked up the receiver. Perhaps because the ringing seemed so insistent—as if the caller knew I was there.

"Hello?" I said hesitantly.

There was a pause; I thought the line was dead, but then a voice said, *"Pick it up."* It really spooked me. A **Peter Lorre** voice, tinny and high as if strained through a metal colander. He spoke again: *"Pick it up."* My heart was thudding, unnerved by such direct contact. I said, "Who is this?"

The voice said, *"If you're there, pick it up."*

So I did.

1967. Night. Elvis and the secretary walking side by side on a quiet street. She seems to want to hold his hand, but his arm dangles uselessly between them, somehow missing the connection. Staring straight ahead, she says, "I'm going away."

He turns. "Going away? When?"

"Soon."

"On holiday?"

"No. To live. I've handed my notice in at work."

Taken aback, he stops walking and turns her towards him. "Where are you going?"

"Tregonhawke. It's a little seaside village on the Cornish coast."

"What are you going there for?"

"My Auntie Irene has a little cottage there, but she keeps forgetting things so she's had to go into a home. I said I'd go and look after it for her.—It's right on the beach."

4,800

"In Cornwall?"

"Yes, why not? It's beautiful there."

"How long for?"

She shrugs.

"What about us?" he says.

"What *about* us?"

Unable to come up with an answer, he looks at the pavement. She touches his arm. "You could come too."

"To Cornwall? What would I do there?"

"You'd live with me."

"Wouldn't you miss London—your friends and everything?"

"Not if you're there with me."

He stares at her for a moment, trying to take it all in. "Just like that?"

She nods. "Just like that."

What had I done? I thought about throwing the cigarette card away without looking at it, but I knew it was too late for that. By picking it up I was already committed. I waited until I got round the corner into a quiet street and then pulled it out of my pocket just far enough to sneak a look. It was the worst thing I could have imagined.

As I approached my flat I saw two men sitting outside in a parked car. Were these the two royal protection officer thugs who had called on me the day after the royal visit? I slid into the doorway of the fitness centre across the road, watching from the shadows. After a few minutes, the car started up and nudged back and forth before easing out of the space. Then, instead of going forwards, it reversed fifty yards up the road, paused, and swung into another parking space under a tree. The engine stopped, the headlights faded and the two men sat in the darkness, waiting. I knew then that I couldn't go home.

"Riley. What are you doing here?"

"Can I come in?"

"Yes, yes. What's the matter?" Amy stood aside to let me in.

"Nothing. I just thought I'd stop by."

"It's late. I didn't think you were coming over tonight." Something was distracting her. "Do you want a coffee? I was just..."

I followed her through to the kitchen where I was surprised to see a man leaning against the kitchen counter. He had the cheeky dark curls of a young **David Essex**, though his wardrobe was more **Adam Ant**. I would have assumed he was in the wrong house, but he was holding a glass of wine and seemed very much at home.

"Riley, this is my ex-husband, Bruno."

"Bruno?"

He nodded. As we shook hands, his leather jacket creaked and a cluster of thin bracelets jingled at his wrist. Bruno had the raffish good looks and devil-may-care trousers that might qualify him as the swashbuckling gypsy buccaneer type, but I suspected that this lusty-young-knave look might have taken longer to achieve than he was letting on. His sideburns were honed to a point sharp enough to burst a party balloon.

Amy gestured for me to sit and began filling the kettle.

Bruno reached for the bottle of red wine and topped up his own glass, but not Amy's.

"Nice jacket." He sounded polite, but I was unconvinced by his sincerity.

"Oh, thanks. It's vintage," I said. "I got it…"

Bruno clicked his fingers and pointed at my chest. "Let me guess. The little indoor market in the Catholic Mission?"

Disconcerted, I said I couldn't remember where I'd bought it.

"Yes, I think so. And I'll tell you how I know that. That's my jacket. As was."

"Your jacket?" I said. Amy turned round to look.

"You bought it from Pauline, the vintage-clothes dealer, didn't you?" said Bruno. "She's my aunt."

"My God," said Amy, laughing. "It is, isn't it? It's your old jacket, Bruno."

He turned to me. "I used to wear it a lot. I just got tired of it."

Amy corrected him: "It didn't fit you."

I said, "I don't think it's the same one. I got this…"

"Oh yeah. It definitely is. There's a button missing on the left sleeve. Lift your arm up." He didn't wait. He plucked at my cuff, holding it under my nose. "There you are. Look."

"It is," said Amy. "I remember that missing button."

"Told you," said Bruno.

I felt humiliated.—More than that. I felt violated.

"Well, it looks great on you," said Amy, trying to make me feel better. "I always liked that jacket. It fits you really well."

Bruno agreed, smugly. "Yeah. Looks great."

He started telling Amy about a mutual friend who'd been called for jury service or something, deliberately excluding me from the conversation. As they chatted, she would glance in my direction from time to time, as if trying to bring me in, but it was clear that I was not part of it. Amy seemed different—less confident, almost apologetic. When she did speak, Bruno was dismissive of her opinions or would interrupt her to correct her on a small matter. When there was a break in the conversation I said, "Is Bruno your real name?"

Bruno nodded. "Yeah. Why wouldn't it be?"

"No reason. My nan had a dog called Bruno. He was vicious. I think she took pity on him because his previous owners wanted to get rid of him. You could see why. When I was a kid he bit me on the finger so after that—whenever I visited, Nan would have to shut him out in the garage."

Bruno cocked his head knowingly. "Well, you know what they say. Once bitten…"

"He was quite smelly." I said. "I love dogs, but he was horrible really."

Bruno nodded. Amy gave me a look.

"No offence," I added.

Nell was just letting herself in when I got there. She'd had a night out with 'the girls'. She calls them girls, but like her, they're really women. She was a little unsteady on her feet. Once inside, she took off her shoes and poured the last two or three inches of wine from an opened bottle she took from the fridge, dividing it equally between two glasses.

We sat together on her sofa; she sat lengthways with her legs across my thighs. I didn't say anything about the men who were watching my flat. I'm sure she'd have told me I was imagining it. Perhaps I was, but recent events had really spooked me. I'd yet to mention Amy so there was no point in telling her about Bruno. I didn't want to think about that little situation. Nell was great. She didn't ask why I had turned up so late; she just accepted that I was there.—No mention of the cards or our little falling-out over the cha-cha-cha.

"We can watch the tape of Barry on *Des O'Connor* if you like," she said. "You still haven't seen it, have you?"

"Yes. Great." It was actually the perfect thing to take my mind off everything. It had been a troubling day.

"Is Barry your cousin on your mum's side or your dad's?"

"My dad's. Why?"

"He's dead, isn't he, your dad?"

"Probably."

"Probably?"

"I don't really know."

"I thought you said your dad died when you were young."

"Well, he walked out on us, me and my mum. Nobody knows what happened to him. He just disappeared."

"So he could still be alive?"

"Could be, I suppose."

"Don't you want to know?"

I shook my head. Amy had suggested the exact same thing. I felt like I'd already had the conversation before.

"He might have had amnesia or something," suggested Nell.

"No. There was another woman, my mum said."

Nell shook her head knowingly. "So he just left without saying anything?"

"Went out for a block of Wall's ice cream. Never came back."

"Oh, Riley. You never told me all this."

"Well—all water under the bridge."

"I don't know how anyone could do something like that. It's not right."

"She's just as much to blame—the woman. Selfish little tramp. She thought nothing about destroying our family. As long as she got what she wanted."

"Such a shame. Did you get on with him all right?"

"When he was there I did, yeah."

"What did he do for a living, your dad?"

"He was a printer."

"Printer? Was he? Where did he work?"

"He worked at a few places. He was at some little place that did letterheads and envelopes. Later on he worked for a company called Greenwood and Sons in Stoke Newington."

"Greenwood's? I used to work there."

"Did you?" I was surprised. I'd never imagined Nell working anywhere other than the café.

"That was years ago, mind."

"What did you do there?"

"Admin. Secretarial stuff. Typing and that."

"Really? Is that where you learned to type?"

"No. I took a course at night school. A lot of us girls did in those days. Ninety words a minute, me. Used to be, anyway. I'd be a bit rusty now." Nell got up to get more wine from the fridge. "When was your dad there?"

"Ooh, I don't know. The sixties, I suppose. Sixty-five? It would have been **nineteen sixty-seven** when he left. I know that because I've been writing about him for my magazine article.—Indirectly."

"I'm trying to think when I was there. It must have been around that time. What was his name?"

"Brian."

"Oh, bugger it."

"What's the matter?"

"I've broken the sodding cork."

"It's that opener, Nell.—It's useless."

I've told her before. She's got one of those ones that looks like a little man you screw in and then move his outstretched arms down by his side, but the spiral bit is too thick and she never screws it in far enough.

"You want the Waiter's Friend," I said. "I'll get you one. Here, I'll do it." I took the bottle from her and began to dig out the remaining piece of cork.

"Brian Richardson," she said, tapping her upper lip as she tried the name out loud. "Can't remember anyone called Richardson. I used to do the wage packets so…"

"He wasn't called **R**ichardson. His name was Pincus."

"Brian Pincus? —Brian was your dad?"

I sat down with the bottle and topped us up. "Did you know him?"

She took a moment to answer. "No. Not really. I didn't know he had a son. He never told me that." She began fiddling with something in the kitchen, speaking over her shoulder. "How come your name's Richardson?"

"Richardson is my mum's maiden name. She changed hers back after he left and changed mine while she was at it. Not much of a name is it, Pincus?"

"No. Not much."

Nell had to go to the bathroom. When she came back she said, "I didn't really know him, your dad. It was a long time ago."

"Still. That's quite amazing that you worked at the same place. Small world, huh?"

She nodded, but looked away.

"So you probably knew the woman he ran off with?"

She shook her head.

"It was someone from work. Some cheap little slag from the office, according to my mum."

I'd seen the VHS tape sitting on top of the television so I got up and fed it into the slot of the video recorder. Nell had labelled the tape neatly: *Barry on Des O'Connor*. Once it was in, I pressed rewind on the remote.

"So your real name is Pincus?" said Nell.

"Yes. Same as Barry. Didn't you know his real name is Pincus? **Barry Manilow** is really **Barry Pincus**. Barry Alan Pincus."

"Pincus?"

"Yes. That's how I know we're related. Barry changed his name from Pincus to Manilow, his mother's maiden name. I thought you knew that."

"No. How would I know that? You never said anything." Nell seemed a bit cross. I don't know why she was getting upset about it. It doesn't matter what his real name is, he's still a great entertainer.

"**R**iley **R**ichardson is a much better name, don't you think? There are lots of film stars with double **R** initials: **R**osalind **R**ussell, **R**onald **R**eagan, **R**oy **R**odgers, **R**alph **R**ichardson."

Nell nodded. She was looking down at her hands, fidgeting with a gold ring which she teased back and forth over the knuckle of her little finger. We sat down to watch, but she seemed distracted.

Barry engaged in a bit of light banter with **Des O'Connor** on the sofa before he went over to the piano to do his song. He was charming and witty—talking about his wonderful legion of British fans. It's funny—you don't notice so much when he sings, but when he talks, the strong Brooklyn accent and his slight lisp make him sound a little like **D**affy **D**uck. He wore a shiny slate-grey suit with a lilac shirt and tie that matched the studio décor so perfectly that at times his shirt and the walls became one and it was as if you could see right through him. Everything about him seemed perfectly polished. His lustrous hair had been teased into a casual-looking bonnet of stiff blond peaks. His skin was cosmetically smooth and I think he may have been wearing a little shimmer of pale lipstick. That's showbiz—they all do it. Des too was sporting a rusty orange glow that looked like he'd been painting himself with Peruvian Mahogany wood stain.

'I Made It Through the Rain' is one of Nell's favourites. Barry took time out in the middle of the song to reflect on his humble beginnings in Brooklyn, and the subsequent highs and lows in his career. As the piano tinkered with chords from the verse, he told the studio audience how his grandfather, the patriarch of the family, had always encouraged him to sing, taking him across the **B**rooklyn **B**ridge each week to a 25-cent record-your-own-voice booth in Manhattan. His grandfather knew that one day Barry would be a star. And twenty-five years later, when 'Mandy' went to number one and Barry found himself appearing at Carnegie Hall, his proud grandfather was there in the middle of the front row to give him a standing ovation. It was a touching story, made more poignant because all his fans know that Barry was abandoned by his father, just like I was. It gave added fervour to the rest of the song: Barry balling his determined little fist to deliver the final chorus—triumphant in his struggle against adversity. Nell always gets emotional when he sings this song so I wasn't surprised to see her wipe away a tear—but when I looked across at her towards the end of the performance I could see that this was something different. She wasn't even watching the screen; her head was bowed low on her hands and she was sobbing deeply. I'd never seen anything quite like it. It was as if all the sadness in her life had suddenly come at once. This was more than just Barry making it through the rain.

"Nell? Are you OK?" She wasn't, of course, but I couldn't think what else to say.

I pressed the remote button to stop the tape, inadvertently turning off the VCR recorder, causing the television to revert to *Newsnight* with **Jeremy Paxman** in the midst of an interview. I scrabbled for the mute button to silence the presenter's hectoring voice and when I looked up, Nell was heading back to the bathroom again. Why was she so upset? If it wasn't about

Barry, it must have been something about remembering her time working at Greenwood's as a secretary. And then it all came rushing towards me like a bully in a school corridor, all big and obvious, and I wondered how I had somehow managed not to see it coming.—The one **connection** I had failed to make was suddenly staring me in the face, making me breathless and panicky. I stared for a moment at the blankness of the bathroom door, imagining behind it—not Nell, not even Dusty or Annette André, but a complete stranger. Looking around me, it was as if I didn't recognize where I was any more. Everything I knew had gone.

1967. The mother is in the kitchen with her neighbour.

"Well, what time did he go out?" asks the neighbour.

"Around half past eleven. He always goes to Morrissey's to fetch the paper on a Sunday morning.—Always has done. He was getting a block of ice cream to go with the pie.—I usually make an apple pie on Sunday."

"And he's not been back since?"

The mother shakes her head. "I've had his dinner in the oven since half past one. It's ruined. We ate ours, thinking he'd be back. Something must have happened."

"No. He'll probably be back in a minute."

"But he's been gone all day. Where could he have got to?"

"He's probably met a friend and gone drinking. You know what men are like when they've had a few."

5,000

She doesn't. She checks the clock and wrings her hands nervously. "No. He wouldn't do that.—The ice cream would melt."

"Perhaps he never went to Morrissey's. Did you check with the shop to see if he's been in?"

"I can't. They close at one on a Sunday. I rang the bell, but there was no answer."

"So you've been out looking for him?"

"Yes, I've been out a dozen times. Backwards and forwards to that bloody shop. I've searched everywhere, checked with all the neighbours. No one's seen him. I don't know what to do."

"Do you think he's had an accident? Got knocked down by a car?" suggests the neighbour brightly.

"Oh, Jean. Don't say that."

"Well, he might have got a bump on the head and lost his memory. Perhaps someone's taken him in and they're trying to find out where he lives. Would he have had his name and address on him?"

"No, he was in his Sunday clothes."

"Well, that's what happened to Ronald Colman in *Random Harvest*, isn't it? He got knocked down by a taxi and lost his memory. Greer Garson found him and looked after him. He's probably with someone like that."

"Greer Garson?"

"Somebody kind, I mean. When his memory comes back he'll come home again, I'm sure."

"Well, when's that going to be?"

In the front room the women's conversation is barely audible. The boy stands at the curtains and nudges his head into the gap between them, letting them drape on either side of his face. He rubs a viewing square in the window's condensation with his finger. Outside, the street is quiet and still. Unusual for the time of year, a light frost has begun to settle.

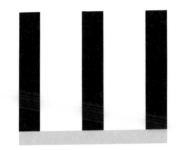

SIXTEEN

IN *THE PRISONER* TV SERIES, when **Patrick McGoohan** abruptly resigns his job as a British secret service agent, he wakes to find himself held captive in a mysterious seaside village isolated from the mainland by mountains and sea. The Village is further secured by numerous monitoring systems and security forces including a huge, menacing white balloon that captures those who attempt escape. My own trip was entirely voluntary— I could leave any time I wanted and, unlike in *The Village*, there was no Number Two controller trying to extract 'information' from me. No one knew where I was so there'd be no repercussions about my sudden resignation.

My room was on the third floor and overlooked the beach. The hotel had barely changed since I used to stay there with my parents. It was like going back in time. It felt good to get away from the mission and the change of location made it easier for me to turn my back on the cards. I'd had enough of all that. Besides, I had more important things to think about.

After leaving Nell's I had sneaked back to my flat to pack a few things. The men outside seemed to have gone, though by then I had other reasons for wanting to disappear. I had no real plans about where I was going, but I could no longer imagine being able to look Nell in the eye and I felt the need to get as far away as possible. A hundred and seven miles. I suppose it's not such a great distance, but it was enough.

For the first two days I didn't do anything much and spent most of the time in my hotel room. I kept thinking about Nell—trying to get it all straight in my head. The realization that she was the woman who had stolen my father from me had completely swept away the foundations of our friendship and I wasn't sure now what was left. I had every right to hate her, but for some reason I couldn't. In my story of **card 19** I had assumed that the secretary made most of the running—flirtatiously enchanting my father with her womanly charms—but maybe it was all Dad's idea. Nell would have been young and perhaps more vulnerable than the woman I had described. I kept having to re-imagine the 1967 scenario I had created, replacing the image of Annette André from *Randall and Hopkirk (Deceased)* with a youthful version of Nell. Like pasting a cutout head from a photograph on to someone else's body, it just didn't seem to fit. I wonder if it's true what she said—that Dad never told her he had a son. Was he so taken with her that he suddenly forgot his family responsibilities? Did Nell even know he was married? Perhaps he neglected to mention that too. There were lots of questions, but I couldn't imagine ever being able to ask them and, as far as I was aware, Nell was the only one who knew the answers. Even with this new discovery, I still had no idea what became of my father. I remember Nell saying that her husband died young, in a car crash I think, but she must have been referring to someone else—someone who came later. She can't have been legally married to my dad unless he somehow got divorced from my mum. Perhaps there *was* a divorce and she never told me about it. I believe that in the case of a missing person the spouse can apply for an abandonment divorce. Christ. If he'd married Nell, that would make her my stepmother.

When I thought more about it, I realized that my overriding emotion was not anger towards Nell for what she had done, or even anger towards my dad for his part in the affair, but more a feeling of betrayal. And if I'm honest, there was an element of jealousy. Even though they were clearly no longer together, somehow my dad was still a bigger part of Nell's history than I was; she belonged more to him than she did to me. And now our friendship had been spoiled—it was just one more thing he had taken away from me.

Another sighting of **ELVIS** in the morning paper. (I refer to the king of rock and roll, not the two-timing north London printer who callously abandoned his family in 1967.) This time he was spotted travelling on the commuter train between Chester and Holyhead. Of all the conspiracy theories going, the *Elvis is Alive* hypothesis has to be the daftest. Even Steve would find it hard to subscribe to that one. I expect the 'sightings' offer comfort to those Elvis fans still finding it hard to accept that their hero is no longer with us. (A bit like it is with Jesus.) These sporadic manifestations of '**the king**'—mending a flat tyre in a lay-by on the A39, or working in the Ipswich branch of WH Smith—act as living proof that their hero's death is nothing more than an ugly rumour.

People handle bereavement in different ways. **McCartney** fans, for example, could never be accused of being 'in denial' about death. When, thirty years ago, a rumour began to circulate that the outwardly alive-and-well Beatle had been killed in a car crash, and as a cover-up had secretly been replaced by a lookalike (who, by chance, could sing and play the bass left-handed like his predecessor) his supporters were quick to accept this as the truth. Unlike the **Elvis** fans who were unable to believe that their idol was really dead, **Paul McCartney**'s fans were all too keen to believe that theirs *was*. And if there were any doubts about his demise, there was an abundance of evidence to verify this. On the *Abbey Road* album cover it was noted that Paul was walking out of step with the other Beatles and was also not wearing shoes—the ancient Eskimo symbol for death, or something. And when the voice at the end of *Revolution 9* was played backwards, it seemed to be saying *Turn me on, dead man*. At the time I, for one, needed no further proof. **McCartney** was clearly deceased. The walrus was Paul.

On the front pages there were blurry pictures of **Princess Diana** gadding about in France—Monaco or Saint-Tropez, somewhere like that—with her new love interest, the Egyptian playboy **Dodi Al Fayed**. The report talked of dream villas, luxury cruises on billionaire yachts, sun-kissed beaches, private jets and romantic dinners, and Diana apparently having found true love, looking radiantly happy, carefree and joyful. Not quite the distressed cry for help as described in last week's newspaper. It was just as well I was no longer needed.

The headline for the Holyhead sighting was *ELVIS LIVES*, the journalist (knowingly or not, it was hard to tell) using the rearranged letters of the subject's name to describe the pop legend's miraculous recovery from death. It occurred to me that if **Desi Arnaz**, the Cuban bandleader husband of **Lucille Ball**, and her co-star on the *I Love Lucy* show, had happened to die on the same day as the **Elvis** sighting, the headline could have used the same anagram system to announce his fate:

ELVIS LIVES; DESI DIES.

Do other people see these things, or is it just me?

ELVIS LIVES; DESI DIES
PRINCESS DIANA DANCES IN PARIS

When he disappeared, we didn't know whether Dad (only the people at work called him Elvis) was dead or alive. There were no mystical clues, no records to play backwards for a hidden message. For a while I clung to the *Random Harvest* amnesia theory, romantically picturing him wandering the streets, not knowing who he was or where he had lived, trusting that one day everything would come back to him and he would return to us with his memory fully restored and his love for his family as strong and as real as the day he left.

About a week later, I was shocked to see his face in the window of the greengrocer's on Cooper's Road. Mum must have had a poster printed. Perhaps Dad's friends at work did it for her. The details were sparse: *Missing Person. Name: Brian Pincus. Height 5ft 10in. Age 30.* And that was it, apart from a bit at the bottom with the contact details. The photo was one Mum had taken on holiday in Bournemouth the previous year. Dad was sitting on a low wall by a fountain and in the original photo I had been sitting next to him. I remembered it because he was holding my hand, and at the time I was a bit embarrassed; it was shaming for a nine-year-old to be seen holding hands with a grown-up. The blurry original had been enlarged for the poster; in the process I had been cut out of the picture, but my small, disembodied hand, severed at the wrist by the brutal cropping, could still be seen resting in his. As the days passed, I noticed more of these posters appearing in the local shops. There was even one in the phone box on Lloyd Road—the same scant information repeated over and over again: name, height, age. Nothing about the date, the location or the circumstances of his disappearance; no description of what he had been wearing. Police on TV always worked from a description. Did Mum think

that was the most significant thing about him, his height? *Hmm.*
Five foot ten, you say? No, Madam, we've seen no one that would fit
that description, but we'll keep on the lookout. Don't worry; a man of
medium height shouldn't be too hard to find.

1967. The wife enters the printing works, nervously clutching her
handbag. She looks around for someone to help her. A young
man speaking on the telephone pauses in his conversation to
offer assistance and points towards Mr Greenwood's office. She
knocks tentatively on the outer office door. When there is no
reply, she turns the handle and peers inside. The secretary's desk
is unoccupied; her in-tray is full and her typewriter is covered. The
wife takes this in as she approaches the inner door marked *G.*
Greenwood, Managing Director. She is about to knock, when she
notices a framed photograph on top of the filing cabinet. Posing
against the grassy background of a golf course is the young
secretary holding a modest trophy. The wife picks up the picture
to take a closer look, her attention focused on the young woman's
smiling face.

5,380

After breakfast I went for a walk on the beach. The strong breeze
blustering in from the sea felt fresh and was starting to clear my
befuddled head. My new jacket would have been just the thing
to keep out the chill, but instead it hung in the little wardrobe in
my hotel room. I still loved it, but after the humiliating meeting
with Bruno, I no longer felt that I could wear it. Did he think he
was being subtle using his discarded garment as a metaphor to
allow him to talk so disparagingly about his former wife—telling me he had grown out of it, that it no longer suited him, and
pointing out what he perceived as flaws that only he, through experience, had discovered?—Referring to Amy as a tossed-aside
hand-me-down for someone else to use. Well, that's not how I

saw it. There was nothing at all wrong with the jacket; the jacket was perfect. The fault was with him. He was the wrong shape for it.

On the promenade, I came upon a woman who claimed to have all the answers. Her home, with its back turned to the sea, was less of a gypsy caravan and more of a garden shed. It was festooned with coloured light bulbs that were not currently working, and its weathered walls had been repeatedly repainted in red gloss, their surface thick and sticky like old nail varnish. Both front and sides were covered in hand-painted signs, the messages written in urgent block capitals.

GYPSY ANGELINA, TV AND RADIO SPIRITUALIST AND CLAIRVOYANT. SHE HAS TOLD THE FORTUNES OF THE RICH AND FAMOUS AROUND THE WORLD—STARS OF THE SCREEN, PAST AND PRESENT—AND SATISFIED THEM ALL. SO WHY NOT LET HER LOOK IN YOUR PALMS TOO? YOUR VISIT WILL CONVINCE YOU SHE IS A TRUE ROMANY GYPSY. CRYSTAL BALL READINGS. TAROT CARD READINGS. PALM READINGS. YOUR HAND IS THE MIRROR OF LIFE. IF YOU HAVE EVER DOUBTED OR BEEN AFRAID, NOW IS THE TIME TO TAKE ONE BIG STEP FORWARD. ALL READINGS IN PRIVATE. NOTICE TO THE PUBLIC—THIS LADY IS KNOWN FOR HER TRUTHFUL PREDICTIONS. CONSULT HER NOW. YOUR HAND TODAY HOLDS THE FUTURE OF TOMORROW. PLEASE WALK IN. SHE WILL GIVE ADVICE ON HEALTH, BUSINESS, MATRIMONY AND OTHER REASONABLE MATTERS. GUARD YOURSELF BY SEEING HER AT ONCE.

I wasn't looking for answers. Not from Gypsy Angelina, anyway. What interested me was the cavalcade of stars from yesteryear with whom she had been photographed. Mostly printed as black-and-white ten-by eight glossies, the pictorial evidence of her celebrity clientele was proudly displayed behind glass in crudely constructed frames. There was **Bruce Forsyth**, looking alarmingly youthful, his face long and thin like an ironing board; **Bob Monkhouse** circa 1962—years before I met him—mugging for the camera as he stared, mesmerized, into Gypsy Angelina's crystal ball. There was **Shirley Bassey**, **Tommy Cooper**, and Irish songstress, **Dana**—winner, if you remember, of the 1970 Eurovision Song Contest with 'All Kinds of Everything'—a woman in a fur coat I didn't recognize; a wrestler that I did, but couldn't put a name to. One, a little more recent, possibly from the eighties: ventriloquist **Keith Harris** with his inexplicably popular green duck, **Orville**. The pictures would have been taken, I imagined, during summer-season variety-show engagements in the town. Among the newer ones was that barmaid off *Coronation Street* who I think left the series about ten years ago, and a handful of younger soap stars who, having started out in full colour, had now turned pale blue in the sunlight—the more recently photographed, seemingly the quickest to fade. In every picture, Gypsy Angelina, a squat woman with earrings and thick, unruly black hair that looked like a Scottish terrier had landed on her head, was pretending to study each celebrity hand while the stars themselves directed their attention towards the camera.

Sitting, incomprehensibly, among these sometimes forgotten faces from the world of light entertainment was a similarly posed black-and-white photograph of Gypsy Angelina reading the palm of **Jimi Hendrix**. Yes, **Jimi Hendrix**. What on earth had the legendary psychedelic-blues, guitar-playing virtuoso, with his pioneering heavy distortion sound and astral-quality feedback, been doing in Bournemouth? I could only guess that he had been on tour at the time, playing one of the big theatres, and had been persuaded by some opportunistic pressman to pose for the shot. The picture must have been taken around the **1967** release of *Are You Experienced?* because he was wearing the same military jacket as the one on the record cover. Jimi's jacket, more traditionally worn by the Royal Hussars, was resplendent with wide loops of ornate frogging down the front and fancy swirls on the forearms—much more decorative than the one I'd recently bought, but appropriate for his flamboyant stage persona. Here in the photo, though, without his guitar, Jimi seemed lost, and while Gypsy Angelina contemplated his short future, the wildman of pop was turned to the camera looking shy and uncomfortable.

The shed entrance had a stable-door arrangement with the bottom half closed and the top half open, and a glass bead curtain parted down the middle and clipped to the sides like a schoolgirl's hair. I was just trying to get a peek inside when a woman appeared in the archway, tossing the dregs of a teacup out on to the pavement.

"Do you want a reading, love? I can do the cards," she said.

"Cards? No. No cards, thank you."

"Or a hand reading? Special today. Five pounds both palms."

She undid a catch and opened the stable door and waddled back to the table to sit down. "Come in," she said.

Thirty or forty years on, Gypsy Angelina's hair was still black, but an inch of grey parting suggested some assistance, though none too recently, from the **No Gray** dye bottle. The colour was flat, with the reflective properties of soot.

Inside, the shed was richly decorated in 'true Romany gypsy' style: floral rugs and patterned fabrics smelling of damp and air freshener. A small, phrenology head sat on a shelf along with a grapefruit-sized glass ball on a stand and a tall aerosol can of fly and wasp killer. Pinned directly to the wall were more photographs, this time showing traditional gypsy caravans being pulled by blinkered black-and-white horses wearing furry moon boots.

On the table, there was a glass lamp with an orange bulb, its thin cord trailing off to a cluster of plugs and adaptors jammed into a single socket.

Once Gypsy Angelina had my money tucked away in a tin box on the shelf, she took hold of my hand between her own and flopped it this way and that, as if breading a pork cutlet. She laid it face up on the table, lightly pressing the ends of my fingers to stop them curling up, and then launched straight into a speech so well-worn it had lost all its punctuation, the sentences trotting out nose-to-tail like performing ponies in a circus.

"I get the vibrations that you're troubled at times... You think a great deal... When you find yourself in one situation you get straight back into another... You don't like to listen to advice—follow rules... you've got to see things your way. You are an easy-going, comfort-loving person and not very hard-working—but you are always able to cope with hard work as a necessity. If needed you can work hard, eight, ten, twelve, any number of hours and other durations—longer days—otherwise you work comfortably in a relaxed manner... Younger days you were very ambitious—there were flights of ambition—but now you are more realistic... whatever can be achieved is being thought about rather than undertaken... Whatever work you do, you want to excel in your performances—if you lag behind you feel uncomfortable... Family ties are very strong, but there are some communication difficulties... You like your food and drink too—and about your health—everything is good except that sometimes you have headaches..." She looked at me and twiddled the fingers of her left hand, presumably trying to summon a response. With nothing forthcoming, she started up again. "...occasional, rare, very rare headaches. Number one. Number two—sometimes you feel a little low, low in energy, low in spirit..." A phone rang, which she fished from the pocket of her skirt, extending the aerial while still talking. "… At those moments…" she looked at the buttons on the phone and stabbed one of them with her thumbnail, "…you do not feel like you have the… hello, who's that?" She stared at me blankly, her mind on whatever was being said to her. She looked away to answer, not because she felt awkward about taking the call, but because she was somewhere else now, and I was no longer present.

"Yes, she's coming down after work… I don't know… well, can't he?… Is… why can't he get Christine to do it?… She is, I've just spoken to her… You what?… No, this afternoon. He hasn't been out this morning… All right, love. I'll… yeah. All right. What?… No, I've got to go back next week for another one… God knows. Anyway… Yeah, all right. I'll see you later, love. OK. 'Bye then. 'Bye." She held the phone out in front of her again and terminated the call with her purposeful thumb. She looked at me and said, "So, were you happy with your reading?"

I didn't know what to say, so I nodded and smiled.

"Do you have any questions?" she said.

Before I went in, I'd imagined I might ask her something about my dad. I don't normally go in for fortune-telling or anything 'spiritual' but I thought it might be interesting to hear what she had to say. I'd even considered how I might word my question. *Will I ever see my father again?* or *Is my father dead or alive?*—Something like that. But now, having listened to my fortune, I wasn't sure that Gypsy Angelina had earned the right to offer her insights on this matter. Still, my 'reading' had lasted no more than a minute, and I'd already paid my five pounds, so I thought I might as well get my money's worth.

"Yes, I do have one question," I said. "What was it like meeting **Jimi Hendrix**?"

SEVENTEEN

1967. Elvis and the secretary raise their faces to the setting sun as they walk arm-in-arm along a beach. Long shadows stretch out behind them. In the distance, the orange glow is reflected in the windows of the beachside property she has inherited, which, as it now turns out, is actually a little café.

As they reach the narrow steps heading up to the cliff-top, they wait for a man on his way down to pass them. He has a mop of shiny dark hair and wears wraparound sunglasses—one of the younger generation. Orange shorts, open shirt and a necklace of small white seashells. He carries a transistor radio playing a jangly Top Twenty tune. He nods his thanks to the couple as he steps down on to the sand. The secretary watches discreetly as he passes. When he's out of earshot, she turns to Elvis.

"Did you see who that was?"

"Who?"

"Him. With the flowery shirt. That was Davy Jones. You know—the little one from The Monkees."

"The singer? Was it?" He turns to look at him. "Are you sure? He only looks like a kid."

"No. Definitely. It was him."

"I wonder what he's doing here. I thought he was American."

"No, no. Davy Jones is the English one. He was in *Coronation Street* when he was younger; he played Ena Sharples's grandson. I should have asked for his autograph."

"What for?"

"I don't know."

Elvis notices her quiet disappointment.

"We haven't got pen and paper, have we?"

She smiles resignedly.

"Too late now, anyway," he says.

5,719

On the third night I rang Amy.

"Bournemouth?" she said. "What are you doing there?"

"Having a holiday."

"On your own?"

"I needed to get away."

"From me?"

"No. From… everything. The cards. The mission."

"So you've definitely abandoned your Diana quest?"

"Definitely. I can't be involved in that. Besides, it seemed like it was getting in the way."

"In the way of what?"

"Us."

"You're a sweet man."

"Am I?"

"Yes. Very sweet. I've never been to Bournemouth. Is it nice?"

"It is, actually. A good old-fashioned seaside town."

"What hotel are you staying at?"

"The Majestic. It's right by the pier and from my window…"

"The Majestic. Right. I'll see you in the morning."

"You're coming here?"

"Don't you want me to?"

"Yes. Of course, but…"

"But what?"

"Will Bruno be coming?"

She laughed. "Bruno? No, of course not. Is that what all this is about?"

"No. I just wondered."

"Just wondered what? If I'm still involved with him?"

"Are you?"

"No, Riley. I'm not."

Next morning I felt so liberated that I ordered the full English breakfast: sausage, bacon, egg, tomatoes, mushrooms and hash browns. Every single thing on my plate began with a different letter. It tasted wonderful.

I had no idea when to expect her, so after breakfast I sat on the bench at the front of the hotel with a pot of tea and a newspaper someone had left in the lounge. I wouldn't normally look at the *Express*, but it does have the Target word game, 'a fun way to test your word power', which I rather enjoy. It was extremely pleasant just sitting there, squinting at the sun and watching people go by, then gradually surrendering to the glare and closing my eyes, letting the gentle breeze bring with it distant smells of the sea, suntan lotion and something sweet, donuts possibly, from a kiosk on the pier. Then, as the wind dropped, identifying smells closer to home: the hot tea in the metal teapot, the parched wood of the bench and the pungent tang as the sun stimulated the impurities in the newsprint. Today's score targets were 38—Excellent, 31—Very Good, and 25—Good. With a score of 35, I was nearly Excellent and certainly much better than Very Good. The nine-letter Target word, which, ironically, I solved straight away, was **ENIGMATIC**.

Amy arrived just after eleven. I looked up to see her wheel-ing a small suitcase behind her. She was dressed for the sun in a classic, possibly vintage, summer dress and sunglasses. I was so pleased to see her. I'd had time to imagine how our meeting would be, the long embrace, charged with longing and affection, the meaningful gazing into each other's eyes, but when it came to it I felt a little shy and it wasn't like that at all. I couldn't see her eyes and the exchange was brief and somewhat casual.

"This is cosy." She looked up at the front of the hotel, sliding her sunglasses on top of her head. "Did you book me a room?"

"No, I didn't know…"

"What…?"

"If you… how long… and if you wanted a sea view…"

"Don't worry. I'll do it in a minute." She plonked herself down on the bench and I sat beside her.

"It's good to see you," I said.

She smiled and squeezed my hand. "You too… So you've stopped picking up cards?" It was as though she was checking up on me before committing to the weekend.

"Yes. I've given up on all that. I have officially resigned from the mission. *I am not a number; I am a free man!*"—I don't think Amy understood my reference to *The Prisoner*, so my loud, forth-right **Patrick McGoohan** voice might have startled her.

"Well, that's good," she said, a little uncertainly.

We waited at Reception to get Amy checked into a room.

"How long can you stay?"

"I'm back at work on Tuesday."

It was four days. The four-day honeymoon.

After that, I didn't mention the cards and my mission. I could see that it was spoiling our relationship and I didn't want that. I also had to shut the whole thing about Nell and my dad out of my mind. It was too much to think about. Instead, I settled down to enjoy a traditional seaside holiday with Amy.

While she dropped off her luggage I nipped to my own room to fetch my jacket in case it turned colder later. I felt like it was mine again.

When I met Amy coming out of her room she said, "I'm glad you're wearing that. You look very handsome in it."

"I know," I said.

We went straight out, playing a few slot machines on the pier, followed by fish and chips on the seafront. After my earlier rule-breaking breakfast I was happy to mix my F's and my C's. As we were waiting to be served, I noticed the handwritten menu on the board behind the counter. At the end of a long list of available choices, I saw that they offered **X**tra Chips, **X**tra Peas and **X**tra Gravy—spelled just like that. The **X**-alliterated dinner conundrum was finally resolved, and I didn't even feel the need to order it.

Afterwards we lay on the beach, using my rolled-up jacket as a pillow. Then, as the sun was hot and I'd already caught it a bit that morning on the bench, we went for a wander along the front, stopping to drink tea in one of the cafés and chatting easily about anything that came into our heads.

"So Bruno was your husband, then?"

Amy looked at me. "*Was.* Yes, why?"

"Nothing. He seemed nice."

She laughed. "You didn't think he was nice. You were rude to him."

"Me? How was I rude to him?"

"You said he was like a vicious, smelly dog who should be kept in a kennel."

I couldn't help sniggering. "Did I say that?"

"Yes, you did. You're terrible."

"So you still see him then—Bruno? —Take him to the park now and again?" Amy gave me a look. I tried to sound more serious. "Sorry. So what ended it?"

"He—he did something that was disrespectful."

"What did he do?"

She bit her lip. I could see her weighing up whether or not she was going to tell me. "Mmm. Let's just say it turned out that he wasn't a very nice person—though I think I probably already knew that when I married him. He's quite selfish. Still, he's got what he wanted now."

"But he hasn't got you?"

She shook her head.

"Then he's an idiot."

Amy smiled, but looked away as though trying to make light of the compliment. "Anyway," she said, "the marriage is completely over. Has been for ages. He's with someone else now. And so am I."

"Are you? You never told me." I was being playful, presuming she meant me, but suddenly worried that I might have got it wrong.

Amy must have detected a trace of self-doubt on my face; she smiled mischievously. "Ah, well, it's quite a recent thing."

"I see. So, is it serious then, this recent thing?"

"Hmm. Don't know yet. Could be. Could be."

Amy bought a postcard of a donkey wearing a straw hat to send home to her family. I bought one too, but couldn't think who to send it to. I'd normally write something silly to Nell, but I realized that now I wouldn't know what to say.

Back at the hotel, Amy produced her special scissors and offered to restyle my hair. We both agreed that on this occasion Mr Vann had failed to achieve his usual high standard.

After washing my hair over the bathtub, she made me sit on a straight-backed chair in the middle of the room. With no mirror in front of me, I couldn't see what she was doing, but I was able to visualize the *hairstyle* she was going for. From time to time, I could feel her soft breath on my neck, and whenever she touched my head, I experienced the most exquisite charge of pleasure tingling through my body. I wondered if she was aware of the effect she was having on me. Perhaps so. When she came to work on my fringe, she sat down on my knees to face me, straddling my legs as though riding a donkey. I was fairly sure that this was not customary in the *hairdressing* profession. Mr Vann had certainly always taken a much more traditional stance when dealing with my fringe, but I could see the benefit for Amy in being able to get up close for detailed work. As she busied herself with the job in hand, the warmth of her flesh radiated through the thin fabric of her dress. Concerned that she might slip backwards off my knees, I put my arms around her waist to hold her firmly in position, interlacing my fingers in the small of her back. To facilitate the extra safety measure, Amy slid her hips closer to mine, wiggling her pelvis as she settled into a more comfortable position. It was the official start of our honeymoon.

1967.

"I haven't got a birth certificate."

"You must have. You were born, weren't you?"

Elvis and the secretary sit facing each other across a table in the beach café. She is holding an application form.

"I've never seen it. Must have got chucked out or something."

"Chucked out? You can't apply for a provisional driving licence without proof of ID." She looks down at the form. "National Insurance card?"

Elvis shakes his head. "It's probably still at work."

She tuts and shakes her head. "Have you got a passport?"

"Yes, but it's at… home." He seems hesitant about using the word. "You know, at the—at my old home."

"Well, you'll just have to go back and get it."

"Go back? I can't do that."

"You'll have to, my love. You can't expect me to do all the driving in this relationship. Now, can you?"

The miniature golf course in the park was small, more like crazy golf really, green asphalt instead of grass, with curves and bumps as obstacles. Just the thing to work up an appetite before dinner. Unfortunately, there was no one in the ticket office. We didn't know if whoever was in charge was coming back or whether he'd shut up shop for the day so we decided not to hang around. There were plenty of other things to do.

It was quiz night in the little pub round the corner from the hotel; we'd seen the sign in the window the previous evening. Turning up at the specified time, we paid our two pounds and settled down to play. There were only two of us in our team, but I thought we stood a chance because the quiz had a 1960s theme and I'm quite good on that period. Popular culture, anyway. I'm no good on sport… Or politics… Or geography… Or science…

It took a while for things to get started, but then a woman with an over-amplified bingo-caller's voice began roaming the tables with her cordless microphone and a set of questions. The first was an easy one to get us started. *Which popular sixties film took place in and around 17 Cherry Tree Lane, London, in 1910?* We were pretty sure it was *Mary Poppins*. There was quite a pause between each question while people tried to come up with the answers. *What name was given to the iconic single-colour UK postage stamps used since 1967 that show only the Queen's head in profile and the denomination?*

"I know this," I said, covering my mouth so that none of the others could see. "Machin."

"How do you know that?"

"Ah. I know that because I was at school with a boy called Jonathan Machin who was always telling everyone that his grandfather was the Royal Academy artist who did the sculpture of the Queen's head that appears on the stamps. I was never sure whether to believe him—Jonathan himself was crap at art—but I know the stamps are called Machins because my dad told me it was true. He was a printer so he knew about stuff like that."

"How do you spell it?"

"Like machine without the e."

Amy wrote it in the appropriate space.

Which famous celebrity wedding took place at the Aladdin Hotel in Las Vegas on May lst 1967? Amy answered straight away. "**Elvis,**" she whispered. "He married Priscilla what's-her-name. Bow-lee-o-lee-o. Something like that." We both laughed at her pronunciation. I had actually thought it might have been **Frank Sinatra** and **Mia Farrow,** but deferred to her certainty.

Elvis? Mayday? Marriage? 1967? Nothing more than coincidence. For the sake of the relationship I resolved not to give it another thought.

Next was a question about the song 'I Can't Let Maggie Go', asking which consumer product it advertised. There were a lot of blank faces around the room, but I knew the answer. Nimble—'Real bread, but lighter'. We were sizzling; Amy giggled excitedly and clutched my knee. She was a good player; she got a lot right that I didn't know, in spite of the fact that she wasn't even born until the 1970s. She correctly suggested Botswana as the answer to one question and she knew that **Jim Callaghan** was the Labour Chancellor of the Exchequer between 1964 and 1967. *How did Spurs player John White die in*

1963? We had no idea, so we put 'struck by lightning'—which we later discovered we had guessed right. Only a few we weren't sure of. *What was the name of the little dog that found the missing World Cup in 1966?* It was on the tip of my tongue but I just couldn't think of it. I wanted to say Sparky but I knew that was wrong. Nipper? No, that was the dog on the His Master's Voice logo. Amy was willing me to remember, but it had gone. Even my repeated finger-snapping technique couldn't bring it to the surface, and anyway, by then we were on to the next question so regretfully we had to leave that one blank. (It was, of course, Pickles. I could have kicked myself because at the time I remember cutting his picture out of the newspaper for my scrapbook.)

There were several rounds of questions. At the end, everyone swapped their answer sheet with another team for marking, just like at school. The table next to us, a team who called themselves The Jammy Dodgers, got more than we did, though the Machin stamp question had stumped them. They'd taken a stab-in-the-dark guess and written, 'The one-eyed queen'.

There was a delicious breeze blowing in off the sea as we walked back along the beach to the hotel. Amy was feeling the chill so I took off my sweater and wrapped it round her shoulders. It's what leading men do in films, but once I'd taken it off, I thought I might freeze to death. I didn't let on. Leading men don't say, *Can I have my jumper back, please? I'm cold.*

I would have worn my jacket, but when I went to my room to get ready to go out I realized I'd left it hanging in Amy's wardrobe when I had visited her room the night before, so instead I decided to go for the casual knitwear option. Amy seemed appreciative of its comforting warmth, bunching the wool in her fist and pulling it close to her chin.

We edged nearer the sea, sidestepping the waves as they dashed in and out. I picked up some pebbles and threw them

into the water, another cliché, but we were already feeling pretty romantic. I wondered if it was like this for Nell and my dad once they'd run away to their seaside café, or wherever it was they went. Perhaps they were deeply in love with each other.

I'd spotted a bit of coloured cardboard riding in on the crest of the breaking waves and used that as my pebble-throwing target. The card survived the assault, eventually floating in on the wide, sweeping skirt of the sea, and coming to rest on the frothy wet sand at our feet. It lay there like a shipwrecked survivor, exhausted by the long journey to shore. We weren't supposed to be finding any more cards. Not here. I stared down at it, craning my neck to make out what it was. The surface of the card was damaged, but it seemed to be a picture of a snooker player.

Amy saw that I was looking at it. "Riley. It's not for you."

"No, I know."

"It's just a piece of litter."

"Uh-huh. I think it is a card though."

"Maybe. But you have to realize that not every card in the world is meant for you."

I was quick to agree; I didn't want anything to derail our honeymoon. "You're right. It has nothing to do with me. It can't have, can it? No one knows I'm here."

"It's just a bit of rubbish that washed up."

I put my hands in my pockets. "Exactly. Let's just leave it."

Although we had separate rooms, on the previous night we had lain on Amy's bed together watching an old movie on TV. We were planning another midnight viewing —in my room this time because it was bigger. Amy said she wanted to take a shower first and 'change into something more comfortable' so she stopped off at her own room further down the corridor. How long would that take her? At least fifteen minutes, surely?

Luckily for me, the tide must have been on its way out. Within ten minutes I was back in my hotel room, sitting on the bed and pressing my hand hard against my thigh; beneath it, the soggy card was sandwiched between sheets of toilet paper. For stage two of the process I held the card by one corner and teased it with the little wheezing *hairdrier* that was wired into the top drawer of the dressing table. The card held together surprisingly well, gaining rigidity as it dried, but I had no idea what it meant. As I wiggled the warm blast against its surface, I tried to figure out how snooker fitted into all this.

I didn't hear her knock at first, or rather I did, but thought it was a noise from the room next door.

"Were you drying your hair? I've been knocking for ages."

Amy was wearing a soft, clinging cardigan in pale grey—cashmere, I surmised—and a pair of tartan shorts. No shoes. I was distracted by her shapely legs and prettily painted toenails; I wanted to put my hand on her thigh—to feel the soft skin and discover whether it was warm or cool to the touch.

"Drying my hair? No."

"I could hear the hairdrier." She moved towards the dressing table, and saw it sitting there. I should have put it back in the drawer. She picked up the damp card that lay beside it. "Oh my God. Have you just been back to the beach to fetch this?"

I didn't know how to answer.

"What are you doing, Riley? If you seriously think a card that washes up on the beach holds a personal message for you, you are absolutely insane. It has nothing to do with you. How could it? Do you honestly believe that MI5, or the KGB or the CIA, or whoever you think you're working for, somehow put it in the sea, hoping that it would wash up on the beach right at your feet, just at that very minute? Did they drop it from a helicopter into the water, or toss it over the side of a boat in the middle of the English Channel—or launch it from the shores of some far-off land? Is that what you think?"

"No, that's not what I think."

"Then *why* did you go back for it?"

I shrugged.

"It was in the sea, Riley. There was no grey-haired man; you said the cards are always facing down—this one was facing up. It's not from the fifties or sixties like the others, and even if it was, it doesn't fit your daft hypothesis. *Prepare to execute snooker.*"

"Ah. No. There's something I didn't tell you," I said. "I did find another card. In London, before I came down here. It was in the phone box that day I was ringing you at work. I was determined not to pick it up, just like you said. I even walked away from it—left it there on the ground. I don't know why I went back, but when I did, the phone rang and a voice told me to pick it up."

I opened my wallet and took out my mission cards. I dealt off the top card and showed it to her. I hadn't looked at it myself since the night I found it. I had nearly thrown it away on several occasions.

"Oh Riley. I thought you'd stopped all this."

"Look at it."

"A racing driver?"

"No. Look at the name. *S. Prince.*"

"*S. Prince?*"

"Or to put it another way, *Prince S.*"

"Who's Prince S?"

"Prince S is *Princess.*"

"That's not a princess, Riley. It's a racing driver."

"A racing driver called **Prince S**."

"No. He's not. He's called S. Prince."

"Well, it seems pretty clear to me. Maybe you're just not very good at making connections."

"What's that supposed to mean?"

I had to let it go. "Nothing. I just don't know why you can't see it."

She eyed me suspiciously. "And you really found this card?"

"What do you mean?"

"Are you sure it isn't one from your collection?"

"What are you suggesting—that I'm the one leaving the cards on the street for myself to find?"

"Well then, why is it so old?"

"I don't know."

"All right, so you're supposed to execute Princess Diana. So how does your snooker card fit? *Prepare to execute Prince. S snooker?*"

"I don't know. Maybe it means something else."

"What? What could it possibly mean?" She was rapidly losing patience.

I tried to think. "Er… snooker. Pot black. Billiards. Cue. Like the letter Q. The **queen of hearts** has a letter Q in the corner of the card."

Amy stared at me, shaking her head incredulously. I could feel her unhitching herself emotionally. She was right about the card. It didn't fit. Not yet, anyway. My knack for deciphering picture puzzles had temporarily failed me.

"I haven't had a chance to work it out yet," I said.

"Well, maybe you need some time to think about it. —On your own."

So that was that. No midnight movie. But with Amy back in her own room, at least I had time to think properly and find a rational explanation for the snooker-player card. It took me less than half an hour to figure it out. Like Archimedes, I rushed down the corridor to Amy's room and knocked excitedly, anxious to share my eureka moment. When the door opened, the security chain was on. She had never used that before. She stood in the gap, looking at me warily.

"I've got it." I said.

"Riley. Let it go."

"No, listen. Look at the player taking the shot. What's he using?" I held the card up for her to see, but she didn't even look at it.

"I don't want to have this conversation, Riley."

"Just look at the picture. What's he using?"

She sighed resignedly. "What's he using? I don't know. A snooker cue."

"No, not that. The long thing with a cross at the end they use to rest the cue on for a long shot. What's it called?"

"I don't know—and I don't care."

"You do. It's called a rest cue."

"A rescue?"

"No. A *rest cue*," I said, enunciating the words. "But you get my point? **Rest cue** equals **rescue**."

"Rest cue? What are you on about? Listen to yourself, Riley. You're crazy."

"No. Think about it. **Prepare to execute princess rescue**. See? I got it wrong the first time. It's not *execute* as in 'put to death'; it's *execute* as in 'carry out or put into action'. My job is to *rescue* the Princess, not to *execute* her. This is it, Amy. I'm back on my mission."

She met the news with a derisive smirk. "Well, good luck," she said. "Let me know how you get on."

With that, she calmly but firmly closed the door, signalling quite clearly that the honeymoon was over.

EIGHTEEN

AMY WASN'T THERE at breakfast so I ate alone. Tea and Toast—it was all I wanted.

The waitress who checks the room numbers off the list said that Amy hadn't been down yet. I waited for a while and then went upstairs and knocked on her door. The silence from within seemed cold and still. She could have been out taking a stroll on the beach, but in my heart I knew she had gone. The front-desk clerk confirmed it: Miss Truelove had checked out earlier that morning. She'd left a note: *Had to go back to work early. Sorry. A.*

I went up to my room and sat on the bed wondering what to do. Then I remembered my jacket. I presumed it was still hanging in the wardrobe in Amy's room where I'd left it—unless she had packed it along with her own clothes and taken it back to London with her, which under the circumstances seemed unlikely.

When I enquired at the desk, the reception clerk said, "Unfortunately, we can't give room keys out to anyone whose name isn't on the registration. Besides, I told you, the guest has already checked out."

"Yes, I know. She's my friend, she had to go back to London, and I left my jacket in her wardrobe."

"If Housekeeping find that a guest has left something behind, it will be brought to Reception, and we'll keep it safe. If your friend wants to contact us we can arrange for it to be forwarded to her home address, but we wouldn't be able to hand it over to anyone who isn't registered to the room."

"But she's my girlfriend." I wondered if that was any longer accurate. "Well, sort of girlfriend," I added.

"I've no doubt she is, but you understand our position."

"Yes. I suppose so." I looked down despondently. She seemed to take pity on me then.

"Listen," she said. "Why don't you get your friend to give us a ring and confirm that the jacket is yours and that she's happy for you to claim it? Meanwhile, I'll get Housekeeping to check her room."

"No, I can't do that. I can't speak to her."

That put the lid on it. The receptionist stiffened slightly and crossed her hands neatly in front of her. "Well, I'm afraid there's really nothing I can do then."

I sighed. "So you'll post the jacket to her home address?"

"If she contacts us. We can arrange for it to be sent to her."

"Right," I said, resignedly. "Thank you."

I packed my bag and left shortly afterwards, taking the next train back to London to resume my mission. The sky was overcast and it had turned cooler so I wore my sweater. I could still smell Amy's perfume on it, but during the journey home I had held the garment to my face so often, trying to breathe it in, that by the time I got back to London her fragrance had all but faded.

With a new man in her life, **Princess Diana** appeared happy and carefree, but beneath the surface she was obviously still deeply troubled and under constant threat from dark forces. How do you rescue someone like **Princess Diana**? With a drowning man it's fairly straightforward: you throw him a life preserver and haul him back to shore. When someone's trapped in a burning building you send a fireman up a ladder or you gather on the pavement below with a group of people, holding an outstretched blanket as a makeshift safety net on to which the imperilled victim can jump. But when the specific nature of the threat is unclear, it's difficult to know just what to do. Steve had highlighted the feasibility of an assassination attempt from a deranged fan, while both he and Amy had hinted at the possibility of a conspiracy from within. Were they seriously planning to murder her? Why? Was it, as Amy suggested, because **Diana** was regarded as an embarrassment and a liability? Had she really become such a threat to state security? Surely no one would go that far; it would be the biggest scandal in history. Isn't her problem more likely to be of a psychological nature, something related to the depression she recently suffered over the break-up with her heart-surgeon lover, **Hasnat Khan**, who, like a patient undergoing one of his less successful transplant operations, ended up rejecting the donor heart? What if this new Dodi chap ends up rejecting her too? Perhaps the Princess is really just fed up with being extremely wealthy, famous and universally adored, constantly hounded by the press slavering over every juicy morsel of insider gossip in their quest to make her personal life seem important—and thereby newsworthy. Perhaps it wasn't a death threat as such, but a royal princess in grave and imminent danger of being not very happy. A few sessions of sensitive counselling might help to alleviate the emotional suffering caused by not always getting exactly her own way. According to the book, she has on several occasions sought solace from New Age healers and spiritualists, though not, I would think, from the seaside clairvoyant Gypsy

Angelina whose phenomenal insights, such as 'You think a lot', may not offer a tenable solution to **Diana**'s plight. I'm not a professional therapist, and I'm certainly no expert on bulimia, but I am a good listener and I'm always ready to offer a sympathetic ear when someone's in trouble. Still, how would I ever persuade her to talk things over with me?

Amy had apparently been home to drop off her things, then gone out again to meet a friend. The Trueloves seemed oblivious of any rift in our courtship, so I assumed Amy hadn't said anything to them about it. Uncle Derek was keen to invite me in to wait.

"You must tell us all about your trip. Did you have good weather? We were just about to have a cup of tea, weren't we, Mummy?"

While Uncle Derek was pottering about with the tea things in the kitchen, Mrs Truelove put her hand on my arm, looked at me with great tenderness and said, "Did you and Amy have a really lovely time together?"

There was such warmth in her words. I translated them to mean: *Did you fall deeply and passionately in love? Are you surer now than ever before that you were meant for each other and that you intend to spend the rest of your lives together in blissful union?*

"Yes," I said. "We had a really lovely time, thank you."

Uncle Derek came in with the tea tray, saying, "Oh, Riley, I forgot to tell you. You had a visitor while you were away"

"A visitor?"

"I'd spotted him once before, watching the house from across the road. He was there for about half an hour. He looked suspicious. I thought it might have been the man who stole Amy's bag so I called the police, but naturally they took bloody ages so by the time they finally showed up, he'd scarpered. I saw him again yesterday. He was in the front garden, trying to look in the window, so I went out to confront him. I said, "What do you think you're doing?"

"What did he say?"

"You should have seen his face. I don't think he knew anyone was at home. It turned out he wasn't casing the joint; he was looking for you, Riley."

"Who was he?"

"He said he was a friend of the family."

"A friend of the family?" That phrase again. "Whose family?"

"Well, yours, I presume."

"So, apart from that, he didn't say who he was?"

"No, he didn't leave his name," said Uncle Derek. "I told him you were away for a few days and asked him if I could pass on a message, but he said it was a personal matter. —Said he'd track you down."

"What did he look like?" I said.

"Ooh, I don't know. Ordinary chap. Medium height…"

Just then, from out in the hallway came the sound of keys in the door. Uncle Derek tilted back in his chair to look through the doorway. "Here she is," he said. "Miss Bournemouth 1997."

I couldn't see who it was yet, but I assumed he was referring to Amy and not to some bathing-beauty-contest winner visiting from the Dorset seaside resort. I sat up nervously and tweaked my hair with my fingers the way Amy had taught me to do, in order to maximize my *hairstyle's* potential. I caught Mrs Truelove looking at me, smiling to herself.

Amy seemed surprised and not exactly pleased to see me. "Oh, Riley. What are you doing here? I can't see you tonight. Sorry. I'm meeting a friend. I just came back to change."

"Oh, that's a shame, Amy. Riley's come all this way," said Mrs Truelove.

"That's fine." I said. "Just stopped by. I'm going in a minute. Things to do."

Amy leaned in to kiss me on the cheek. At the same time I got up to go, which made the exchange clumsy and awkward. Mummy was on to it immediately. She could see that something was wrong. Her eyes darted between us, trying to read the signs.

I wanted to ask Amy about my jacket, but this wasn't the time to bring it up.

Uncle Derek was fetching Amy a teacup from the cupboard. "I was just saying, Amy. That man who was watching the house—the one I thought had stolen your bag—it turns out he was looking for Riley. He's a friend of the family."

"Oh, *is* he?" She said it condescendingly, in the way one might humour a child telling you that submarines can go underwater. The mocking tone was, of course, for my benefit. "Ah. So he *isn't* a spy after all. —Just someone trying to get in touch. *That's* why he's been hanging around. Nothing to do with MI5."

"MI5?" said Uncle Derek.

"Well, it's a long story," she said. "Riley thought the man was a secret agent from MI5 sent to deliver him a coded set of instructions."

"Good heavens," said Mrs Truelove, cutting a slice of cake.

"He kept finding cards on the street and thought they had something to do with—can I tell them, Riley?" She glanced at me for approval, but didn't wait to get it. "He thought he was being recruited to rescue **Princess Diana** from imminent danger."

Everyone laughed. It wasn't meant maliciously, but it was humiliating just the same.

"What sort of cards? Playing cards?" said Uncle Derek.

Amy nodded. "Cigarette cards, bubble-gum cards. Any kind of cards. They all hold secret messages, don't they, Riley?" Amy knew she'd gone too far so made some attempt to spoon a little of the scorn back into the jar. "It seemed to make sense at the time," she said. "I was starting to believe it myself. That's the funny thing; once you start looking out for cards, they turn up wherever you go."

"Really? I don't think I've ever found a card on the street. Have you, Mummy?"

"Well, I've no doubt Riley has much keener eyesight than *we* have," said Mrs Truelove helpfully. "And I'm sure he had every reason to believe whatever he did."

"Absolutely," agreed Uncle Derek, leaning in to pour the milk. "So, if he's not from MI5, any ideas who this friend of the family might be, Riley?"

Amy was clearly convinced she already knew the answer to that one. She'd suggested before that the **Silver Fox** could be my estranged father trying to make contact with me, an idea that, in spite of all the MI5 evidence I had shown her, she refused to relinquish. She cocked her head to one side, teasingly. "Yes, Riley. Any ideas?"

On the way home I kept mulling it over—what I could have said, should have said. If the Trueloves had read *The Spy Handbook*, or even just glanced at the glossary of terms at the back, they would know that a **Friend of the Family** is the code name for an undercover agent working for the government. And that's who the Silver Fox was; he was not my long-lost old dad appearing out of the blue, hoping for some kind of reconciliation with the son he'd abandoned. No. I think after what he'd done, even he would realize that, using the phrase in its literal sense, he could no longer refer to himself as *a friend of the family*. That epithet was stripped from him the day my mother came home and told me bluntly that he'd run off with another woman and that he didn't give a damn about either of us. Shortly afterwards I became a **R**ichardson.

"There'll be no Pincus in this house," she had said. Then she turned to the fireplace and, with one hand resting on the mantelpiece, she bent over and spat into the fire burning in the grate. Her saliva hissed with contempt as it sizzled on the hot coals. "That's what I think of the name Pincus," she said.

At the time, I was shocked—partly by the extent of her hatred, but mostly by the sight of my mother spitting. It was something I'd never seen before and have never seen since.

From then on she rarely spoke of him. When she did, she referred to him as 'your father'; it was never 'your Dad', which she must have felt held too much affection. In the company of others, he was always 'Riley's father' and certainly never 'Brian' or 'my husband' as he had once been. I noticed that she would only ever mention him to talk of him disparagingly—to point out some particular flaw or weakness. "Of course Riley's father was hopeless at mental arithmetic," she'd say, or "Riley's father never learned to drive a car; he had absolutely no sense of co-ordination." I wanted to ask how then did he manage to play golf so well, and how, one Christmas, had he taught himself to juggle tangerines from the fruit bowl? Even though I couldn't forgive him for what he had done, I couldn't be so cruelly dismissive of him either—he was still my Dad—so I clung onto the idea that perhaps my mother, who had a tendency to jump to conclusions, had got it wrong and that there was no other woman.—Perhaps he had other reasons for walking out like he did.

As far as the mission was concerned, I had to go it alone. There was no point in confiding in Amy about it any more. I'd gone as far as I could in trying to convince her. I had to see it through now and prove to her that I was right. Diana was in danger and it was my job to save her. Somehow. Her whirlwind romance was clearly spiralling out of control. It was fortunate that the rescue card had washed up on the beach the previous night. Without it, the message would have remained misleadingly incomplete, with its heavy full-stop falling like a death sentence at the end of the subject's name: *Prepare to execute Princess Diana.*

Steve was there on the doorstep as soon as I got back, wanting to know everything that had happened on what he referred to as my 'dirty weekend' with Amy. I refused to discuss it, of course.

"Where are you off to tonight then?"

"Nowhere."

"You're not seeing her?"

"Not tonight, no."

"Oh-oh. You haven't worn it out, have you?"

His big, clumsy hands were all over everything. I squirmed a little, instinctively trying to shrug him off.

"So how's the mission? I suppose you've been too busy to find any more cards?"

"No. I have found more, actually. Three."

"Really? What do they say?"

"Prepare to execute princess rescue."

"Christ. That seems pretty serious. There's no arguing with that, is there?"

"It took me a while to work it out."

"Have you formulated a plan?"

"A plan. No, not exactly. I thought I'd…"

"You've got to have a plan. We should sit down and discuss it."

"I can't now. I've got to… be somewhere." I was reluctant to let Steve bully me into a course of action.

"When then? Are you going to the café tomorrow?"

"I don't know." I wasn't sure what I was going to say to Nell after the dreadful revelation at her flat, the night I skipped town.

"I'll nip off work," said Steve. "What time? Shall we say half ten? Eleven?"

"I suppose so."

"Eleven then. Don't be late. And keep your eye out for more cards."

When I got inside, there were two messages from Nell on my answering machine. In the first she'd tried to sound casual, with an informal invitation to 'grab a Chinese takeaway' and watch a movie over at her place. In the second, left the following day, there was an audible note of concern, asking me to let her know if I'd received her message. I didn't want to telephone. I had no idea how she felt about it all and was nervous of making the call. I decided it would be easier to wait until I saw her at the café and see if I could read any clues from her manner.

Someone must have guessed that Nell's would be one of my first ports of call upon my return. Four cards had been prominently placed no more than a few feet apart outside Moody's wine bar, a couple of doors up from the café. It was as if, while I'd been away, the messages had been stacking up like milk left on the doorstep. Frustrated by my absence, the Silver Fox was apparently trying to make up for lost time by dumping the backlog of cards in the most obvious place possible. I picked them up in the order I found them; I felt it was important not to get the message parts jumbled. *Good Husbands Make Cakes* is not the same as *Cakes Make Good Husbands*—not that these cards had anything to do with cakes or husbands. With the new quartet, some of the subtlety of the previous coding had gone; the clues now seemed much more straightforward. It was as if time had become an issue and the control officer in charge of the operation couldn't risk the delay of any possible misinterpretation of the instructions. I sensed the clock was now ticking.

WORLD
FIRSTS

A series of 50 cards. No 48

FIRST LIVING CREATURE IN SPACE

A Soviet dog called Laika was the world's first living animal to journey into space. She was a passenger on Sputnik 2, launched into Earth's orbit on November 3rd, 1957. A special pressurised cabin allowed her enough room to stand, sit or lie down. Laika was fitted with a harness and electrodes to monitor her vital signs, but died when her oxygen supply ran out. The little dog's heroic act provided Soviet scientists with the first data on the behaviour of a living creature in the space environment, paving the way for human space travel.

WORLD FIRSTS
ISSUED BY J.WIX & SONS LTD. LONDON

Ben Stevenson

GOALKEEPER
6ft 3ins, 12st 7lb

CRYSTAL PALACE
Born Oakley

Started with Norwich City, then joined Crystal Palace for £35,000 in December 1964. He has since played more league games than any other goalkeeper in the club's history. Known as 'Big Ben', Stevenson has been capped for England and Football League. Especially safe in the air, he also possesses brilliant reactions to close-range shots.

FOOTBALL QUIZ
Which club plays at Bramall Lane?

SHEFFIELD UNITED

© CHAD CHEWING GUM LTD

FOR MAGIC ANSWER. Rub coin over blank space

Printed in England

16

A SERIES OF 50

HISTORY OF THE MOTOR CAR

No.39

AUSTIN MINI 850 Mark 1

Launched in 1959, the Mini was designed for the British Motor Corporation, a collaboration of Austin and Morris. At its debut, the Mini was being produced in both the Austin and the Morris factories. Both factories produced identical cars, except for badges. From 1961, two similar new variants were available, the 'Wolseley Hornet' and 'Riley Elf'. Despite the exterior length of just over 120 inches, the Mini offers enough interior space to seat four adults comfortably. This is the result of the revolutionary drivetrain and the position of the wheels at each corner of the car. The driver is seated very upright and the steering wheel mounted almost horizontally, which allows adequate space for an adult in the rear seat. Rear seat access is made possible with tilting front seats. Every aspect of the Mini's design is dictated by efficiency, including the exterior. The end-result has proved quintessential to its success.

MERRIDOWN
CONFECTIONERY

Merridown Confectionery Ltd, Merridown House, Gloucester

1967. From across the road, Elvis is watching the family home. The front door opens suddenly and he has to duck down behind a car to avoid being seen. His ex-wife emerges wearing her coat and carrying a shopping bag. She sets off down the street. With the coast clear, Elvis moves towards the house. At the front door, he discovers that his key no longer fits in the lock. Tugging open the garage door, he slips inside.

Upstairs, the boy is in bed reading. On his bedside table, Kleenex and Veno's cough mixture suggest that he is off sick from school. At the sound of the back door opening he looks up.

Downstairs, Elvis enters the kitchen and makes his way towards the front room. Over the banister, the boy catches a glimpse of the intruder's shadow as he passes through the hallway. Shock registers on his face. The sound of drawers opening in the bureau, papers being sorted. Frightened, the boy creeps back to his room.

6,000

Elvis rummages through the bureau drawer and locates the passport. As he flicks through it, the bubble-gum card falls to the floor. He bends to pick it up, shoves it in with the other papers and slides the drawer shut. At the door, he thinks better of it and returns for the card, tucking it back between the pages of his passport, which he slips into his inside coat pocket.

Upstairs, the boy stands behind his bed in his pyjamas, brandishing one of his father's golf clubs, listening intently. To his relief, he hears the uninvited visitor make his way out again, closing the back door behind him. The boy rushes to the back bedroom window. Keeping himself hidden behind the curtain, he peers out, hoping to catch sight of the man in the garden below, but Elvis has doubled back and left through the garage door at the front of the house. By the time the boy figures this out and moves to the front window, Elvis has mingled with other passers-by on the street and been lost to view.

FIRST • SAVE • MINI • GOLF

Hang on a minute. **First save mini-golf?** Were these my new instructions? *Your mission is to save the life of a royal princess, but first you must do something to revive the popularity of miniature golf.* This was not what I'd expected. At first I thought I'd made a false reading, but then I remembered the woman who had waylaid me the first time I saw the Silver Fox—the one who had got me to sign her petition objecting to the closure of the mini-golf course in Mirfield Park. Casting my mind back, I could picture the heading of the petition on her clipboard using those same words: *Save the Mini-Golf.* As a mission, it seemed something of an anticlimax after the edict to rescue the most important woman in the world. I'm all for a game of Pitch-and-Putt, and my sympathies are with the campaign to preserve such recreational amenities in our public parks, but the focus of my mission seemed to have shifted to a comparatively trivial cause and I no longer felt the same sense of urgency to fulfil my patriotic duty. Perhaps I was missing something. I decided that later I would head down to Mirfield Park to investigate further.

Steve suddenly appeared from nowhere and was peering over my shoulder.

"What's all this then? More cards? I suppose this is the next part of your instructions from MI5?"

"Four cards together this time."

"Really? Must be important. Have you worked it out yet?"

"I've only just found them. They were just here on the pavement, but I think I've figured it out."

"Go on then. What do you think they say?"

"I have a bit of investigating to do first," I said, slipping the cards into my pocket.

Just then I noticed a familiar blue sports car pulling up at the kerb. Uncle Derek got out and dashed into the newsagents. I waved, but he didn't see me. I would have shouted his name but I didn't know what to call him. 'Uncle' Derek sounded silly. He emerged again just a few seconds later holding a packet of cigarettes. This time he caught sight of me and made a beeline towards us.

"Hello, Riley," he said, touching my shoulder. "I've just been looking at a car on Essex Road. Pile of bloody rust. You managed to find him then?"

"Who?"

"Your 'friend of the family'." He removed the cellophane wrapper and lit a cigarette, offering the pack to Steve, who declined.

"**Friend of the family?** You mean this is the man who was skulking outside your house?"

"Yes, we met the other night. I wouldn't call it *skulking* exactly." He smiled at Steve. "I gave Riley your message."

"Oh, cheers." Steve nodded, looking a bit sheepish.

"He's not a friend of the family," I said. "He lives in my building. I was expecting someone else: an older man, with grey hair."

Uncle Derek was distracted by something over my shoulder. "Blimey, is that a traffic warden? I'd better get going. You don't need a lift anywhere, do you?"

"No thanks," I said. "I'm just going to the café."

"Right, lads. See you later." And he was off.

"What were you doing at their house, lurking in the front garden?"

"Nothing. I just wondered when you'd be back. Come on. I'll join you for a cuppa. Help you work out the message."

"No. If you don't mind, Steve. I want to talk to my friend."

"What friend? Not the woman in the café? Aye, aye. What's

going on there then? Chasing older women as well now, are you?"

"Don't be ridiculous. She's upset about something, that's all. I need to talk to her. Alone."

"Ah, diddums. What's she upset about?"

"It's a personal matter. Please."

Steve reluctantly agreed. "Go on then. I'll see you back home later."

m 1967. A deserted car park near the seafront. Learner plates attached to the front and back bumper of the red Mini. Elvis is in the driving seat; the secretary, as passenger, is nervously watchful of him as she guides him through his first lesson.

"OK, so remember what we said. Neutral... ignition... clutch down... and into first... Let the clutch out... slowly... slowly... a bit more gas."

The car lurches to a stall.

"OK. Start again. Neutral... ignition..."

Elvis takes up the commentary: "Clutch... first gear... mirror, signal, manoeuvre."

"Very good. Now, just a bit more acceleration... Now let the clutch out."

The car moves off.

"That's it. Now. Clutch down and into second. Yes, now let the clutch out. That's it. Look, you're driving. OK, now, into third. Across and up. No, across and... get it in neutral... and over into third. Take your foot off the gas. Cover your brake. Brake. Brake!"

6,350

In a panic, Elvis takes both hands off the wheel and makes a grab for the handbrake.

"No, your foot. The middle one. Brake! Brake!"

She looks up to see that the car has veered off track and is trundling slowly towards a concrete bollard. She makes a grab for the wheel, but it is too late. The car rolls into the bollard with a gentle bump, and stalls. They relax back in their seats.

"There's nothing to it really, is there?" he says. "How did I do?"

"Congratulations, Mr Pincus. I'm pleased to inform you that you have passed your driving test."

"Thank you, nurse."

Nell was stacking the fridge with cold drinks when I arrived. She turned to look at me for a moment, then carried on with her work, talking over her shoulder.

"Where have you been? I was worried." She affected a non-chalant tone, but she still sounded a little hurt.

"Sorry. I went away for a few days. I should have sent a post-card but I hadn't got any stamps."

"Secret mission abroad, was it? A bit of espionage?"

"No. Nothing like that." I was tired of the teasing and it must have shown in my voice.

Nell decided to back off. She glanced over her shoulder. "You didn't have to go, you know."

"You seemed upset. I thought perhaps you wanted to be alone."

"It was nothing. I was a bit tipsy, that's all."

Nothing? It didn't seem like nothing to me, but I didn't say anything.

"It's an emotional song. It always gets me when I've had a few."

"I know," I said. "Me too."

Our eyes met for a moment before she looked nervously away. She knew that I knew and she knew that I knew that she knew, but if we didn't talk about it we could pretend that neither of us had figured it out: she had once run away with a married man; my father had abandoned his family for another woman.—Two separate events that could remain unrelated so long as we chose not to make the connection. It was the only way we could continue our friendship. Of course, it meant that I could never ask her any questions about what happened between them, but I wasn't sure I wanted to know.

Nell busied herself tidying the cardboard packaging from the drinks into a bin bag, then went to wash her hands in the little sink behind the counter. I probably should have left it at that, but while her back was turned I felt more able to speak.

"About my dad and the woman he ran away with. I said some cruel things about her. I don't really blame her. I'm sure she didn't mean to hurt anybody."

Nell wiped her hands on her apron. "She probably didn't even know he had a family. Men don't always tell the truth."

NINETEEN

STEVE WAS BACK on the case with his interpretation of the most recent cards, but it didn't make any sense to me.

"Why would I have to save **Minnie Driver**? Who's Minnie Driver anyway? I don't even know who she is."

"Yes, you do," he said. "I've already told you who she is."

"Why would I be saving some actress who's been in a Bond film? Saving her from what?"

"Maybe it's a practice mission before you go for the big one. Sort of like a test to see if you're up to the task. If you can save a Bond girl, you can save anybody. I can come with you if you like—give you some advice."

"No thanks. I'm not going to save a Bond girl. It's ludicrous. Anyway, I still don't think you've got it right. Minnie and driver. Why is that driver?"

Steve held up the card with the golfer on it. "Look at it. **William Hollydean**, right? He's demonstrating the swing when teeing off. He's got something like a five iron there. That's called a driver."

"It's a picture of a golfer. It's not Minnie Driver, it's **mini-golf**."

"Save mini-golf?"

"Yes. There's a mini-golf course in the park and they are threatening to close it. It's been there for years; it would be a shame to see it go."

"You've got to be kidding. Is that what you think they do at MI5? Let's have a look, shall we?" He picked up *The Spy Handbook* from my coffee table and turned to the introduction. "Ah, yes. Here we are. Agenda: to protect the UK from foreign espionage and other covert foreign-state activity; to thwart sabotage attempts by enemy agents and suspected militants intending to overthrow or undermine parliamentary democracy; to frustrate terrorism and the procurement by proliferating countries of weapons of mass destruction; and, last but not least, to campaign against the closure of mini-golf courses throughout the nation's recreational parks."

I still wasn't convinced. **Minnie Driver**? Silly name.

1967. The beach café. The secretary and Elvis in the bedroom of their flat above. He is fastening his tie in the wardrobe mirror; she sits at the dressing table in her slip, studying his passport photo. She starts to laugh.

"What happened to your hair in this picture?"

He looks up. "Hey. Give it here."

"No, I want to look."

He makes a grab for the passport; she pulls it away, teasingly. He tickles her and she eventually surrenders, throwing the it across the room. While he picks it up, she retrieves the card that has fallen from between its pages. She studies the picture.

"Who's she?"

"Oh, nobody."

"Why is it in your passport? Do you fancy her, or something?" Her tone is kittenish.

"You know I only have eyes for you, my angel. Actually it's the card that got withdrawn. Remember?—From the *Mission: Impossible* bubble-gum cards we printed at Greenwood's."

"It was supposed to be destroyed, wasn't it? How did you get hold of it?"

"That one was cut from the proofs."

"Does Mr Greenwood know you've got it?"

"No, does he heck. I sneaked a proof sheet home for my... nephew, and he cut it up into cards." The swerve goes unnoticed.

6,666

She makes a dramatic face. "You took a proof sheet? Mr Greenwood was really nervous about that."

"I know."

"You're bad."

"I know."

"Why's it so special, anyway?"

"Beats me."

"So why was it withdrawn?"

"No idea. There was a rumour that there was something, you know, rude on it."

"Let's see." She studies the card more carefully.

"What's rude about it? I don't get it."

"Neither do I."

"So why have you kept it?"

"I confiscated it from my nephew. I was worried that he'd swap it at school or something and that it would get into the wrong hands. I thought Greenwood might trace it back to me. I didn't want to get into trouble."

"That still doesn't explain why you've kept it."

"I just shoved it in with my passport and forgot about it."

"Oh. I thought it might be because it reminds you of me?— Our first date after you came into my office trying to find out the card number."

"Of course that's the reason I kept it."

"And?" she says dubiously.

"Well, it's unique, isn't it?—The only one in existence. It might be worth something one day."

"Who to?"

"I don't know. A collector?"

Is this all a bit too convenient? I need to steer my story towards a conclusion, but I can't be sure if Nell ever knew that my dad took the proof sheet, or that he subsequently seized the contentious card from his 'nephew's' collection. If she had chanced upon it one day—lying between the pages of his passport or amongst letters and papers in an old shoebox—would it have meant anything to her? Would she recognize it as the same card I have been looking for all these years? She must have heard me talk about **card 19** a thousand times, but when I'm telling her about bubble-gum cards I'm never sure how much of it she listens to. **Barry Manilow**'s a different matter. If I'm talking about him, she's all ears. I might need to go over some of the early parts of my story again. I still need a good ending. It's over 6,800 words so far. How many words are there in a book?

The last time I played **P**itch-and-**P**utt in the park there was an old man giving out the clubs and balls from a little hut. The hut was still there with its serving-hatch opening, hinged along its top edge and propped open with a hook and hasp fastener to create a little porch. The old man had been superseded by a skinny student-type with a mass of tight **Leo Sayer** curls. He was reading a battered paperback copy of *Catch-22* and eating a Cornetto. I paid my money and he handed over two clubs and a ball plus three plastic golf tees in assorted colours, a ticket that doubled as a scorecard, and a little pencil with which to tally my score.

It was a sunny afternoon, but there wasn't a soul on the course—which may have explained the Parks Committee's decision to call it a day. I was there *under cover* to see if any further instructions had been left for me, but after a couple of holes I'd got so involved in the game, I'd forgotten the real reason for my visit. By hole four I'd really started to get my eye in. I'd never had that much success with golf before, generally frustrated by the shortfall between my expectations and my performance. I could never seem to get it to go straight at the teeing-off stage. My club—not the putter, the other one, what's it called, the pitcher, the wedge, or is it, as Steve says, the driver?—tended to slice the ball wildly or sometimes miss it completely. This time, though, there was a crisp, satisfying 'tink' as the ball connected with what I believe is called the sweet spot, which lifted it gracefully into the air, sending it soaring in a perfect arc and dropping with a soft thud on to the green. I watched as it trickled wilfully towards the flag and then disappeared from view as it was swallowed up by the hole. I couldn't believe it. **A hole in one.** I'd never scored a hole in one before—in any area of my life.

I looked around for a witness to confirm what had happened, a passer-by willing to testify to my extraordinary feat, but I was alone, like a tree in the forest with no one to hear it fall. Except I hadn't fallen; I had reached the highest pinnacle of golfing achievement. I felt an overwhelming sense of satisfaction and suddenly I understood people's all-consuming passion for the game. Nell used to play quite a lot in her younger days (though the significance of that had never consciously occurred to me) and I remember her once telling me that the first time you hit the ball correctly, you were hooked for life. The rest of your golfing career, she said, would be spent trying to recapture that perfect moment of success when, instead of the usual jarring shudder along the shaft and up through your arms as your club fell short and slammed into the rubber teeing-off mat, you felt that solid ringing resonance as the weight of the club head connected with the ball. I wasn't exactly sure if I was hooked for life yet, but I was certainly eager to get to the next hole to see if I could do it again.

I was just about to tee off when I noticed a woman up ahead on the green, scooting her ball backwards and forwards in an attempt to sink her putt. I don't know where she had come from; she looked a bit mad to me. I was getting impatient. My recent accomplishment had left me very much **in the zone** and ready to play my next driving masterstroke before the spell was broken. By pure chance the woman's ball eventually found its way into the hole and I wondered whether she would own up on her scorecard to the embarrassing number of strokes she had taken to get it there.

Looking back now, I realize I probably didn't wait long enough for her to clear the area, but it was really her own fault for dawdling to the next green. Where my previous hole-in-one technique had been to swing the club both confidently and forcefully so as to chip the ball with sufficient uppercut lift, on this occasion I must have struck it more squarely in the centre, which sent it at impressive but alarming velocity at what would soon turn out to be head height. It's amazing how fast one of those balls can go. I once remember seeing a golf ball dissected, its innards apparently made up of a million rubber bands.

Of course, I knew what was going to happen even before I made contact with the ball, but once the club was in full swing there seemed to be nothing I could do to stop myself following through. I remembered there was something you were supposed to call out to warn people, but I couldn't think of the word in time. The ball skewed slightly to the left like a Scud missile seeking its target, striking the hopeless amateur squarely on the back of the head. The woman fell instantly to the ground, just as surely as if she'd been shot by an SAS sniper. Oh, Lord. I'd killed a complete stranger with my new-found golfing prowess. I stood hesitantly, hoping she'd get up again, but she just lay there, motionless. I know I should have gone over to deal with it myself, but I've never been very good in this kind of situation so I convinced myself that it would be more practical to report the incident to **Leo Sayer** in the hut and get him to summon an ambulance. On my way down the slope I tried to calm myself. No one dies from being hit on the head by a golf ball, do they? Surely she'd just conked out and would come round upon receiving a light shake of the shoulder or a whiff from a smelling-salts bottle.

The serving hatch was open but the young **Leo Sayer** wasn't at home. There was a loud, splintering crack against the wooden boards of the shed, the same sound repeated just a few seconds later. I found him round the back with a basket of golf balls, taking practice shots at an assortment of empty drinks cans lined up for target practice on a low bench against the back wall.

"Have you got a phone?" I said.

He nodded and produced it from the thigh pocket of his combat pants.

"There's been an accident. A woman on hole five. She's unconscious. She must have had a seizure or something. Call 999."

I felt proud knowing I'd done the right thing, because you can never be too careful with a head injury. I hurried back to the course, thinking that I might venture near enough to reassure the woman that help was on its way, but when I got there she'd gone.—No sign of her anywhere. She must have woken up and toddled off. As I stood there thinking about it, I slowly became aware of a little boy of about four years old standing alone at the edge of the bushes.

"Where did the lady go?" I said.

He just stared at me.

"Did you see the lady lying on the ground?"

He nodded.

"Where did she go?"

"She went to heaven," he said.

After I'd told Leo Sayer to cancel the ambulance, I tried to get back in the swing of it, starting again at the fifth hole, but the incident had rather put me off my stroke. He was just a kid; he didn't know what he was talking about—nevertheless I found it somehow unsettling. After that, there were no more holes in one; for the rest of the game I was at sixes and sevens.

I took the bus home and sat upstairs at the front. I like looking out of the big window though I always feel slightly vulnerable there. I imagine the bus in some kind of collision that will cause me to lurch forward and smash my face on the glass. There's a horizontal metal bar to hang on to, but that's no protection. They should provide seat belts.

Someone had shoved a copy of the *Daily Mirror* down the side of the seat. It wasn't my newspaper of choice, but traffic was slow so I thought I'd look through it—perhaps tinker with the quick crossword. When I finally found the right page I discovered it had already been completed. All but two or three of the answers were filled in with a series of blobby letters in red ink. On page five, a heading caught my eye: *Driver Stalker.* Above it, there was a small publicity photo of **Minnie Driver.** She wasn't quite what I had imagined. She was good-looking, I suppose—even glamorous—but to me her face looked hard and muscle-bound, her sharp, dark features like a handful of currants pressed into a weightlifter's thigh. Beneath the picture was a short article highlighting the threat of which Steve had spoken.

Actress and singer Minnie Driver has been granted a tempo-
rary restraining order against a man recently arrested outside
her London home. In documents filed at Highbury Corner
Magistrates Court, the Good Will Hunting *star claims*
Charles Stephen Corrigan, 34, is an 'obsessed, mentally ill
and delusional stalker' who believes he's in a relationship
with the actress.

Corrigan is alleged to have bombarded her with 'ominous
frightening letters and items' including a bag containing a
knife, a screwdriver and a roll of duct tape. In the papers,
the star states, 'I am in fear that Mr Corrigan may pose an
immediate threat to my well-being and the well-being of my
family.'

A judge has ordered Corrigan, who was arrested for
trespassing at Driver's Islington home earlier this month, to
stay at least 100 yards away from Driver and her family
until September 4th, when a hearing will be held to decide
whether the restraining order should be made permanent.

Beneath the news article in an apparently unrelated footnote:
Go Camping for 95p! Vouchers collectable in the Daily *and* Sunday
Mirror *until 1st September.*

When Steve looked in on me later I showed him the piece from
the paper.

"Looks like you were right about her needing protection," I
said. "This Corrigan guy sounds creepy."

He snatched it from me and read it through. The words
seemed to make him angry.

"What's the matter?"

He stared at me for a moment. "You've got to devise a plan,"
he said, folding the paper shut.

"Plan for what? What am I going to do?"

"Save **Minnie Driver** from this stalker pervert. That's what the cards are telling you. I told you it wasn't about mini-golf."

I had to admit he was right on that score. Apart from revealing a hitherto latent gift for the game, the afternoon at the Pitch-and-Putt had been a waste of time.

Steve produced a Post-it note from the breast pocket of his shirt. There was an address written on it.

"Is this where she lives?" I said. "I can't go to her house. It wouldn't be appropriate."

"You can bet this Corrigan bloke doesn't care about appropriate. I bet he's there right now, hanging about, waiting for a chance to strike."

"But if it's in the newspaper, the police must know all about him. They must be providing some kind of protection."

"Nah. They can't do fuck-all. That's just it. Stalkers generally aren't technically committing a crime. The police are powerless. So is the victim. The police only move in once the stalker strikes, but by then it's usually too late. Look at **John Lennon, Sharon Tate**. Fans that got a bit too close."

"What about the restraining order?"

"Pfff. Restraining order? Waste of time. OK, so the court says he can't come within a hundred yards of her. He's only got to get himself a good sniper rifle. The Barrett M107 has a range of well over a mile. It can cut a man in half at fifteen hundred feet."

"Do you think he's that dangerous, this guy?"

"Fuck, yes. Typical behaviour pattern. That's why you've got to do something—stop him, before he gets to her."

"Why me? Why don't *you* do something?"

"It's not my mission, is it?"

"You're the one who likes **Minnie Driver**; she's nothing to do with me. I'm supposed to save **Princess Diana,** not some actress with a daft name."

"Well that's what I'm telling you. It's all part of your mission—a dry run to get you primed and ready to save Princess Diana. Or who knows, this Corrigan bloke might be stalking both of them. They might want you to nab him now before he gets too close to the royal target. And you'd be saving **Minnie Driver** too, of course."

"*Nab* him?"

"I don't mind lending a bit of moral support."

"What would we do?"

"Get hold of the bloke and tell him in no uncertain terms to back off. Frighten him a bit."

"I can't do something like that."

"Course you can. Princess Diana's life could depend on it."

I still don't know how he got me to go along with it. I feel such a fool now.

TWENTY

"Steve what?"

"I don't know his last name."

I tried to think. Steve... McQueen? Steve *May Queen*?

"And where is this Steve person now?"

"I don't know. He must have run off when you came."

"And you say he lives in the same building as you?"

"Yes. Flat Six."

The interviewing officer—Sergeant Kyle, I think he said—
looked down at the notes he had made. "You said you'd read in
the newspaper that Miss Driver had a stalker and your aim was
to protect her from him?"

"Yes. Well, sort of."

"By doing what?"

"I don't know. By stopping him, I suppose."

"Who?"

"The stalker."

"But there wasn't a stalker, was there? Only you. You're the
stalker."

"No. It's not me. It's this man Corrigan. But he didn't show up. I'm not the stalker. I didn't even know who she was, this **Minnie Driver**."

"You must have known it was her house; you were in her garden. How did you know where she lived?"

"I told you. My neighbour, Steve…"

"The one who ran away?"

"He got the address from someone at the post office. I wasn't really interested but he persuaded me to get involved."

"Have you been to Miss Driver's house before?"

"No, but Steve has. He went there to talk to her about window grilles. He's in home security."

"What were you planning to do with the gun?"

"Nothing. It's not a proper gun, anyway. It's only an air gun. I wasn't going to use it. It was to frighten the stalker. I read about it in yesterday's paper: it said Corrigan was dangerous, that he had a fixation about her. The idea was to protect her, not to harm her."

"You see how this looks from where I'm sitting, Riley? You're caught in the garden of this film star wielding a gun…"

"I wasn't *wielding* anything. It was Steve's. He gave it to me to hold. Look. I know how this must look, but I promise you've got it all wrong. I'm not interested in **Minnie Driver**."

"But you do like to lurk in celebrities' gardens at two in the morning?"

"No. No. No. That was Steve's idea. He put me up to it. I'm just a patsy."

"A patsy?"

"Like **Oswald**."

"Oswald who?"

"Doesn't matter. Forget it. What I'm saying is, Steve's the one with the knives and guns and army stuff, not me. I'm not a stalker. I've never stalked anyone."

The sergeant massaged his chin, trying to weigh me up. It began to dawn on me that before long someone was bound to dig out my record and discover the **Kylie Minogue** incident at the Dorchester Hotel and the misunderstanding with the threatening letter to **Princess Diana**. I was sunk. My only option was to tell him about my mission. I knew I'd have my work cut out explaining the full story. Steve had said that Special Services don't have anything to do with *uniforms*, as he calls the regular police, whom he describes as 'a bunch of thickos', so it would be no surprise if they didn't know anything about it.

Sergeant Kyle didn't look like the kind of man who would be open to such a fantastical idea. Still, there was nothing else I could do. The evidence was stacking up against me and I had to get myself vindicated.

"Look, I wasn't going to tell you this, but I'm on a secret mission."

"Really?"

"Yes, a mission to save **Diana, Princess of Wales**."

"I see. Save her from what?"

"I'm not exactly sure, but she's in grave and imminent danger and it's my job to protect her. I have been selected."

"Selected? By who?"

"By *whom*," I corrected him. He rolled his eyes. I lowered my voice to answer. "MI5."

He raised one eyebrow. "MI5?"

"Or six, possibly. —Which is why you wouldn't know anything about it."

I could see he was irked. As Steve says, the rivalry between Mr Plod and MI5 is legendary.

"Are you a secret agent then?"

I fluttered my fingers. "Let's just say I'm a friend of the family."

"So if your 'mission' is to save Princess Di, what were you doing in this actress's garden? Did you get the wrong house?"

"No. It was a practice run to see if I was up to the task."

"Of protecting the Princess? So first you have to protect this actress, Minnie Driver?"

"Exactly."

"Is she in grave and imminent danger too?"

"Of course. She has a stalker, a deranged fan."

"Yes, she does. You."

"Why do you keep saying that? It's not me; it's Corrigan. There's a restraining order against him."

"Is there?" he said, dismissively. "Well, we'll check on that. But if there is, how do I know your name's not Corrigan?"

I shook my head in frustration. I had no ID on me; we'd been through that already. I patted myself down again, but this time felt something stiff in the breast pocket of my jacket. It was my library card. Ha! I held it out for him to see. He pointed at it while he checked the name. I've noticed ticket inspectors on trains often do that—point at your ticket while they check the details.

"See? I'm just carrying out instructions," I said.

"From who? Who told you to do this?"

"They've been leaving me secret messages, telling me what to do."

"MI5?"

"Naturally, they're not going to say who they are."

He winced. I could see he thought I was crazy and that this had gone far enough. Who could blame him? My story sounded preposterous.

He put down his pen and laid his hands flat on the table. "Listen to me," he said. "You're mistaken about these messages. They're not real. Princess Diana has professional bodyguards— people specially trained in these matters."

"Yes, but can she trust them?"

"Of course she can. She's in perfectly safe hands. It's not your job to protect her. I'm sure that your concern for the Princess and Miss Driver is appreciated, but your services are not required. Understand?"

I didn't say anything.

"*Do. You. Understand?*" he said, enunciating the words as if he were speaking to someone from another planet. I sensed that with my acquiescence, he was about to let me off with a warning, so I nodded submissively. Perhaps it was better to leave it at that. —Let the policeman have his say, take the reprimand full on the chin, promise to behave and get myself off home like a good lad.

Just then, another policeman poked his head round the door, beckoning Sergeant Kyle over to him with a little jerk of his head. He lowered his voice and turned away as he spoke, in an attempt to keep their conversation private. I averted my eyes, but I could hear most of what they said:

"Can't get hold of anyone, Sarge. She's away for the weekend, according to a neighbour, but she's made several complaints about a fan who's been harassing her. There's a temporary restraining order."

"Name?"

The policeman looked down at the piece of paper in his hand. "Charles Corrigan."

The sergeant looked round at me and shook his head. "It's not him."

"So who's he? Another one? Blimey. She must be popular, this Minnie Driver. I've never even heard of her."

"He claims his mate was the one who put him up to it."

"Have we got a name?"

"Says he doesn't know the surname, but he's given an address.

They live in the same building. We'll try and get hold of the other one in the morning."

"So what do you want to do with this one? Charge him? Trespassing without reasonable cause while in possession of a loaded firearm?"

"Airgun. It wasn't loaded."

"It's still an offence."

The sergeant tilted his head this way and that as he mulled it over. "Actually, he's a bit of a crackpot. He thinks he's working for MI5."

1967. The red Mini parked in front of the Driving Test Centre. Elvis gets out of the driver's seat while a man in a raincoat with a clipboard emerges from the passenger side. He makes a couple of marks on a form, unclips the sheet and passes it to Elvis. The two men lean over the car to shake hands. While the man heads inside the building, Elvis studies the paper he has been given. He gets into the car, then, moments later, gets out again. He removes the learner plates from the front and back bumpers before getting back in and setting off. At the gate, he slows down and leans out of the window to dump the L-plates in a litter bin. He turns confidently into the stream of traffic and heads off down the road. 7,000

The policemen left me on my own for a while. In television dramas they usually have an officer who remains in the interview room with the prisoner; he stands guard by the door, eyes straight ahead, pretending to be detached from it all. I didn't get one of those. I noticed that the sergeant had left his pen on the table. Was it a recording device? Were all the other policemen gathered round in another room, ears cocked to a radio speaker, waiting to hear if I'd blurt out a confession?

Was there a two-way mirror enabling them to study my body language? If they weren't going to release me, why had they left me unguarded? Were they testing me? Seeing if I'd make a run for it? I knew they didn't believe me about MI5, but did they really think I was the stalker, or were they just applying pressure as a matter of routine? They probably get the occasional result from their *Look, we know you're guilty, so you'd better tell us what you've done* approach, but surely they could see that Corrigan was the one they wanted and that I had merely been caught up in Steve's mission to ward him off.

If it hadn't been for the airgun they might have seen it as a bit of high jinks and let me go. God knows what had happened to Steve. He must have sensed trouble and legged it over the garden wall. Following his instructions, I had been lying low in the bushes waiting for Corrigan to show. There were lights on in the windows overlooking the garden of the Driver residence—a charming, but more modest house than I had imagined, situated in a square off Rosebery Avenue—but I couldn't see anyone inside. I should never have listened to Steve. Imagine if **Minnie Driver** had been found dead in her home that night, murdered by a jealous lover, or, having tripped on her nightie, fallen down the stairs and broken her neck. My being discovered in her garden with a Walther CP88 airgun would have placed me in a far more serious situation. As they say in cop shows, they would have thrown the book at me, locked me up and thrown away the key. **Oswald** caught red-handed with the service rifle on the fourth floor of the Book Depository: *I had nothing to do with the shooting, Officer. A man called Steve told me to come here and look after his gun for him.*

How did I let myself get involved? I've no doubt Miss Driver is a marvellous actress, a delightful singer and a wonderful person, but she isn't anybody I'd go out of my way to meet. Steve was the one who really liked her and thought she was 'a babe', not me. It was all his idea. Suddenly it dawned on me. Perhaps I did know Steve's surname after all. Perhaps it was Corrigan.

Steve's innate geekiness had always been there for all to see, but if he was the stalker I'd read about in the newspaper, this new evidence betrayed a disturbingly sinister element to his character. What on earth had he been doing hanging around Minnie Driver's house with a knife? And duct tape? What was he planning to do with that? Then I remembered him mentioning a videotape of her taken at the local swimming baths and worried that it might have inadvertently (or otherwise) found its way into the slipcase of one of the tapes he had lent me.

Steve's unwelcomed interest in Minnie Driver had obviously landed him in seriously hot water. With one arrest in relation to her already on record, and who knows how many other convictions and outstanding restraining orders filed against him, it made sense that he'd be looking for a way to pin the blame on someone else. He didn't have to look far. By steering me off course, he saw a way to hijack my mission for his own needs. His thinking was obvious: if he could get me caught red-handed in **Minnie Driver**'s garden with **Lee Harvey Oswald**'s smoking gun, the police might concentrate their efforts on me rather than on him. Classic misdirection.

From the newspaper report, I'd pictured Corrigan as short, dark and pudgy with wire-framed glasses and bad teeth. It had never occurred to me that the stalker I was reading about might be Steve. I recalled how he had snatched the newspaper from me. At that point he must have realized that I had failed to make the connection and he was thereby able to sidestep all blame by encouraging me to project the stalker profile on to the Corrigan character I had created in my mind. That's how I ended up in **Minnie Driver**'s garden with Steve's air pistol. My vision of the stalker had provided him with the decoy he needed to lure me into the supposed stakeout, putting myself squarely in the frame for his recent misdoings.

I *knew* there was something funny about those last four cards, the way they were so perfectly laid out on the pavement for me to find. He must have gone to Hector's and picked out cards that he thought would spell out his message. *First Save Mini Driver.* (Except I still maintain it was mini-golf. If he'd wanted me to get driver, he should have used a card featuring a racing driver, **Stirling Moss** or **Nigel Mansell**, not **William Hollydean**. It would have spared an innocent amateur golfer a nasty bump on the head.)

I was tired and wanted to go home. I'd been at the police station for nearly three hours and outside it would be starting to get light again. I needed to tell Sergeant Kyle that I had remembered Steve's surname. That would put the lid on it and get me released without charge—but I needed to do it quickly, before he started delving too deeply into my own record.

At 3.45 a.m. I stepped out of the interview room in search of the sergeant. There was no one outside and no sign of anybody in the adjacent offices. At one end of the corridor was a door with a glass panel. Through it I could see the reception desk and the front door leading to the street beyond. The glass-panelled door was locked but then I noticed a green door-release button on the wall, so I touched it and let myself out. It wasn't exactly Colditz.

Behind the reception desk, a policeman in a short-sleeved shirt was writing a report in longhand and it was requiring all his concentration. On the other side of the desk, a man was providing details for him to take down. I only wanted to ask where I might find Sergeant Kyle, but as a suspected felon, I didn't feel it was my place to butt in so I waited my turn. (From what I overheard, I deduced that the victim, a well-dressed man in his early thirties, had been mugged in the park by some boys on bikes. Perhaps mugged isn't the right word. They had told him to give them his mobile phone and he had complied.) I could see it was all going to take some time so I asked for a pen and some paper and wrote a short note for Kyle, giving Steve's full name and address in relation to the **Minnie Driver** stalking.

I had just handed the note to the officer when shouting erupted outside. Shortly afterwards, a woman burst through the doors, saying, "You don't own me, right?" She was probably not yet twenty but already heavily set, with thick arms and a broad back like one of those cheap sofas from DFS. She wore a short skirt and a skimpy top that proudly displayed a bulging roll of midriff. The skinny man who followed her in, and to whom the remark was addressed, was suitably attired for a night out: neatly ironed casual shirt, professionally distressed denim jeans and box-fresh white trainers. He was trying to calm the woman.

"Sharon, Sharon, Sharon."

"Can you take your hands off me, please?"

"Sharon. Just..."

"Can you take your hands off me, please? Can you take your hands off me, please?" Sharon was becoming increasingly insistent.

The officer and the recently mugged businessman looked up to see what was going on. They both watched for a few seconds, taking it in. The policeman made no effort to intervene. His pen hovered over the paperwork as if he was searching for a specific word and thought the spectacle before him might provide the inspiration to find it.

"Excuse me, can you arrest this man, please. He's assaulting me. You're assaulting me. Yes you are. Can you take your hands off me, please? Can you take... your... fucking... hands... OFF!"

She shrugged her arms to free herself and then tried to kick her partner in the groin, but her skirt was too tight to get her leg high enough. Instead, her stiletto came off and sailed through the air, clattering against a partition screen and landing on the desk in front of the surprised police officer.

Hurrah! The British escape committee had come to my aid with a perfectly timed diversion. During the earlier commotion I had been sidling nonchalantly towards the exit to test the waters, but now all eyes were on Sharon's shoe, nobody seemed to even notice I was there. Seizing the moment, I was quickly under the perimeter fence, stealing silently into the night and heading for the Swiss border.

TWENTY-ONE

1967 TO 1997. IT'S QUITE A JUMP in my story, but what can be said about the intervening years? Thirty years on, 'Elvis and the secretary' have long since parted company. Something went wrong. Who knows what? Without asking Nell, I can never find out what happened between them. Somewhere along the line, 'the secretary' took an unexpected career path and became owner/manager of a café in north London. **'Elvis' lives**… where? Somewhere else. Maybe he stayed on at the seaside where, on his day off, he plays golf alone, hoping one day to score a hole in one and dreaming of a *This Is Your Life* type of family reunion. Or perhaps he died tragically young in a car crash, like the pop star **Marc Bolan**, precipitating the secretary's return to London to start a new life without him.

I could pick up the story again in the more recent past.

1997. A London café. A signed copy of *Manilow Magic: The Best of Barry Manilow*. The café owner holds the record cover against the wall behind the counter, trying various positions to decide which looks best. The card collector, last seen in his bedroom brandishing a golf club, is no longer a boy, but a man. He occupies a table near the counter, where he sits with a cup of tea and an open notepad, his pen poised as he gathers his thoughts. On the table beside him is an empty John Lewis carrier bag folded neatly into four.

At an adjacent table, a group of pensioners, three men and a woman, sit playing cards. There is an open bag of Werther's Originals between them and the group suck contentedly on the sweets as they study the cards they have been dealt.

The café owner interrupts the collector, setting a plate of food in front of him: Pork, parsnips, potatoes and peas. No gravy.

"What are you writing? A love letter?" she says, clearing his empty cup.

The man slides the writing pad to one side and takes up his knife and fork. "Far from it," he says. "It's a letter of complaint. Somebody sold me a fake card."

The pensioners next to him are playing a shedding-type card game whereby cards are being put down and picked up in turn as each player attempts to be the first to get rid of all his cards. Sitting with his back to the card collector, one of the players, a grey-haired man in a smart Prince of Wales check jacket, eyes his fellow players furtively. Confident that no one is watching, he pretends to sort his hand while surreptitiously sneaking one of the playing cards into his lap. He lets the palmed card rest briefly on his thigh, safely hidden under the table. He glances up at the group to see if anyone has spotted the move. Nobody's suspicions appear to have been aroused so he slips the card discreetly into his jacket pocket, adding a little cough to divert the focus away from his duplicitous act. At the next table, his attention divided between his lunch and the writing pad, the card collector fails to notice any of this deceit.

The card game finally ends and the grey-haired man is

declared the winner. The others groan good-naturedly as they lay down their remaining cards in defeat. Claiming his ill-gotten gains, a handful of pennies in the ashtray, the victor gets up to leave. Bidding his companions farewell, he exits the café, stepping out on to the street and crossing the busy road where he stands looking anxiously for a bus. Meanwhile, the card collector at the nearby table lays down his knife and fork in the half-past-six position on the plate of half-finished food, signalling that he has had sufficient. He looks up from his letter and notices that a window table has opened up. He decides to move to it, transferring his empty carrier bag and notebook to the preferred spot.

7,500

The café owner sweeps by, delivering plates of fried food to workmen on a nearby table. The collector is about to resume his writing when he happens to glance out of the window. Across the street, standing with his back to the café, is the grey-haired pensioner.

"Here, quick, Nell," he says, calling the owner over.

"What?"

"Come and see who's outside."

"Who?"

"Look."

Her hands are full and she is reluctant to join him.

"It's that bloke off *Mission: Impossible*," he says.

"Where?"

"There," he says, pointing.

She peers out of the window at the man.

"That's not him, you daft sod," she says.

Fifteen minutes later. The man he has taken to be the *Mission: Impossible* star is marching along the streets at a brisk pace. Following at a safe distance, the card collector sees him heading into an alleyway. Unsure where the man is leading him, the collector hangs back and watches cautiously. Halfway along the

alley, the grey-haired man halts in his tracks. He appears to have
remembered something. Dipping his hand into his jacket pocket,
he pulls out the recently concealed playing card and lets it drop
to the ground.

The tubes had long stopped running so I decided to walk home
from the police station. I was hungry and vaguely on the lookout for a twenty-four-hour garage where I could find something
ready-to-eat in the convenience food section, so I ended up
taking the road that runs down from the Highbury and Islington
roundabout. It was really quiet. One or two cars trundled by
from time to time, but the street was otherwise deserted.

I wanted to presume that Sergeant Kyle had got my note
and was already investigating Steve rather than delving into my
file; if he didn't, the police might decide to pursue their original
line of enquiry and demand to search my flat again. Being found
in possession of a big pile of Steve's weapons-of-war-themed
reading matter might provide fuel for the fire they had been
trying to get started. I needed to douse those kindling flames
before they took hold.

In the distance I could hear an engine revving wildly. When
I looked round I saw a car speeding towards me down the hill.
My first thought was of joy-riding teenagers out for some late-
night thrills. I turned away and carried on walking, but as I heard
the car getting nearer, I checked again. It was going at such a
speed that at first I thought it might be heading straight for me
so I backed away from the kerb, ready to leap to safety over the
nearest garden wall should the reckless driver look set to mount
the pavement. As the car shot past I saw that it was a red 1960s
Mini Cooper, like the one on the Merrydown Confectionery
card. From the glimpse I caught of him, the driver seemed—not
young and reckless, but middle-aged and responsible, although

his head was bowed forward slightly as if he might be looking at something on his knees. A hundred feet down the road, near the traffic lights, he ploughed headlong into a lamppost. No change of speed, or any attempt to brake; he just piled straight into the concrete. I simply stood and watched him do it. There was a hefty crack, but no big explosion or anything. The back end lifted and dropped like something you might see in a cartoon and the car skewed round in the road to face me before it came to rest. The entire front had squashed flat. The misaligned headlights and dented grille made it look like the crumpled face of a recently smacked child. My initial reaction was to think: *What an idiot. What did he do that for?* And I waited for the driver to get out and acknowledge his foolish mistake, but he didn't. The traffic lights waited too and then changed through red-and-amber to green as if signalling him to make a move, yet there were still no signs of life from within the car. What was he waiting for?

I looked around to see if there were any other witnesses; but as with my **hole-in-one** achievement at the mini-golf course, there was no one. The world is full of people, all jostling to stick their noses into other people's business until something important happens, then they all disappear. Everyone suddenly has something better to do.

I couldn't see anybody through the front of the car; the windscreen seemed to have frosted over. The engine must have stalled because everything was quiet now except for a hissing from under the bonnet and the rhythmic shudder of rubber across dry glass as the windscreen wipers continued to sweep back and forth. Why did the driver have his windscreen wipers on? It wasn't raining.

I edged nearer and peeked through the side window. I couldn't help noticing how basic the controls were. Pedals, a steering wheel, a speedometer with a couple of switches on a tiny dashboard panel, and that was it. It looked like a toy. At first I thought there was no one inside, that the driver had somehow escaped, but then I saw him slumped sideways over the gearstick with his head in the passenger foot-well, as if he were searching for something under the seat. What was he doing? I knocked lightly on the window, but he didn't move. When I tried the door, I found that it was stuck and I had to yank it open. I asked the man if he was all right, though by then I was beginning to suspect that he wasn't. What at first had seemed almost comical had turned serious and at that point I began to feel the ground shifting under me and I could no longer trust my legs to support me.

The driver's seat belt dangled uselessly from the door column. He didn't look the type to ignore **Sir Jimmy Savile**'s 'Clunk Click Every Trip' safety warning, but it explained the round impact mark on the windscreen. With his face tucked under the seat, all I could see was the back of his head—or at least, when I think back, that's all I can remember seeing—but the familiar grey hair verified what I had somehow suspected. As further confirmation, he was wearing his trademark Prince of Wales check; and, inexplicably, there was a shoe on the front passenger seat, a treacle-toffee brogue, just sitting there, showered with turquoise crystals of broken glass from the passenger window.

The windscreen wipers were struggling—more laboured now, like someone with a breathing obstruction. I kept thinking a passer-by would come along or that another car might arrive at the scene, a police car preferably, or an ambulance full of caring, capable professionals who were used to dealing with this sort of thing.

Somehow I knew the man was dead, but I couldn't bring myself to check for the vital signs. I wasn't even sure I knew how to. I looked at his back to see if I could detect the rise and fall of breathing. Nothing moved.

FIRST • SAVE • MINI • DRIVER

Steve had been so nearly right, but so completely wrong.

I thought about what Amy had said and wondered if the man I was looking at was actually my dad. Could that really be him, just a few feet away from me, hiding his head in shame? It somehow didn't seem possible. I'd grown used to the distance between us and this man was too close—so close that I could easily have reached out and touched him, put my hand on his back and given him a shake like I used to. *Dad, Dad. Wake up, there's someone at the door. Dad, Dad. Can I get the hosepipe out? Dad, Dad. My ball's gone in next-door's garden.* He'd always respond, even if it was to tell me to go away.—*Later, Riley, I just want to let my dinner go down.*—*In a minute, son, I'm just having forty winks.* Dad lying on a towel on the beach at Bournemouth. Dad with his head under the kitchen sink, fiddling with the U-bend. Dad asleep on the sofa on a Sunday afternoon. *Dad, Dad. Wake up, Dad. Dad! Dad! Dad!*

TWENTY-TWO

I COULDN'T BRING MYSELF to touch him. I stood there for a bit, but in the end I just left him.—I didn't know what else to do. There seemed to be nobody else on earth. As the only witness, I knew it was my duty to report the accident, but what would have been the point? It wasn't anybody else's fault; he had no one to blame but himself. If questioned about it later—asked why I had walked away, I'd just say I was in shock. Who knows, perhaps I was. A lot of people say that—*I was in shock*. In a moment of crisis it's a handy excuse for anyone found guilty of selfish or cowardly conduct.

Sometimes, in the middle of the night, I find myself still caught up in the dream from which I have just awoken. Even though I'm fully conscious, it can take a while to shake myself free from the anxieties and responsibilities of the other world. I usually find a trip to the bathroom or fetching a glass of water from the kitchen settles me back down. The long walk home from the accident should have laid the ghosts to rest, but back at my flat, I found that the footage was still running in my head. I kept seeing the slumped figure, with Prince of Wales check all bunched up round his shoulders, his shirt riding high in the saddle to reveal a little soft bulge of pale flesh at the hip and the word *Jockey* sewn into the elastic waistband of his underpants. Whether or not the fallen rider was my father, it was an undignified conclusion to the race.

Those who have lost their fathers expect there to be a grave somewhere, a headstone inscribed with a few basic details that they can visit from time to time. It's a place to 'pay their respects': lay flowers and shed a tear, or to attempt some kind of posthumous reconciliation. For others, it's equally important—simply as a marker to tell them, if not where the dear departed has been, then at least where he ended up.

1997. In the flat above Nell's café, the owner sits on the bed with a drawer of papers on her knees. She is sifting through them—envelopes, postcards, etc. and from time to time she takes out something to inspect it before putting it back. Eventually she finds what she is looking for: a passport—the old kind with the stiff blue cover. She opens it at the photo page where, beneath a teetering crest of slicked dark hair, Elvis sits upright and alert as the camera flash fixes his conscientious gaze. She fetches a pile of colour photographs in a FotoKwik paper envelope. They are recent shots of her and her friends at some kind of celebration. She flicks through them until she finds a photo of her card collector friend from the café. She holds the pictures side by side to make a comparison. In spite of the different hairstyling choices—Elvis Presley/David Bowie—there is a discernible likeness. She flicks through the other passport pages as if searching for something more. Blank. No stamps or visas; Elvis has never been anywhere.

Towards the back of the passport, a card slips from between the pages into her lap. She picks it up and studies the picture

7,900

before turning it over in her hand. The reverse is blank except for a juvenile signature and the cyan-blue-printed border box in the lower portion of the card that reads: *Mission: Impossible, No. 19 in a series of 48. Chad Chewing Gum Ltd.*

When I reached home I read through the newspaper piece again. It mentioned how the stalker had left a plastic bag behind, with a knife and a screwdriver in it. Of course! The screwdriver love token was Steve's preferred ploy for a romantic introduction. Charles *Stephen* Corrigan. I hadn't noticed the Stephen part.

Needless to say, 'Stephen' was not at home. I expect he'll make himself scarce for a while. Unsurprisingly, the spare keys he had given me didn't fit the door to his flat. Who knows what they really did fit?—Some unsuspecting Goldie Locks customer's new door-lock or window grilles?—An extra key he had cut for his own personal use?

I'd never been in Steve's flat—never wanted to. I had always imagined that inside it would look like an ex-army-surplus outlet, the repository for weapons and combat paraphernalia such as my own flat had recently become. I pictured him as someone who might sleep under a mosquito net on an army camp bed with a couple of grenades on his bedside table. When the police came calling, I assumed they would find his inner sanctum filled with all the incriminating appurtenances of the obsessive predator: guns, knives and binoculars; a ghillie suit hanging in the wardrobe; back numbers of monthly publications such as *Gun Lord* and *Task Force Heroes*, and rows of VHS tapes with titles like *Kill Zone* and *The Assassins' Code*. I envisaged dozens of images of **Minnie Driver** pinned to the wall, in a recklessly collaged arrangement over the mantelpiece. I'd seen similar displays in films and police dramas. Detectives search the residence of a suspected serial killer or stalker and uncover a shrine to the victim created from assorted photos and newspaper clippings. As evidence, it's usually a clincher, ostensibly giving insight into the criminal's twisted psyche. In films they generally go overboard with the same clichéd look: daubed paint, roughly torn edges and frenzied scissor cuts—irrespective of the personality of the suspect, who might otherwise be mild-mannered and cautious. I'm not a murderer, but even if I were I would certainly never use drawing pins on my wall—especially since my living room has only recently been decorated with very expensive wallpaper from Fulford Brown Interiors. If I'd been compelled to create an obsessive shrine to my intended victim, I'd have done so with an artistic montage mounted on board, which I would have had properly framed at You've Been Framed. Better still, I would have displayed the best of the pictures as a series and then pasted the loose cuttings neatly into a scrapbook.

What worried me was that since so much of Steve's stuff had been transferred to my flat—presumably to build up a stockpile of evidence against me—perhaps his own flat was now left looking wholesome and innocent. Any residual clues that would have pointed to Steve as an obsessed **Minnie Driver** fan might since have been removed. Would Sergeant Kyle and his men arrive to find a perfectly ordinary one-bedroom flat with the impersonal functionality of a business hotel or a hostel: a neatly made bed, a table-lamp, a small dressing table with a tablet of lined paper and two ball-point pens, the only indications that he or anyone else had ever been living there? This wouldn't look at all like the home of a stalker, whereas my home now did. I had to put things right.

It didn't take more than a couple of trips across the landing. I stacked everything squarely against his door and in doing so felt I had severed all previous association with **Charles Stephen Corrigan**. For good measure I pinned the news piece from the

Daily Mirror to his door, with the same disregard for his paint-work as he had shown for mine.

There had never been a name on the bell to Steve's flat, even when the previous occupant, Mrs Brooks, was there; it just said Flat 6. In case I was out when Sergeant Kyle and his colleagues arrived, I felt I should point them in the right direction so I added a little piece of masking tape and wrote *Corrigan* on it. There's a way to take the cover off and slip a label into the slot, but I couldn't be bothered with that.

Now that Steve's presence in my home had been expunged, things felt more normal again. With everything in its rightful place and the culpability for the **Minnie Driver** violation re-dressed, I went back inside my own flat and shut the door on Steve and his unsavoury world. It was almost as if I were back to where I was before he had managed to steer me off course. The trouble was, I wasn't sure what to think about my mission any more. Now that I had been sidetracked, I'd rather lost my sense of direction with it. I honestly wished I'd never started it; the cards had got me into all this trouble. I should have left the queen of hearts where it was—should never even have followed the grey-haired man in the first place. The one card I *am* glad I picked up—the most important card in all of this—was the **FOUR OF CLUBS**; it was the card that led me to Amy. Without it, I would never have found her. Yet, picking up all the other cards had ultimately driven her away.

There seemed little point in going to bed as the day was already well under way, so I decided to stay up. Had it been a weekday, I would have gone round to Nell's for a hearty breakfast, but she doesn't open on Sundays. I think she heads off early to Mirfield Park to practise her golf swing.—Not on the Pitch-and-Putt: she takes her proper clubs and uses those plastic balls with holes in them, what are they called—wiffle balls? So instead of the full English I'd have liked, I made myself some toast and sat down to try and finish my story. It was time to wrap things up.

1997. 7a.m. The café owner enters the park. She is dressed in tracksuit and trainers and is wheeling a smart golf cart behind her. The patent leather handbag slung across her shoulder is somewhat at odds with the sporty look. It's Sunday, and the park gates have only just opened so the area is more or less deserted save for a few dedicated joggers and dog walkers.

On an adjacent path over by the boating lake, a young woman is taking junior for an early-morning stroll in his push-chair. She wears leggings and a pink hooded sweatshirt; her thin hair is scraped back into a high ponytail. She tugs hard on a long cigarette and huffs the smoke out of the side of her mouth. The boy strapped into the pushchair clutches a handful of cards. Closer inspection would show these to be an assortment of gum and cigarette cards, mostly from the 1950s and '60s, which have originated from the Odds-and-Sods box in his grand-father's collectors' emporium. The little lad is far too young to appreciate them. He is unfamiliar with the *World's Best Cricketers of 1958*, as issued by *The Rover* comic; cares nothing about *Army Badges Past and Present* or *The Story of the Locomotive* as told by Kellogg in their 1963 series. He's never heard of *Danger Man* or Herman's Hermits, and in answer to the question posed by the title of the 1957 Lyons Tea card series, *What Do You Know?* the youngster would be forced to reply, *Not Very Much*. Nevertheless, the cards seem to hold his interest. He singles one out from the top of the pile: Bolivia, no. 17 from A&BC's *Flags of the World* bubble-gum series. He stares at it briefly before flinging it wilfully to the ground. "Da!" he says dismissively, before returning his attention to the remaining cards. His mother fails to spot the discarded card as the pushchair rolls along.

At the fountain, the young mother and the café owner's paths converge. They are casual acquaintances so they stop to chat. The café owner listens attentively, apparently gripped as the young mother imparts some titbit of news. Meanwhile, the boy in the pushchair tosses another card overboard. This time, a rare but badly damaged Hopalong Cassidy bites the dust. Out of the corner of her eye, the café owner sees what has happened. Without shifting her focus too far from the conversation, she stoops to pick up the card and shoves it back amongst the others in the boy's chubby pink hands. Moments later, thinking it's a new game, he throws it down again. "Da!"

Presently, the two women part company and set off in opposite directions. The café owner heads towards the boating lake, taking the path along which the young woman and her son had come earlier. Almost at once she spots a picture card lying on the ground. She picks it up and quickly calls out to the young mother before she gets too far away. The mother turns and sees the café owner holding up the card as if she were a football referee sending someone off the pitch.

"What is it?" shouts the young mother, looking puzzled.

"A card. Is it one of his?"—she points at the boy in the pushchair.

"Oh. Yeah." The mother makes a show of rolling her eyes and shaking her head. "Just chuck it," she says, flopping her hand over at the wrist as though demonstrating how she might do this. "My dad gives him them. He's been dropping them all over the place."

She sets off again with the pushchair to the play area, and the café owner is left standing with the card in her hand. She nonchalantly studies the picture: it is the Bolivian flag from the A&BC series, a tricolour of red, yellow and green. Unsure what to do with it and unable to find a bin to throw it away, she lays the card back down on the path where she found it and continues on her journey. But a little further on she sees another card on the path—this time it's Batman and Robin in the Batmobile. Then another: Dr Kildare. Something has begun to dawn on her. She glances down at the cards as she strolls past them, her smile widening with growing amusement. When she comes to yet another, Lady Penelope from *Thunderbirds*, she puts her hand to her mouth and starts to laugh.

6,500

TWENTY-THREE

THERE WAS A STRANGE atmosphere on the streets. Some people were going about their Sunday-morning routine as normal, while others seemed distracted and confused. When I reached Amy's neighbourhood I saw a girl kneeling on the pavement, crying. Her head was bowed and her hands were cupped together, enclosing her nose and mouth like an oxygen mask. Her hands briefly parted to sweep away the tears that were streaming down her cheeks. Her attention seemed fixed on the grass verge in front of her, as if she were kneeling before a grave that wasn't there, and I wondered if perhaps her cat had been run over. I'd seen a dead cat on the side of the road a few days earlier—such a sad sight—which I suppose is what made me think of it, but I could see nothing here to suggest that this was the cause of her sorrow. Was she the girl I had seen riding her bike when I first went to survey Amy's house? Had someone stolen her lovely new bicycle? Whatever she had lost must have meant a great deal to her. I probably should have gone over to ask if she was all right, but then I wondered if her distress might somehow have something to do with the dead Mini driver and I felt guilty that I was unable to grieve for him in the same way.— The poor girl couldn't stop crying and I couldn't even begin.

As I rounded the bend in Amy's road, I was reassured to see that both the **R**ange **R**over and Uncle Derek's blue sports car were parked in the driveway as usual, so I figured that everything there at least was normal. The Truelove door was slightly ajar so I stepped inside and called out hello. It was Uncle Derek who greeted me.

"Good morning, Riley. You're an early bird. I suppose you've heard the dreadful news?" He was on his way to the sitting room carrying a mug of tea and a plate of toast. Through the open door I could see Mrs Truelove sitting in her dressing gown, smoking a cigarette and staring distractedly at the television.

"The car crash, you mean? Yes." I was confused. How did they know what had happened? Perhaps the schoolgirl was a neighbour and had told them about the accident.

"We're just watching it now. Would you like some tea?"

"Watching it? Is it on television?"

Uncle Derek nodded at the screen, then set his tea and toast down and sat next to Mrs Truelove. They both stared ahead, but they weren't watching anything. It was just the station ident: the BBC logo against a blurry background of swirling colours. No sound. I didn't get it. What were they doing?

With her eyes still fixed on the screen, Mrs Truelove reached out towards me. I'd never seen her without make-up before. Her face was still pretty but she looked pale and fragile; there were smudgy circles of grey under her eyes. I went and sat next to her on the arm of the sofa. She took my hand in hers and pressed the back of it firmly against her cheek. Her skin was damp with tears.

"There was nothing you could have done," she said. "You mustn't blame yourself. Not for a minute." She looked at me and squeezed my hand to emphasize her point.

"No.—I think I was in shock."

"We're all in shock," said Uncle Derek. "It's a terrible thing. It's like losing someone from your own family."

On the television, a woman's voice cut in: This is BBC Television from London. Normal programming has been suspended and we now join **Martin Lewis** in the news studio.

Martin was wearing a black tie and was looking sombre. He said, "This is BBC Television from London. Diana, Princess of Wales, has died after a car crash in Paris. The French government announced her death just before five o'clock this morning. Buckingham Palace confirmed the news shortly afterwards. In a statement, the Palace said that the **Queen** and the **Prince of Wales** are deeply shocked and distressed by this terrible news. Normal programmes have been suspended while we bring you the latest developments throughout the morning."

The picture faded to black and then faded up again to reveal a flag flying at half-mast. The familiar drum-roll intro followed by the thin violin strains of our national anthem. A caption appeared underneath:

Diana, Princess of Wales 1961–1997.

Amy appeared in the doorway. Mrs Truelove released my hand so that I could go to her. We went and stood in the hallway.

"I can't believe it," she said. "It's just so weird, isn't it?"

I nodded.

"Such a tragedy. It's hard to imagine how something like that could happen.—No seat belt, apparently."

I shook my head with doleful respect, not knowing what else to say. We looked at each other for a minute then Amy touched my hand.

"I'm so sorry," she said.

I wasn't sure exactly what she was so sorry about. Sorry that

Princess Diana was dead, or sorry that she had doubted me about the reality of the danger? I didn't ask. I had been wrong about so many other things. "No, I'm sorry." I said.

I squeezed Amy's hand tight and we stayed like that for some time, until she said,

"You know, I have something that belongs to you."

"Have you?" I said. "What?"

Amy turned to the hall cupboard behind her, opened the door and lifted a coat hanger from the rail. On it hung my jacket, looking clean and freshly pressed.

"Are you sure that's mine?" I said.

Amy nodded resolutely. "Oh yes. Absolutely sure."

She slipped the jacket from the hanger and held it up by the lapels as if she wanted me to try it on. I knew it fitted perfectly, but I accepted her invitation anyway, my hands gliding down the cool satin lining of the sleeves as she slid it on to my shoulders.

"There," she said, smoothing the fabric across my back. "Perfect."

I turned towards the full-length mirror on the cupboard door as if seeing the jacket for the first time. Amy stood behind me, studying our reflection.

"And that missing button on the cuff..." she said. "I'm going to sew that back on for you."

I smiled. "You don't have to."

"I want to," she said.

Across the country, families were waking to the news that would send them into paroxysms of uncontrolled grief—the entire nation torn apart by the untreatable trauma. In the light of this, I felt somehow guilty that between Amy and me at least, the wounded area seemed to be healing over nicely.

Just then the phone rang on the sideboard nearby, but she made no move to answer it, seemingly reluctant to acknowledge the interruption. It rang a couple more times before she turned and shouted into the sitting room, "Shall I answer it?"

Uncle Derek responded from within, "No. We don't want to talk to anybody just now."

Amy snaked her arm round my waist and pulled herself closer to me. "No, we don't," she said softly.

After another ring, the machine kicked in and the announcement played: it was Uncle Derek speaking in his most formal voice, but with a hint of jocularity—*You have reached the Truelove residence. Please speak clearly after the tone.* There was a beep and then a voice at the other end—high and scratchy like one that might come from a parrot. *Hello... Hello?... Are you there?....*

Amy sighed and spoke into my ear. "It's Auntie Joan. She's probably ringing to tell us the news about **Princess Diana**. Ignore her."

Suspecting that the Trueloves might be screening calls, Auntie Joan continued to vie for attention: *Are you there?* — And then after a long pause, *Hello?* The voice sounded lost and alone. Amy snorted a little laugh and I laughed too. Auntie Joan refused to give in. *Hello. Pick it up. If you're there, pick it up...*

I closed my eyes and tried to tune out Auntie Joan's plaintive request, but the voice continued to ring in my ears. I found myself thinking about the **Peter Lorre** voice I had heard in the phone box the previous week when I had picked up the S. Prince cigarette card. It wasn't Auntie Joan ringing that night—or anyone connected to the cards—just a stranger dialling a wrong number and thinking he was through to someone's answering machine: *Pick it up. If you're there, pick it up.*

As if in answer to Auntie Joan, I suddenly blurted out, "I've stopped collecting cards. The mission—it's over. I promise."

Amy looked a little taken aback by my sudden burst of

earnestness. She touched my arm. "You don't have to promise anything. I don't care what you do. I just want you."

"Do you? Why?"

She shook her head. "I don't know. I just do."

While it was a shock to the world, many had seen it coming. People were aware that the Princess was **in grave and imminent danger,** yet nobody was given specific instructions on how to save her. And, of course, she was incapable of saving herself. What can you do in these situations? By the time you've recognized the precise nature of the hazard, it's invariably too late. With the benefit of hindsight, and the chance to rewind events, you could go back and issue direct warnings to those in peril.— You might persuade **Janis Joplin** to cut back on the drugs; advise **Buddy Holly** to take a later flight; suggest to **Marie Curie** that exposure to radioactivity might be detrimental to her health; or alert **Terry Kath** (the guitarist out of American rock band, Chicago) to the potential dangers of playing **R**ussian **R**oulette. Yet, without being privy to that same hindsight, you wonder if any of them would have listened.

So you stand at the roadside and watch as the tragedy unfolds before you and it's like watching a rerun of the Zapruder 8-mm movie footage following **JFK**'s presidential motorcade along Dealey Plaza. You know what's going to happen because you've seen the film so many times before. The inevitable outcome is already there between frames 310 and 328 and it's the same every time. Intervention is hopeless, so you wait for the critical moment to play out, then you walk away telling yourself there was nothing you could have done.

Uncle Derek came out of the sitting room just then and put his arms round Amy and me in a group hug. He said, "Mummy's very upset so I think the best thing we can do is to all sit down together and have a proper cooked breakfast. It won't bring **Princess Diana** back, of course, but I think we'll all feel a lot better for it. Now, how would you two like your eggs?"

I decided to end my story with **card 19** lying face down on the ground. I figured that most *Card Collector Monthly* readers wouldn't need much more to explain how it ended up where it did. By now they would assume that once Nell had found the card in the passport and realized what it was, she would have wanted me to have it. But how would she go about getting it to me?—that's what my readers would be wondering. She couldn't just hand it over; it would be too blatant an admission of her involvement with my father. I suppose she could have dropped it anonymously through my letter-box. Or left it on my garden path, as she had done with the **cha-cha-cha** card, knowing that I would be bound to find it. But even that, to her, must have seemed too obvious.

1997. Mirfield Park. Having seen the cards on the path—Dr Kildare and his chums—and chuckled to herself about how they had got there, the café owner now seems more pensive. She opens up her shiny black handbag and takes something out: it is the old blue passport. From between its pages she removes card 19. She regards it wistfully, as one might study a photograph of a loved one, letting it linger in her hand as though wanting to hold on to a memory before letting it go. Then, slipping it into her pocket, she sets off towards the children's playground where she can see that the young mother and her little boy have found the perfect spot for a well-deserved fag break.

The pushchair is facing an elegant Victorian park bench—a rolling curve of strong wooden slats with decorative cast-iron ends. Here sits the mother, a cigarette pinched between her lips

R. Pincus

MISSION: IMPOSSIBLE
No. 19 in a series of 48 photos
© CHAD Chewing Gum Ltd.

as she rummages in the depths of her capacious handbag for a lighter, like a dog digging for a bone. She looks up with a smile to acknowledge the café owner, who rests her golf bag against the fence and sits down beside her. The young woman resumes her search while the café owner leans forward to engage with the child. Taking the card from her pocket, she holds it up discreetly for him to see. The little boy stares at it, but naturally fails to recognize its importance. The café owner glances at the young mother, who is still distracted; then, like a novice sleight-of-hand magician, she tucks card 19 in amongst the fistful of other cards in the youngster's grasp. The boy is unsure what has happened, but looks back at her with a gleeful smile, expressing himself in the only way he knows how: "Da!"

With her cigarette now lit, the young mum leans into the bench, tilting back her head to exhaust her lungs. The escaping swirls of smoke are quickly snatched by the breeze and lost to the clean morning air. On the bench beside her, the café owner unconsciously mimics the gesture. She lifts her face to the sun, deeply exhaling—not smoke, but a long sigh that seems to carry with it a mixture of emotions: regret, relief—completion.

Total word count: 9,097

I'd like to be able to say that on my way through the park to Amy's earlier that morning I stepped right over **card 19** without even looking at it. The truth is—I couldn't help peeking; my eye was somehow drawn to it. Inevitable, I suppose—I'd been searching for the damn thing for thirty years. Perhaps I needed to be sure what I was walking away from.

I paused for no more than a few seconds outside the children's playground, yet it was long enough to take in the slightly wonky scissor-cut edge where my own ten-year-old hands had tried to shape the card, and the cyan-blue printing on the back: *Mission: Impossible, No. 19 in a series of 48.* The legendary, mythical **CARD 19**.

The back had yellowed less than the others in the series; presumably because the card had been stored somewhere away from the light of day. I knew it was real because my name was on it. It was the same *signature* as on the backs of all the others in the series, the writing in blue biro, careful and deliberate with no extra embellishments or flourishes to mark it from my everyday handwriting. Even so, I can't say I recognized the penmanship as my own.—R. Pincus. It wasn't even my name any more.

Had I been unable to resist the urge to pick it up and turn it over, what would have been the image? A glamorous for-your-eyes-only female spy, as suggested in my magazine piece? Or the silver-haired Jim Phelps listening to a recorded message on the miniature tape recorder? *Your mission, Jim, should you decide to accept it is to...* What? Save the life of the most famous woman on the planet? *Should you fail in your mission, the entire world will grieve in perpetuity, treating the death of a complete stranger as if it were the death of a loved one, crying harder and longer than for the loss of their own. And the endless flow of their collective tears shall fall on your shoulders for all eternity. This tape will self-destruct in five seconds.*

Throughout my years of searching, the hardest thing for me was knowing that the card had once been mine—that I had held it in my hand and somehow let it slip through my fingers. I had taken the cards to school, which I had promised faithfully I would not do, and losing it was the price I paid. Now, so many years later, I realize that the card wasn't lost through carelessness or the youthful urge to show off, but that it had been taken away from me when I wasn't looking. That's what happens. Someone sneaks into your room at night and steals the heart of your collection from under your very nose. Your attention is misdirected to the playground scuffle while the real business has taken place elsewhere.

In the summer of 1977 we sold the family house and my mother went to live in Devon with a man she met at night school. He seemed dull, but nice enough. I was twenty by then, living in a shared flat and working part-time as a bar waiter in a hotel in Bayswater.

The hotel had a small off-street parking area for their patrons round the back. On my way through it one lunchtime, I remember seeing some juvenile graffiti on the car park sign. With a blue felt marker, somebody had added a little horizontal dash to the letter **C** in **CAR**, altering it to a **G**. At the end of the word **CAR** he had added a **Y**, making the name **GAR**y. To complete the transition, the culprit had simply crossed out the word **PARK** and underneath it written **GLITTER**. It wasn't **CAR PARK**, it was **GAR**y **GLITTER**—it just needed a little adjustment. At the time, the tenuousness of the link made me laugh; how on earth had someone got **Gary Glitter** from Car Park? To the author it must have seemed perfectly obvious, but it takes a dedicated fan to notice these things. If **G**ary **G**litter is fixed in your mind, it's hard to read the signs any other way.

To another breed of fan, the words **CAR PARK** might have suggested **CAR**y **Grant** or **ChAR**lie **PARK**er, or even Os**CAR PARK**es—the well-known naval historian and editor of Jane's Fighting Ships from 1918 to1935. The latter less likely perhaps, but it depends where your loyalties lie. Someone else is bound to see it as a sign from God. But when all is said and done, it's probably just a sign telling you where to park your car.

Beef, broccoli, beetroot and beans.
Pork, parsnips, potatoes and peas.
No gray. No grave. No gravy.

If you look hard enough, you discover that all things are connected. And once your brain starts making these links, it's
hard to get it to stop. Mini-golf and **Minnie Driver**. **Gordon
Banks** and the one-eyed queen. A May Day wedding for **Barry
Manilow** and the Library Woman. **SOS**, cha-cha-cha, **TTT**.
Paul McCartney, this is your life; **Elvis Presley**, this is your
death. Jim Phelps and the Silver Fox. Psychopath 'patsy' **Oswald**
and 'crazy' **Patsy Cline**. **Bob Monkhouse** and **Dora Bryan**.
They're all related—friends of the family. **Princess Diana** and
Catherine of Aragon. Aragon, tarragon. Oregon, Corrigan.

In the aftermath of the national tragedy, those seeking anagrammatical truths might see Princess Diana **ascend in Paris**.
Others will only see **aspirins dance** and wonder what it all
means. I should have seen Paris coming, but by then my path
had been diverted, my train rerouted at the critical junction by a
weirdo in combat gear intent on making me see things his way.
Rescue snookered; Carry On Regardless.

The trick is in knowing your own mind—knowing how it
works and realizing that the signs always point to where you
were going in the first place. I may never be able to ignore the
connections, but I think I've learned that I have the right to
walk away.

ACKNOWLEDGEMENTS

Thanks to everyone at Atlantic Books for their unfailing support for this project, particularly to my editor Sarah Norman for her tremendous dedication and insight. Thanks also for invaluable advice from Clare Harris, Neil Hunter and, as always, my wife, Margaret Huber.

All of the cards featured in this novel have been fabricated by the author.